BUSY PEOPLE'S LOW-FAT Cookbook

by
Dawn Hall

Published by:
Cozy Homestead Publishing

ISBN# 0-9649950-3-4

Attention Businesses, Groups, Teachers, and Fund-raisers; This book is available at quantity discounts with bulk purchase for business, education, sales promotional and fund-raising uses. For more information call, write or fax:

Cozy Homestead Publishing
**5425 S. Fulton-Lucas Road
Swanton, OH 43558**

**Toll Free: 1-888-436-9646
Fax: (419) 826-2700**

Printed in the USA by
WIMMER
The Wimmer Companies
Memphis

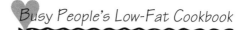

TABLE OF CONTENTS

DEDICATION

I am living with a walking miracle and it is to him that I dedicate this book. He is my gentle hero, faithful best friend, cherished lover, children's loving father and courageous husband, Tracy Hall. I am in constant awe of his steadfast love and dedication to God and life itself.

In November of 1994, the day after his 32nd birthday, Tracy was diagnosed with an aggressive brain cancer the size of a baseball. One pound of the malignant tumor was surgically removed which left him completely paralyzed on his entire left side. Radiation did not make his remaining aggressive cancer any smaller, but left him bald, weak and tired.

Today Tracy is living proof that God is still doing miracles!! His cancer has shrunk approximately 90% on an experimental treatment, he has cycled as many as 32 miles in one day and is able to work part-time! Wow!! Most important, he is a living example of a loving, Godly person.

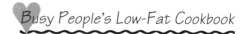
MISCELLANEOUS NOTES TO THE COOK

 When you see this Kids Cookin' logo, it means the recipe is child appropriate. Most children will be able to make it with a minimum of adult supervision.

Budget
Friendly
 When you see this logo it means the recipe is inexpensive to make.
Recipe

SUGAR SUBSTITUTES

I do not encourage the use of Equal and NutraSweet, which are registered trademarks of the NutraSweet Company. None of these products have sponsored or are otherwise connected with this publication. However, I feel it is important to provide an alternative for those who are diabetic. For more information, you might call: NutraSweet Hotline 1-800-321-7254.

BRAND NAMES

Most brand names used in this book are registered trademarks and are thus protected by law.

BUTTER BUDS/BUTTER BUDS SPRINKLES

This is a boxed butter flavored substitute found in the spice section of most grocery stores. To make liquid Butter Buds, simply follow the directions on the box and add water to one envelope of Butter Buds. One Tablespoon of dry Butter Buds Sprinkles is the same as one packet of dry Butter Buds. Butter Buds 1-800-231-1123

THANK YOU! THANK YOU! THANK YOU!

As I take a moment to reflect and gather my thoughts before actually putting pen to paper to write this, (my acknowledgments) I am over-whelmed with thankfulness. Tears are rolling down my cheeks as I try to swallow the big lump in my throat. My body is consumed with goose bumps from the top of my head to the tips of my toes. I am probably one of the most thankful people to have ever lived on the face of this earth.

I wholeheartedly believe my talents are a gift from God, so of course I want to thank Him first. Without a doubt, I know 100%, absolutely and positively that God is using (what I at one time thought were problems) as my talents. It's not uncommon for me to wake-up at 3:30 in the morning with a low-fat, fast and easy recipe idea in my head. I know it is not normal. For years I thought, "What is wrong with me? Is my food addiction consuming even my sleeping?" I was frustrated and hated that I did this.

It wasn't until my students, friends and family kept requesting the recipes I'd created and kept encouraging me to write cookbooks that I realized I didn't have a problem, but rather a <u>gift</u>! To this day I think it is <u>so</u> cool how God works! It is just like Him to use something we think of as "bad" for good! I am forever grateful, and will (to my dying day) give God all of the praise and glory for all of the good He does through me!

Next, I'd like to thank my family which consist of my hero (my husband), and our children, Whitney and Ashley. So often when I'm on a talk show or I'm the guest speaker; people "ooh" and "aah" over the fact that I love to create new recipes and we've practically never eaten the same meal twice. In all honesty, how many of you would like to be a guinea pig every single day of your life? Believe me . . . it's not all peaches and cream! I've had my fair share of flops in my days. (Of course none of the flops are in my books!) I never follow a recipe. It bores me. I love to create! Maybe I'll get an idea from a "high fat" potluck or restaurant. While I'm eating I'll jot down on a paper napkin what I think is in the dish, then when I'm home I try to make the dish as delicious, but extremely low-fat; quickly and easily.

For someone to ask me not to be creative with food would be like asking a flower not to blossom. My family has never done that to me. I am truly thankful.

To my personal assistants (who are my left arm,) I publicly let everyone know how much I appreciate you. Diane Bowman-Yantiss, Karen Schwanbeck, Mable Jackson and Robin Friend are probably sick of me telling them practically everyday how much I appreciate them, but I just can't help it! Every single day I verbally thank God for my assistants! I don't know how I could do it all without them. They are the glue that keeps my business of Cozy Homestead Publishing together!

In all honesty, I wish I looked as good in person as Bert Heindel (from Bert & Associates Photography) makes me look in these photos for this book. Please don't get me wrong. I know I'm not dog meat. Still, I'm no model. None the less, he made me look like one. Thank you, Bert!

A great big warm and friendly thank you to Kitchen Design Plus on Renwyck Drive in Toledo for graciously allowing us to use one of their many beautiful kitchens for the backdrop of the cover. Not only were they wonderful to work with, they were all sweethearts as people to know and became some of my biggest fans after sampling the many foods used for the photo shoot.

Last but not least, my most heart felt thanks and appreciation to the staff of the Wimmer company who did the actual printing of "Busy People's Lowfat Cookbook". An extra special thank you to Freddie Strange (who is anything but strange!), Ardith Bradshaw and Jim Hall. With all of my heart I wanted to be able to hire Wimmer to print my book, because I feel they are among the best in what they do. I literally prayed to God that we could afford to have them do this book. I am so thankful and feel so blessed to have them working with me. They are everything I had ever hoped for!

As you can see, I am very blessed. It's no wonder I consider myself probably one of the most thankful people to have ever lived on the face of this earth!

HELP! I'VE STARTED EATING AND I CAN'T STOP!

It seems like most of us have been there at one time or another. Thanksgiving, Christmas day, all you can eat buffets (we want to get our money's worth!) and those dreadful "P.M.S." times, are just a few situations when a lot of us "overeat." For those of you who never over indulge, "God Bless You!" You can go ahead and move to the next chapter, as this will probably bore you.

I wish I could have been born with that quality also. I am always impressed by a child who says "no thank you" to a special snack because, "I'm not hungry." <u>WOW!</u> Good for you! (Parents don't encourage them to eat it anyway. Simply save it for when they are hungry.) For those of you that are afraid your child will starve to death, don't worry. Most doctors agree, when your child is hungry they'll eat. Make sure it's nutritious, not junk food.

For most of us, it's the opposite. A lot of us don't even know what it feels like to be "truly hungry." Wouldn't it be great if we only ate when we're hungry? (Not starving, but hungry.) We eat for so many wrong reasons:

> —We're happy
>
> —We're sad
>
> —We're bored
>
> —It's time to eat (the clock says)
>
> —And on and on and on!
>
> You know it's true!

<u>THE TRUTH</u> ABOUT YOUR WEIGHT.

The "weight, nutrition and health" issues are complicated. When it comes to "fighting the bulge" the truth is it can be hard! For some of us <u>very</u> hard! If you're thinking, "No joke. Now tell me something I didn't know." Listen up. What you are about to read may surprise you!

The number one reason people are in the hospitals today is because of lifestyle. Heart disease, cancer and diabetes can all be positively effected by a low-fat diet. As I said earlier, there are so many wonderful choices today of low-fat foods that taste delicious. We don't have to eat like a rabbit to eat healthy. If you've never tried "doing the low-fat thing", I strongly encourage you to do so. For those of you who complain and say you don't like low-fat foods yet have never tried it, all I can say is, "Don't knock it until you've tired it!"

Although, many dietitian, health enthusiastic, and other people with good intentions would like to make being healthy seem simple, it is not. What is not true for <u>most</u> people is thinking if they would just change <u>one</u> of the following behaviors their dream of being their ideal weight would magically happen.

Each individual statement, <u>alone and by itself</u> is for <u>most</u> people not true in and of itself.

STATEMENT:

If God were #1 in your life you wouldn't
have a weight problem.   Not True!

If you eat all low-fat foods you'll never
have to worry about being overweight.   Not True!

If you would aerobically exercise daily,
you wouldn't have a weight problem.   Not True!

If you only ate when you were hungry
and quit eating once you felt comfortable
you wouldn't have a weight problem!   Not True!

There must be some hidden abuse, or
emotional reason behind why people are
overweight.   Not True!

If only they had more self-control they
wouldn't be heavy.   Not True!

Yes, some of the statements above do apply to some people, and it can be as simple as changing one bad behavior or attitude towards food. However, for the most part, I feel it is much, much more complicated than <u>just one issue per person</u>. For the most part, for most people maintaining ideal weight is complex and multifaceted. <u>A combination of the comments stated, not just one reason.</u>

MAINTAINING IDEAL BODY WEIGHT

For many of us its a complicated and complex issue that many people have tried to simplify with comments such as,: "If you don't want to be fat, just don't eat fat". Wouldn't it be nice if it were so simple! Then there are those who say, "If you don't want to be fat, just stop eating when you feel comfortable". That's a fine idea for those who are overweight because they simply keep eating even though they are full. What about those of us who already quit eating when we are comfortable and we happen to have a larger appetite than our bodies need? Another way of looking at this is that we don't eat too much, our body is just shorter than it ought to be for the weight we are. It's very frustrating & annoying trying to stop eating once you know you've eaten what is a so called portion when your head, stomach and watering mouth cry out "I'm still hungry!" One way to help calm hunger cries is to drink water before, during and after your meal.

OTHER IDEAS TO HELP SATISFY A HUNGRY TUMMY ARE:

♥ Set your alarm 5 minutes earlier than you need to get up. Think positive, reinforcement thoughts such as "eating healthy is a gift I give myself. I love to eat healthy, etc . . . "

♥ Eat a cup of vegetable soup or a clear broth before your meal.

♥ Eat more salad with fat-free salad dressing or fat-free green vegetables at the end of the meal to help feel satisfied.

♥ Sip on decaffeinated herbal flavored teas. There's something very soothing and relaxing about sipping on flavorful teas. A unique beverage for sipping is placing 8 to 10 tic-tacs per 10 cup pot in the filter holder of your coffee maker instead of coffee. This will create a hot, flavorful beverage that is virtually calorie free. (One calorie per cup.)

♥ Drink a glass of Metamucil (the flavored ones aren't bad.) Not only does it help you feel fuller, but it provides 3 grams of natural fiber per glass full. It is not addictive and is helpful to those with digestive problems. Daily recommendation on box is no more than 3 glasses per day. For those who can't stomach the thought, (thinking you can't bear the taste), the orange flavor is not bad. At night time, before bed when I'm hungry I find drinking a warm glass of Metamusil helpful before I brush my teeth to go to bed. Also, in the morning before eating breakfast I have a glass.

♥ Sometimes we still feel hungry because our "sweet tooth" is not satisfied. With this in mind, try a tic-tac or chewing a piece of gum. If that doesn't work, try a small fat-free cookie, sugar-free jello, popsicle or a piece of fruit. Sometimes all we need is just a little something to satisfy the sweet tooth.

♥ Ask the advise of your family doctor or holistic medical doctor. Explain your hunger. See if there are some natural herbs, vitamins or minerals that maybe helpful in curbing your appetite. For those who say, "It's all in your head . . . that's why you think you're hungry", a part of their statement is true. Hunger signals are released from the brain. However, being overweight usually is more complicated and complex than simply just that. By going to a holistic medical doctor, the doctor can actually test your blood. Sometimes a deficiency in one area or another can make you feel hungry, tired, etc.

♥ My mother, Wendy Oberhouse has lost over 80 pounds, and my stepfather Donald Oberhouse has lost 70 pounds. They've kept the weight off for years. I am so proud of them. Along with the switch to a low-fat, low calorie lifestyle they use herbs to help curb their large appetites. They both feel the herbs help take "the edge off" so they can maintain their healthier lifestyle. For more information you can talk to them personally at #419-867-9907.

Here are photos of my parents then and now.

♥ Out of sight out of mind theory. Sometimes we think we're hungry because the delicious, mouth-watering foods that are leftover from the meal are staring us in the face from their serving bowls. We think we're hungry, when in all reality, we are not hungry. It tasted good and we'd like more. Keeping this possibility in mind, do not serve any food homestyle except vegetables and salad. (Which can be used as filler, if still hungry after meal is eaten.) All other foods place on dinner plates before serving. Do not put into serving bowls or platter, as this encourages overeating.

♥ Learn the difference between the true feeling of feeling "satisfied" without feeling "full". There is a difference. Let me say up front, that it is not necessarily our fault as Americans that we are fat. Years ago when the media stressed: eat 5-6 meals a day not 3, many of us took the media literally. What they should have said is eat 5-6 healthy "snacks" a day and no longer eat big meals. Many of us think of meals as what Mrs. Cleaver (Beaver's mom) used to serve, complete with meat, potatoes, gravy, vegetable, rolls, butter and of course dessert. Please media - eating 6 full course meals a day is a sure fire way to put on the pounds and fast!

♥ The media also encourages "grazing", which if done correctly is absolutely wonderful at helping keep blood sugar levels good and energy levels strong. However, what we graze on is of the utmost importance. Yes, cows like to graze for the most part of the day, and if we grazed on greens such as green leafy salads most of the day we'd be thinner and healthier.

♥ The problem is, just like ranchers do to fatten their cattle for slaughter by feeding them lots of high calorie, low-fat foods such as corn and oats, a lot of us are grazing on high caloric, fat-free foods or low-fat foods such as Light Twinkies and cookies. Beware of "compacted caloric foods"!

♥ Instead of thinking of eating 5-6 meals a day, think of it as eating 5-6 snacks a day. Only on special occasions - like dinner out or a holiday will you eat a full meal. Instead, what I encourage you to do is break-up your regular 3 meals a day into 6. Let me explain:

OLD WAY OF EATING
3 low-fat meals a day

Breakfast
1 slice toast, orange juice, cereal with skim milk

Lunch
Turkey sandwich, Baked Lays Potato Crisp, Apple, Herbal Tea and fat-free cookie

Dinner
Barbecued Chicken Breast, Tossed Salad with fat-free dressing, roll, baked potato and green beans

NEW WAY OF GRAZING
and eating 6 snacks a day

Breakfast
Cereal with skim milk and toast

Snack
Orange (instead of juice because it's more filling & satisfying to chew)

Lunch
Turkey sandwich, Baked Lays, apple and tea

Snack
Fat-free cookie

Dinner
Barbecued Chicken Breast,
Tossed Salad w/ fat-free salad dressing, baked potato and green beans (skip roll)

Snack
100 calorie snack such as fat-free cookies, instead of roll which we skipped at dinner

TOTAL CALORIES AND FATS:

1225 Calories & 8 fats

1225 Calories & 8 fats

As you can see, we simply broke up our meals and used part of our meal as snacks. You never get really full nor do you ever get really hungry.

A lot of my students would skip breakfast and their morning snack. By lunch they were starving. Because they were starving they ended up eating more calories in their lunch alone than if they'd had a small breakfast or snack or both. Even a fat-free 50 calorie slice of toast with 10 sprays of "I Can't Believe It's Not Butter" spray for breakfast totaling only 60 calories and 1 gram of fat can save you oodles and oodles of calories later by helping curb your hunger so you don't feel ravished by lunch. What many do is think, "Well, I didn't eat breakfast so it's okay to go ahead and eat these fries". Those 300 calorie fries just blew your total daily caloric and fat intake for the day out of the water! Whereas if you'd eaten a small breakfast or snack before lunch you probably would have been able to refrain from the fries all together - or at least shared an order with a friend.

I've read books stating "eat whatever you're craving or want, but only eat a little bit. Savor each bite". That too, is good counsel to a degree. However, I think it is important to eat what you are craving for, but of low-fat choices if at all possible. Remember, eating a low-fat lifestyle helps fight countless diseases including heart disease, cancer and diabetes. Why eat a Snickers at 12 grams of fat if a Milky Way Lite will do the trick and satisfy the sweet craving for only 5 grams of fat and almost half the calories? Or how about a bite size Milky Way Lite at 1 gram of fat and 30 calories? Why eat regular french fries at 20 grams of fat and 300 calories when the baked ones are equally delicious and practically no fat and 1/3 of the calories? With todays endless array of wonderful low-fat, lower caloric choices why not make the healthier choice and eat what you're hungry for? I feel so blessed to be able to have the choices we do today regarding food verses 20 years ago. There are a lot more healthier options - and many taste wonderful!

As I stated in my 1st book "Down Home Cookin' Without the Down Home Fat," there are going to be times when we will choose to wander from our healthier lifestyle of low-fat. However, those choices will be special occasions and not the norm. The problem is what used to be a special treat 50 years ago is now in many families the daily norm. A special candy bar from the five and dime store or a hamburger, fries and milk shake at the local diner was a special treat. Nowadays, people think nothing of having an Egg McMuffin loaded down with sausage, cheese and a side of fried hash browns for breakfast; Quarter Pounder with cheese and mayo, fries and a milk shake for lunch; a candy bar for a snack; pizza for dinner and then a bowl of ice cream before going to bed.

That's the problem. It's the norm. In our fast paced, go, go, go world it's eat on the run. Unfortunately it's high fat, high calorie and usually very low on nutrition. Once in a blue moon to splurge on pizza or a real hamburger is fine for a special occasion. Doing it daily is trouble. Sooner or later it'll catch up with you one way or another.

Don't think of low-fat eating as a diet. Think of it as a lifestyle change. What you do to get thinner and healthier is what you need to continue doing after you've reached your goal to maintain.

In the Bible it tells us to "train your children in the way they should go". I believe it is not only about spiritual things but physical and financial also. Wouldn't it have been easier for us as adults if we'd have grown up more conscious of what we were eating? On behalf of baby-boomer parents everywhere, I must admit the healthier choices we have today far out number the healthier choices of yester years. None the less, some things remain the same such as eating habits. I am the oldest of seven. We took great pride in "how much" we could eat. As children, we'd have contests to see who could out eat the other children. You can eat 7 ears of corn, well I can eat 8! It may sound funny now, but to this day I struggle within.

I am a recovering food addict. I tell people there's nothing a hot fudgy brownie can't help make feel better. I've used food like an alcoholic would use alcohol to numb the pain, help me feel better, keep me from being bored or lonely, to celebrate . . . the list goes on and on and on! I know how hard it is. I want to encourage any of you who struggle. There is hope. There is help. All you have to do is ask. Often, when we think we're hungry what needs fed is our hearts, not our stomachs. I know, because I've been there. There is an excellent self-help, 12 step work book I found very beneficial titled "The Love Hunger Workbook" by the Minirth-Meier Clinic. I can not recommend it highly enough. *Account-ability is important for food addicts, just like alcoholics or drug addicts. Unfortunately, food addictions are the unspoken accepted addiction. For those needing accountability, Overeaters Anonymous, First Place and T.O.P.S. are all groups I'd encourage you looking into. You are not alone. There are a lot of people who struggle with food addictions. God wants to help you help yourself, however the first step is up to you. God has created you to be happy and healthy. He wants you to enjoy your life. Release from the bondage of food addiction can be a wonderful thing. If you don't know if you can overcome it, believe me - you can! God says in the Bible, "We can do all things through Christ who strengthens us." Keep believing! You will succeed!

I've heard and read of people who say they can consume 3,000 calories a day and maintain 125 pounds body weight simply by eating a very low-fat diet. For all of us that were "born watching our weight", I know how extremely frustrating that can make us feel. We eat about 1/2 that many calories and weigh more! It's not fair, but the truth is life is not fair. We have to do the best we can with what we've got.

In regards to people who claim they can eat 3,000 calories a day and only weigh 125 pounds, here are some theories as to how they are able to eat that much and be slender.

They may have a lot of muscle mass to maintain. One pound of muscle burns 50 calories a day whereas one pound of body fat burns 2 calories a day. For easy explanation lets say we have 2 people, each weighing 100 pounds, neither of them have any bone, water or internal organ weight. Person "A" is made up of nothing but solid muscle. Person "B" is made up of nothing but solid body fat. Look at the remarkable difference in caloric intake it'd take daily to maintain the 2 bodies of the same weight, but consisting of different body masses.

Person "A" - 100 lbs.	<u>50</u> Calories burned per day to maintain each pound.
Solid Muscle	5000 Calories burned per day.
Person "B" - 100 lbs.	<u>2</u> Calories burned per day to maintain each pound.
Solid Fat	200 Calories burned per day.

Wow!! A tremendous difference of 4,800 more calories needed daily to maintain 100 pounds of muscle verses 100 pounds of fat. (The all muscle body verses the all fat body.) Of course, it goes without saying there are no bodies made of either all fat or all muscle, but it is an excellent example of how 2 bodies weighing the same can very easily have two totally different calorie needs.

Basil Metabolic Rate - Known as metabolism by a lot of people, is the way each persons' body individually burns energy (calories, fat, etc.) to maintain daily survival.

It's important to remember the number one factor in our build and body make-up is genetic. In other words, we're each born with a genetic blue print based on our ancestors. However, in the blueprint there are some things we can somewhat control by our lifestyle.

Graphic example of the exact same body and that persons potential within his blueprint of life depending on lifestyle chosen.

200 pounds plus
(Never exercises, eats what & when- ever desires to.)

175 pounds
(Eats healthy - just too much. Never exercises.)

155 pounds
(Eats healthy - just too much. Exercises moderately - 3 times per week. 20-30 mins.)

140 pounds
(Eats healthy. Exercises 5 times per week. 30-45 mins.)

130 pounds
(Exercises 30-45 mins. 5 times per week. Eats low calorie & low-fat diet.)

Although each of our body types has its own blue print we do have some control as to where in that blue print we want to be. No matter where we choose to be it will have a price. It's also important to remember that body fat percentages is more important than what number is on the scale, because the scale does not let you know if you are at your ideal weight for your frame, etc.

I strongly encourage people to get their focus off the scale and onto overall health. Isn't it a shame how so many of us base our self worth, how we feel about ourselves or even how good our day is, on what the scale says we weigh? In all honesty - isn't it ridiculous? I know. I've been there. Throwing my scale out and asking myself these questions daily has made a world of difference in releasing the bondage and preoccupation of my weight. It also got me to focus on the real issues - was I eating healthy, and was I treating myself healthy? Important questions we can ask ourselves daily are, "Am I treating myself healthy? Did I eat healthy? Did I take time to exercise? Am I getting enough rest?" Not only is physical health important, but our spiritual, emotional and mental health also. Questions such as, "Am I feeding myself positive thoughts? Am I having a good relationship and communication with God? Am I treating myself good." (Often over weight people tend to be "People Pleasers." Often they treat others better than they treat themselves.)

I've been blessed with two wonderful daughters. The one who looks like me, and has my basil metabolic rate, (poor child!) is the healthiest eater of our family and has a voluptuous body build. My other daughter has her daddy's metabolic rate, eats like a horse and would eat junk food all day if allowed. She has a slender, athletic build. The truth is life is just not fair and we have to do the best we can with what we've got. (Read that before?) The goal is to treat our bodies healthy and be thankful for the bodies we have when we are treating them healthy.

*I encourage my students who are switching to a low-fat lifestyle to not have "my food/low-fat" and "your food/high-fat" at home. What is good for you is good for your family and your children. Wouldn't it have been easier for us if we grew up loving to eat low-fat foods instead of having to make the switch later on in life? For those of you who are concerned your children will not get enough fats or calories check with your children's doctor. I have found that most children will make enough "unhealthy" choices on their own and will get more than enough fat. There is enough fat in just one of most school lunches for a few days! Plus there are healthy high-fat foods they may choose to eat which you & I will normally avoid because they are so "calorie dense" such as peanut butter and nuts.

*Think of fat grams as dollars. As a woman, I try to stick to no more than 20 grams of fats a day. It's easy to keep track of in my mind approximately how many I eat, or should I say spend? One fat gram equals one dollar. Your body only needs 10 grams of fat a day for good health. Ask your doctor how many you should try to stick under. Beware! Just because you're eating low-fat doesn't mean you can go hog wild on sugar. You can get fatter eating low-fat if you chow-down on sugar. It's true sugar has 1/2 the calories gram per gram compared to fats. But sugar is fattening because it's so calorie dense. Beware!

Here are some helpful ideas in doing the low-fat thing.

-Purchase an inexpensive complete and up-to-date fat and calorie counting book titled "FAT BOOK". The one I use is by Avery Publishing Group by Karen J. Bellerson. ISBN# 0-89529-483-4. It costs approximately $5.95. This book list over 25,000 food products by name and in many instances by

brand. Highlight items in the book you like that have less than 3 grams of fat per 100 calories. You will be surprised by the countless foods you like, have been eating and can continue eating that are low in fat and fall within the American Heart Association's guidelines of 30% or less of your daily calories deriving from fat. This simple rule of thumb: 3 fat grams or less per 100 calories will help you stay within those guidelines.

-Write down for your own personal reference what items you highlighted in the FAT BOOK in a handy little writing tablet that you can keep with you in your purse, pocket or car. If you are not already very familiar with your very favorite low-fat foods this will be a quick and handy resource for you.

-Keep eating the foods you love, but modify or substitute. Doing the first two ideas listed will be helpful in allowing you to not feel deprived and will allow you to keep eating the foods you love. A perfect example. Let's say you have a sweet tooth. A lot of so called "diets" would not allow candy, cookies, etc.; but low-fat eating is not a so called "diet". It is a lifestyle change. By writing your personal list of low-fat sweet favorites you've opened your eyes to your healthier food choices. So now when your sweet tooth is driving you nuts, instead of going crazy you'll know from your list of your favorite low-fat sweets what are your healthier choices.

Example of my list for:

Low-fat Candy: Peppermint Patty, Sugar Babies, Sugar Daddy, licorice, Milk Duds, Milky Way Lite, Tootsie Roll, Taffy, 3 Musketeers, Kraft Toffee, Skittles, Starburst Fruit Chews, Kraft Butter Party Mints, Mike & Ike, Gum Drops, Jaw Breakers, Jelly Beans, Junior Mints, Hot Tamales, Life Savers, Tic-Tacs, Breath Saver Mints - Sugar Free, Butterscotch Disc, Candy Corn, Chuckles, Milk Maid Caramels, Jellied Candied, Peppermint Kisses, Red Twist & Red Laces, Sweet Tarts, most hard candies, Dark Chocolate Covered Cherries, Marshmallow eggs and Bit-O-Honey.

Surprised? Hopefully you are "pleasingly surprised!" Isn't it nice to know we can still eat the things we've grown to love and not eat like a rabbit in order to be healthier? Some simple substitutions such as a Milky Way Lite candy bar instead of a Snickers candy bar can save oodles of fat and calories (7 fat grams and 110 calories saved!) Yet, you don't feel deprived. You feel satisfied and you've done your body good. (Or at least better!) However, let us not forget sugar is still fattening if eaten too much. Remember, moderation is the key in not ending up a big fatty.

Parents have told us for years, "Eat your vegetables." Nowadays, if someone does not know vegetables are good for us, they must live under a rock. It's everywhere! I have found it helpful to immediately (after arriving home from the market) to clean, cut and prepare all fresh vegetables and fruits for the week. The saying "out of sight, out of mind" falls true when satisfying our hunger pains also. For most of us, the last thing we feel like doing when we're hungry is peeling a carrot! Please! It's no wonder we probably eat more prepackage junk foods now than ever before. Of course, in our moment of weakness, we grab the prepackaged junk food so beautifully prepared and staring us in the face over the fresh carrot which still lies boring, all dirty, not peeled and unappetizing! I've said all that to say this,

"Cut and clean to be appealing!"

Large ziplock, clear plastic bags are absolutely wonderful for storing visually beautiful and prepared fresh vegetables and fruits. Most vegetables last a good 5 days. Cutting vegetables thicker verses thinner helps them stay fresher longer.

If you don't have a good "one hour" extra per week to prepare these delicious delectables then spend the extra money on already prepared vegetable and fruit snacks. You will pay more (at least double) however, you'll find you are eating a lot more vegetables and fruits. Don't store in drawers of refrigerator where they are out of sight. Instead keep on shelves up front where you will immediately see them.

Keep a wide variety of your favorite fat-free salad dressings on hand and refrigerated in an organized, easily visible spot at all times for using not only as a salad dressing but also as a dip for vegetables and marinade.

Keep fresh, whole fruits (apples, oranges, pears, bananas, etc.) out on the counter for snacks instead of sweets. Fat-free cookies, cakes and treats are usually higher in sugars and lower in actual nutritional value than fruits.

EXERCISE

It's important. Not only physically, but mentally and emotionally. When you take care of yourself, you can't help but feel better about yourself.

WHEN YOU EXERCISE:

♥ Your body releases endorphins which help you feel good and better about yourself.

♥ Energy creates energy - by burning energy when exercising you will feel more energetic afterwards.

♥ You build muscle, which in turn burns more calories throughout the day, than if you had less muscle. (Read page 15).

♥ Helps relieve stress.

♥ Helps fight numerous diseases.

Studies show: People who exercise first thing in the morning are more apt to sticking with it, than those who exercise at other times of the day. It seems like it's happened to all of us at one time or another. We have the best intentions of exercising at such and such a time during the day. Before you know it, our day has blown by, we're tired or exhausted and the last thing we feel like doing is exercising.

How Not to be a Quitter and Stick to Exercising:

♥ Do something aerobically you enjoy. If you don't enjoy it, no matter how wonderful your intentions are, chances are you won't stick to it.

♥ Find something to preoccupy your mind during your exercise. Video a favorite show you can watch when you want to exercise, visit with a friend while exercising, listen to something of interest, read, or be in a prayerful state of mind.

♥ Plan it into your day as a priority. Again, remember, exercising first thing in the morning increases your chances of sticking with it for the long haul.

The Cost Factor

Who ever says buying low-fat or fat-free is not more expensive when grocery shopping verses the cost of regular high-fat foods clearly has not been comparison price shopping. Ounce for ounce, dollar for dollar in most cases it is more expensive to eat fat-free or lower fat if you are not consumer wise. Manufacturers take out the fat and charge you more. It doesn't make sense, but you know what folks? It makes for the manufacturers a lot of dollars!

Item	Super Value	Kroger	Sam's	Aldi's
Frozen veggies	0.89	1.20	1.00	0.79
Canned veggies	0.50	.78	N/A	0.29
Chicken breast	1.99	3.99	2.50	2.30
Eye of round	2.49	3.99	4.29	N/A
Ultra Promise Margarine	1.89	1.69	N/A	N/A
Healthy Choice Cheese	2.39	1.99	N/A	N/A
Film developing (36 exp.)	6.20	5.10	3.24	N/A
Eggs - 1 dozen	0.75	1.09	0.80	0.60
Skim milk	2.29	1.89	1.89	1.89
Yogurt	0.35	0.69	0.50	0.29
Baked Lays Potato Chips	3.29	3.39	2.49	N/A
Baked Tostitos	3.59	3.31	2.69	N/A
Fat-free Frozen Yogurt	1.89	4.99	3.99	N/A

N/A = Not Available.

One way I've saved without using coupons is to make a list of the products I like to use the most. One day take time to comparison shop. Make a list of the 3-4 stores you shop most often. Here's a miniature example of my chart.

MAKE YOUR OWN CHART (FILL IN STORE NAMES).

Item	Store #1	Store #2	Store #3	Store #4
Frozen veggies				
Canned veggies				
Chicken breast				
Eye of round				
Ultra Promise Margarine				
Healthy Choice Cheese				
Film developing (36 exp.)				
Eggs - 1 dozen				
Skim milk				
Yogurt				
Baked Lays Potato Chips				
Baked Tostitos				
Fat-free Frozen Yogurt				

N/A = Not Available.

Once you've filled in on the left column the items you usually use, go to each store and write in the appropriate box how much that product cost usually. See what store has the lowest prices on certain items. Once you've completed your chart when you are at that particular store, which has the lowest price on certain items, stock up. Having a pantry, closet, storage space under the bed and extra freezer space can be helpful, but not necessary. You will not shop at each store weekly. You may only shop 1 or 2 times per month. Then stop in for fresh bread, milk, fresh fruits and vegetables when needed.

The key is to stock up on certain items that you know are lower priced on a regular basis at each individual store. Using the mini chart I've made (on the previous page) as an example you can see which items I get at the designated store.

Super Value - Chicken breast, Eye of round and Frozen Yogurt.

Kroger - Ultra Promise Margarine and Healthy Choice Cheese.

Sam's - Developed film, Baked Lays Potato Crisp and Baked Tostitos.

Aldi's - Frozen vegetables, canned vegetables, eggs and yogurt.

Of course, if a store happens to have something on sale, costing less than I regularly pay for it elsewhere than I stock up.

Shopping this way saves me an estimated 20-30% compared to if I did all of my shopping at one location, plus a lot of time! For busy people - time is something many of us wish we had more of. We can make more money, but we can't make more time. It's important to be smart with both time and money.

SAVING MONEY WITH COUPONS

For those who like doing the "coupon thing" I am going to reprint from my first book, "Down Home Cookin' Without the Down Home Fat" how I've done my coupons. Also the name and phone number of a woman who sells $100.00 plus worth of the coupons you want for only $14.95. If you shop at a store where the coupons are doubled, you just saved yourself $185.00. The neat thing about this, is you get coupons for products you use because you tell them what coupons you want. Again, this saves you time in not having to hunt for the coupons you want.

TURN YOUR GROCERY BILL INTO $AVVY $AVINGS!

How? With Grocery Coupon Certificate Books, YOU SELECT THE COUPONS YOU WANT FOR THE GROCERIES YOU BUY! (from a list of over 1,000 national name brand products). Grocery Coupon Books contain certificates valued at $10 each and the coupons you selected can be redeemed at your favorite grocery store. (Note: these coupons are worth even more if your store doubles or triples coupons!)

FREE BONUS GUIDE: When you order Book II, receive the "Guide to Savvy Savings" absolutely FREE. The Guide offers many valuable shopping tips on how to add value to your coupons, avoid impulse buying, market with children, enjoy stress-free shopping, plus get FREE food - and much more! A $12.95 value FREE when you order Book II!

Complete order form on next page to save on groceries including meat, produce, grains, and dairy.

ORDER FORM

[X] Yes, I want to SAVE BIG at the grocery store!

Please send me:

Book I _____ Grocery Coupon Certificate Book(s) Good for $100 of face value grocery coupons, at $14.95 each. PLUS receive $10 bonus certificate.

Name: _____

Address _____

City: _____ State: _____ Zip: _____

Even greater savings

Mail this order form along with payment to:

Savvy Saver
c/o Dept. C.H.
P.O. Box 205
Portage, OH 43451

Book II _____ Grocery Coupon Certificate Book(s) Good for $200 of face value grocery coupons, at $24.95 each. PLUS receive $20 bonus certificate and "Guide to Savvy Savings" - a $12.95 retail value, yours FREE!

Please add $.75 shipping fee your order. Ohio residents add 6% sales tax.

For the most part, fat-free products are more expensive than their counterparts. I feel it's worth peace of mind and better health to pay the extra cost. When I have time, I do "the coupon thing." For a $5.00 investment, my coupon book has saved me a lot of grief, time, and money. I get so many compliments on my coupon organization and it is a lot less stressful than sorting through them, so I'm sharing it with you. Here's what you'll need:

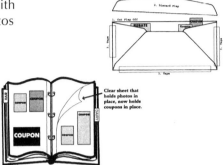

- ♥ 100-page large photo album with clear film sheets that hold photos in place

- ♥ 1 envelope with flap cut off

- ♥ tape

- ♥ coupons

- ♥ tabs (used for filing)

Label tabs individually for easy finding. I label mine: Dairy, Breads, Meats, Fish, Chicken, Cleaning Supplies, Hair Care, etc. Each section will have its own title page. Tape labeled tabs onto outside edge of photo album pages so that you can easily go to any section desired. (Only one tab per page. There will be numerous pages without tabs in each section following title page.)

Put coupons in proper sections.

Cut flap off the envelope. Tape the envelope to the front inside cover of the photo album. Put coupons you've pulled from the designated sections in an envelope for easy storage until check-out time. I also put rebates into the envelope.

Another way to stay within budget is to spend only cash for groceries. On payday keep out in cash exactly what is set aside for your grocery budget until next pay period. This helps our family live within our means. It saves time when picking up only a few items at the grocery store because you don't have to write a check.

Also, for those times when you only need a few items, do not take a cart. Carry the items in your arms or basket. You will be a lot less tempted to impulse buy if your arms are full. Also, select the heaviest thing first. A gallon of milk weights 8 pounds, it's a good first choice. Not only does this idea save you money from spending less on impulsive buying, but it will also save you from possibly purchasing oodles of empty calories you don't need.

WHAT I LIKE TO STOCK IN MY KITCHEN

There are literally hundreds (if not thousands) of fat-free and very low-fat products on the market today. The problem (as I'm sure a lot of you know) is that many do NOT taste good! Once I tried a new fat-free potato chip. Yuck! I'm telling you, the bag it was packaged in had to taste better than the product! It was terrible!

Eating low-fat really shouldn't be a tasteless, boring experience. My motto regarding low-fat foods is, "if it doesn't taste good don't eat it." There are too many delicious choices available for any of us to waste calories on food that doesn't taste good.

Have no fear! The following is a list of products I enjoy using. An asterisk (*) in front of the product means the generic brands of these items are less expensive and good. Look for them in your grocery store, and have confidence they will taste better than the packaging!

An easy rule of thumb when reading labels: if it has more than 3 grams of fat per 100 calories, don't buy it, don't use it, and pitch it! The only time I break that rule is for super lean beef such as:

Type of Beef	Serving Size	Fat Grams	Calories	% Fat Calories
London Broil/Flank Steak	3 oz.	6	167	32%
Top Loin (Lean Only)	3 oz.	6	162	33%
Eye of Round	3 oz.	5	150	30%

(As a steak, roast or have butcher grind for super lean hamburger)

If you enjoy eating red meat and do not want to refrain, then I encourage you to make the switch to ground eye of round. You'll be doing your heart, health, and waistline a lot of good!

The second time I break the rule is when I "choose to wander." An example might be a small piece of chocolate. Remember, this is done very rarely!

(Note: I am not a big fan of fat-free cheeses or margarines, but in my recipes, they taste good.)

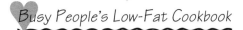

Butter & Margarines

Butter Buds (found in spice or diet section)

Butter-flavored Pan Spray

Non-fat cooking sprays (generic brands are fine)

I Can't Believe It's Not Butter Spray

Ultra Fat-free Promise Margarine

Breads & Grains

Aunt Millie's breads & buns

*Enriched flour

Father Sam's Kangaroo Bread

Flour tortillas fat-free (El Paso and Buena Vista are good)

*Graham crackers

Health Valley fat-free cookies

Health Valley fat-free granola (I use for my homemade granola bars)

*Italian seasoned bread crumbs

Lite breads with 40 calories and no fat per slice (Aunt Millie's, Bunny, and Wonder are good)

Nabisco Reduced Fat Ritz Crackers

*Oyster crackers

*Pastas (except egg noodles; pastas from whole durum wheat are best)

Pillsbury Buttermilk Biscuits

Pillsbury Pizza Crust

Quaker Rice Cakes (caramel and strawberry flavored)

Rice (whole grain enriched)

Rightshape Biscuits (buttermilk flavor)

Vegetable bread

*Whole grain and white rice

*Whole wheat flour

Beverages

*Bottled water (don't be fooled by flavored waters; a lot of them are loaded with sugar and calories)

*Cider

Country Time Lemonade (sugar free)

Crystal Light (sugar free)

Dole fruit juices (100%)

*Grapefruit juice (100%)

Kool-Aid (sugar free)

*Orange juice (100%)

*Prune juice (100%)

Tea (instant or tea bag)

*Tomato juice

Virgin Mary juice

Cheese

(To be honest with you, I do not like fat-free cheese, but used properly in recipes they can taste delicious!)

Borden Fat-Free cheese slices-Sharp Cheddar flavor

Healthy Choice fat-free cheese

*Italian topping (grated)

Kraft Fat-Free cheeses - all flavors

Kraft "Free" Parmesan cheese

Krogers brand of dairy products including frozen

*Parmesan (grated)

Sargenta Fat-Free Ricotta

Condiments

A1 Sauce

*Almond extract

Barbecue Sauces (all - I haven't found one high in fat)

27

Condiments continued

Braum's fat-free fudge topping

*Cocoa

Coconut extract

*Cornstarch

Equal

Evaporated skim milk (Lite)

Heinz 57 Sauce

Hershey's Lite Syrup

Hidden Valley Fat-Free Salad Dressing

Hidden Valley Reduced Calorie Dry Salad Dressing Mix

*Honey

*Karo Syrup

*Ketchup

Kraft Free Mayonnaise and Miracle Whip

Kraft Fat-Free Tartar Sauce

Kroger Fat-Free ice cream toppings

Liquid smoke

*Lite soy sauce

Lite teriyaki marinade

*Lite syrups (I like Mrs. Butterworth's)

*Mint extract

Mrs. Richardson's fat-free ice cream toppings

*Mustard

Not So Sloppy Joe Mix

NutraSweet

*Pam non-fat cooking spray

Preserves and jellies (low sugar)

Seven Seas "Free" Ranch Salad Dressing

Seven Seas "Free" Red Wine Vinegar Salad Dressing

Seven Seas "Free" Viva Italian Salad Dressing

Condiments continued

Smucker's fat-free toppings

T. Marzetti's Fat-Free Raspberry Salad Dressing

*Taco seasoning mix

*Tomato sauce

*Vanilla

Western Fat-Free Salad Dressing

Dairy

Buttermilk (non-fat)

*Cottage cheese (non-fat) (I like all of them)

*Dry powdered milk (non-fat) (best used in recipes - I don't care to drink it)

Eagle brand Fat-Free condensed sweetened milk

Flavorite Fat-Free yogurts and non-fat cottage cheese

Fleishmann's Fat-Free Buttery Spread (comes in a bottle)

Fleishmann's Fat-Free Cheese Spread (comes in a bottle)

Healthy Indulgence (Kroger grocery stores' name brand fat-free cheeses, yogurts, etc.)

Pet Fat-Free evaporated canned skimmed milk

Reddi Wip Fat-Free Whipped Topping

Skim milk

Sour cream-Fat-Free (I like Light & Lively or Land O Lakes)

Yogurts - Fat-Free (watch labels)

Junk Food

Baked Tostitos, Salsa & Cream Cheese, Cool Ranch, and regular flavors

Junk Food continued

*Caramel corn (krack-o-pop (most brands are only 1 fat gram but high in sugar content which is still too much sugar or bars salt to eat a lot of)

Dole fruit & juice bars

Entenmann's fat-free baked goods (Beware! These babies are loaded with sugar!)

Fat-free ice cream

Frito Lay Potato Crisps (new potato chip substitute) (They're delicious - if you like Pringles you'll like these! Only 1.5 grams per 100 calories - about 12 chips)

Frozen fat-free yogurts (T.C.B.Y., Healthy Choice & Kemps)

*Fudge Bars (most are low-fat or fat-free)

Health Valley fat-free tarts

Hostess "Lite" twinkies, cupcakes, brownies, and muffins (all flavors) (It's hard to believe they're really low fat.)

Jello fat-free pudding and pudding cups

Keebler Elfin Delights

Little Debbie's Lite Oatmeal Pies and Brownies

*Marshmallows

*Marshmallow Creme

Pepperidge Farm Fat-Free Brownies and Blondies (too good!)

Pop Secret Popcorn Bars

*Popsicles - all

*Pretzels

Quaker low-fat granola

Rice cakes (Quaker strawberry, rice, corn & caramel flavored)

Richard Simmons cookies

Junk Food continued

Smart Pop microwave popcorn (Orville Redenbacker)

Snack Well's cookies, tarts and breakfast bars

Super Pretzels - soft pretzels

Sweet Escapes Candies (by Hershey's)

*Welch's frozen juice bars

Meats, Fish, Poultry

Beef (eye of round, London broil, flank steak, top lion)

ButterBall Fat-Free sausage, turkey breast and lunchmeats

Canadian bacon (usually very low in fat)

Chicken breast (no skin; dark meat has twice as much fat!)

Crab meat flake or stick (imitation)

Eckrich fat-free meats (hot dogs, lunch meats, smoked sausage, kielbasa)

Fish (the white ones are lower in fats; i.e., flounder, grouper, pike, sole, cod, orange roughy, monk fish, perch, scallops)

Healthy Choice lunch meat, hot dogs and smoked sausage

Hillshire Farms Fat-Free smoked sausage & kielbasa

Hotdogs - Healthy Choice - 1 fat gram; Hormel Light & Lean - 1 fat gram; Oscar Mayer Fat-Free

MorningStar Ground Meatless (for chilis, pasta sauces, etc., but not alone as a burger)

Shellfish (Lobster, Crab, Shrimp)

*Tuna (packed in water)

Turkey breast (no skin; dark meat has twice as much fat!)

Pre-Packaged Items

*Applesauce (sugar-free is lower in calories)

Betty Crocker "Lite" Cake,

Brownie, Bread & Muffin mixes

*Bouillon cubes (chicken, beef, and vegetable flavors)

Healthy Choice low-fat frozen meals

Hot chili beans (I like Brook's)

Nestle's Fat-Free, sugar free

hot chocolate

Simply potatoes shredded hashbrowns (found in refrigerator section)

Swiss Miss Fat-Free, sugar free hot chocolate

Fruits and Veggies

*Canned vegetables - no salt added

*Canned fruits in fruit juice only

*Cranberry sauce

Fresh vegetables - all (except for avocado - major fat!!)

*Frozen vegetables and fruits - all - with no sugar added

*Lite fruit cocktail

*Lite pie fillings - cherry, apple, and blueberry

Other Items

*Bac-O's (imitation bacon bits)

Betty Crocker Reduced Fat Sweet Rewards Cake Mix

Campbell's Healthy Request low-fat & fat-free soups

Chef Boy-R-Dee Spaghetti O's

Cool Whip Free

Dream Whip

Eggs (use only the whites)

Other Items continued

*Egg Beaters

Gold Medal Fudge Brownie Mix

Healthy Indulgence (Kroger's name brand) fat-free cheeses, yogurts, etc,)

Health Valley Chili and Soups

Healthy Choice soups and sauces (low- and no-fat)

*Instant mashed potatoes

Jiffy cake mixes

*Legumes (Beans - canned or dry variety and lentils)

Martha Whites's Lite mixes (muffins, etc.)

Nabisco's "Royal" Lite Cheesecake mixes

Old El Paso fat-free refried beans

*Pancake and buttermilk pancake mix

*Pasta

Pillsbury Lovin' Lites frostings

Progresso "Healthy Classics" soups

Special K Fat-free Waffles

*Stuffing mixes (look for brands that have only 2 fat grams per serving as packaged)

Sauces

Campbell's Healthy Request low-fat & fat-free sauces

Healthy Choice Spaghetti Sauce

Heinz Homestyle Lite gravies (in a jar)

Hunts "Light" fat-free pasta sauce

Pepperidge Farm Stroganoff Gravy

Prego spaghetti and pizza sauce (Lite ones)

Ragu Lite "Garden Harvest & "Tomato & Herb"

Ragu Pizza Quick Sauce

Ragu Today's Recipe spaghetti sauces (low fat)

Back To Basics

So many of my students don't have a clue how to convert many of their old "high fat" favorites to delicious "low-fat" favorites. Everyone is absolutely correct when they complain many fat-free products don't taste good. However, there are many that do!

This section is chock full of "Back to Basic" recipes you might have thought you could no longer enjoy while following a low-fat lifestyle! Hopefully, you'll be pleasingly surprised - even amazed - at how delicious these simple basic foods can still be even while low-fat!

SCRAMBLED EGGS

Budget Friendly

Recipe

*Every bit as good as the high fat ones
you remember your parents making as a child.*

4 egg whites plus 2 drops yellow food coloring (or ½ cup Egg Beaters)
1 tablespoon skim milk

1 teaspoon dry Molly McButter (or Butter Buds Sprinkles)
dash of lite salt
dash of pepper

♥ Spray a non-stick skillet with non-fat cooking spray.

♥ With a fork, briskly beat all ingredients together until well blended. Pour into prepared pan and cook over medium heat, stirring constantly with a spatula until fully cooked.

Yield: 1 serving

Calories: 78   Total Fat: 0 grams (0% fat)
Cholesterol: 0 mg   Sodium: 247 mg

Total preparation and cooking time: 5 minutes or less.

FRENCH TOAST

A sweet tooth breakfast favorite.

Budget Friendly
Recipe

1 cup Egg Beaters (or 8 egg whites with a couple drops of yellow food coloring)

²/₃ cup skim milk

8 slices fat-free bread (I use Aunt Millie)

♥ Spray a non-stick skillet or griddle with non-fat cooking spray and preheat to medium-high heat.

♥ With a fork, briskly beat Egg Beaters (or egg whites with yellow food coloring) with skim milk until well mixed.

♥ Dip bread slices (one at a time) into egg mixture.

♥ Arrange dipped bread slices on prepared griddle (or skillet) making sure edges of bread do not touch. Cook until bottom is golden brown. Turn over and continue cooking until golden brown. Serve hot (2 slices per serving) with 1 teaspoon powdered sugar, 1 tablespoon light maple syrup, and up to 10 sprays of "I Can't Believe It's Not Butter" Spray.

Yield: 4 servings

Calories: 185   Total Fat: 0 grams (0% fat)
Cholesterol: 1 mg   Sodium: 444 mg

Total preparation and cooking time: 7 minutes or less.

Menu ideas: ¹/₂ grapefruit, fruit cup or orange slices, coffee or herbal tea.

People read newspapers - not minds. So tell each other your wants, needs and desires.

GRILLED CHEESE SANDWICH

Budget Friendly

Recipe

If you like a "cheesier" sandwich, use 2 slices of cheese.

10 sprays "I Can't Believe It's Not Butter" spray

2 slices fat-free bread (I use Aunt Millie)

1 slice fat-free cheese (Kraft and Kroger brands are good)

♥ Preheat a griddle or skillet to medium-high heat and spray with non-fat cooking spray.

♥ Spray 5 sprays of "I Can't Believe It's Not Butter" spray on one side of each slice of bread.

♥ Lay buttered side of bread on griddle or skillet.

♥ Lay cheese on top of bread.

♥ Lay second slice of bread on top of cheese with buttered side facing up.

♥ Cook on medium-high heat until bottom is golden brown.

♥ Turn over. Continue cooking until bottom is golden brown.

Yield: 1 serving

Calories: 156   Total Fat: 0 grams (0% fat)
Cholesterol: 0 mg   Sodium: 478 mg

Total preparation and cooking time: 3 minutes or less.

Menu ideas: A piece of fresh fruit, Baked Lays potato crisps (taste like Pringles potato chips) and fresh vegetable sticks. Or tomato soup, made with skim milk, and fresh vegetable sticks.

*GRILLED HAM & CHEESE OR GRILLED TURKEY & CHEESE:
Cook exactly the same except heat extra lean ham or turkey on griddle just enough to warm. Place on cheese before putting second slice of bread on top of cheese. Continue cooking as directed above.

Yield: 1 serving

Calories: 193   Total Fat: 1.4 grams (7% fat)
Cholesterol: 13 mg   Sodium: 883 mg

ALL AMERICAN HAMBURGER

Budget
Friendly

Recipe

*One bite of this and you'll never want to
eat another "fatty" burger again!*

3 ounces ground eye of round
beef, lean meat only (this is not
ground round!)

♥ Cook as you would a regular hamburger on the grill, broiler or skillet
to your desired doneness. Or ½ pound ground eye of round combined
with ½ pound ground extra lean turkey breast (no skin or dark meat).
Make into 3 ounce patties. Cook thoroughly.

Ground eye of round, cooked:
3 ounce serving = 4 grams of fat per 141 calories, 27% fat

Verses regular ground beef, cooked:
3 ounce serving = 17 grams of fat per 248 calories, 60% fat

WOW!!! Save 13 grams of fat and 107 calories per sandwich!
Simply substituting a leaner beef can make a big difference in saving
fat grams!

Yield: 1 (3-ounce) burger (using eye of round beef)

Calories: 141   Total Fat: 4.0 grams (27% fat)
Cholesterol: 59 mg   Sodium: 53 mg

(using turkey and eye of round beef combination)
Calories: 126   Total Fat: 2.6 grams (19% fat)
Cholesterol: 62 mg   Sodium: 48 mg

*CHEESE BURGERS:
Same as hamburgers and top with Kraft fat-free cheese slices.

Yield: 1 (3-ounce) burger (using eye of round beef)

Calories: 171   Total Fat: 4.0 grams (22% fat)
Cholesterol: 61 mg   Sodium: 343 mg

(using turkey and eye of round beef combination)
Calories: 156   Total Fat: 2.6 grams (16% fat)
Cholesterol: 65 mg   Sodium: 338 mg

Total preparation time: 10 minutes or less.

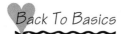

OMELETS

Budget
Friendly

Recipe

A hearty breakfast that is good for the heart!

4 egg whites plus 2 drops yellow food coloring (or ½ cup Egg Beaters)

½ teaspoon dry Butter Buds Sprinkles (or Molly McButter Sprinkles)

1 tablespoon skim milk

dash of lite salt

dash of pepper

1 slice fat-free cheese - your favorite flavor (I use Kraft or Kroger brand)

♥ With a fork, beat all ingredients (except cheese) until well blended but not frothy or foamy.

♥ Spray a 6- to 8-inch non-stick skillet with non-fat cooking spray. Add egg mixture and cook over medium heat.

♥ As eggs set, run a spatula along the outside edge of where the eggs touch the skillet, lifting the eggs just enough to let the uncooked egg mixture flow underneath. When eggs are set but still shiny, remove from heat.

♥ Place cheese slice on half of the omelet. Fold the other half of the omelet over. (Onto the first half with the cheese on it.) Cover for one minute to allow the heat of the omelet to melt cheese.

Yield: 1 omelet

Calories: 90   Total Fat: 0 grams (0% fat)
Cholesterol: 0 mg   Sodium: 392 mg

Preparation time: 2 minutes or less.

Cooking time: 3 minutes or less.

Total time: 5 minutes or less.

Menu ideas: Fat-free toast and fresh fruit cup.

HAM & CHEESE OMELET:
Microwave 1 ounce of fat-free ham lunchmeat, chopped, for 10 seconds (or until warm). Place cooked ham pieces over cheese before folding in half.

Yield: 1 omelet

Calories: 111   Total Fat: 0 grams (0% fat)
Cholesterol: 9 mg   Sodium: 706 mg

(Omelets continued)

MUSHROOM OR VEGETABLE OMELET:
Microwave ¼ cup any combination of your favorite vegetables (onion, green peppers, mushrooms, etc.) for 20 seconds in 1 tablespoon chicken broth. Drain off any excess juice from vegetables before placing on cheese and folding omelet in half.

Yield: 1 omelet

Calories: 101   Total Fat: 0 grams   (0% fat)
Cholesterol: 0 mg   Sodium: 414 mg

FRENCH FRIES

Budget Friendly

Recipe

Childrens' favorite way to eat their vegetables!

4 potatoes - your favorite type of potato   Non-fat cooking spray

- ♥ Preheat oven to 425 degrees.
- ♥ Spray cookie sheet with non-fat cooking spray. Set aside.
- ♥ Cut potatoes into long strips, ¼-inch thickness.
- ♥ Lay potatoes on cookie sheet. Do not let edges touch.
- ♥ Spray tops of potatoes with non-fat cooking spray.
- ♥ Bake at 425 degrees for 20 minutes. Turn fries over. Bake another 15 to 20 minutes. Fries will be crispy and golden when done.

Yield: 4 servings

Calories: 133   Total Fat: 0 grams   (0% fat)
Cholesterol: 0 mg   Sodium: 10 mg

SEASONED FRIES:
Make the same but sprinkle with Lawry's seasoned salt after you have sprayed the tops with non-fat cooking spray.

Yield: 4 servings

Total preparation time: 40 minutes or less.

37

HOT DOGS

Budget Friendly

Recipe

Now this is how an "All American Hot Dog" should be!
Fun to eat and healthy, too!

Healthy Choice hot dogs
Aunt Millie fat-free hot dog buns

Fat-free cheese (Kraft and Kroger brands are good)

♥ Cook as you normally would a regular hot dog using a grill or microwave, or boil. Top each hot dog with ½ slice of cheese.

♥ Add mustard, relish, onions, ketchup and/or sauerkraut.

Yield: 1 hot dog

Calories: 162   Total Fat: 1.5 grams (8% fat)
Cholesterol: 20 mg   Sodium: 723 mg

*CHILI DOG:
Top with 2 tablespoons Healthy Valley fat-free chili

Yield: 1 chili dog

Calories: 192   Total Fat: 1.5 grams (7% fat)
Cholesterol: 20 mg   Sodium: 763 mg

Preparation time: 5 minutes or less.

SUNDAES

Budget Friendly

Recipe

If only grandma could've known it could be so good -
and not terribly bad for you either!

½ cup fat-free ice cream or frozen yogurt
1 tablespoon fat-free ice cream topping (Hershey's light is good)

2 tablespoons fat-free Reddi Wip
1 maraschino cherry

♥ Top ice cream (or frozen yogurt) with topping, Reddi Wip and maraschino cherry.

Yield: 1 sundae

Calories: 205   Total Fat: 0.3 grams (1% fat)
Cholesterol: 0 mg   Sodium: 85 mg

Preparation time: 5 minutes or less.

Breakaway Breakfast Items

PREFACE FOR OATMEAL RECIPES

♥ When it comes to serving something deliciously warm and smooth on a cold winter's morning, there's nothing like a bowl of hot oatmeal. My flavored oatmeals just give those morning moments an extra special touch!

♥ The fat content of these recipes is very low, most of the fat coming from that naturally occurring in the oatmeal itself. So go ahead, treat yourself to a nice, warm bowl of oatmeal without any guilt and enjoy!

CHERRY OATMEAL

Budget Friendly Recipe

The slight tartness of the cherries is a pleasant fruity surprise. Children especially like this fruity oatmeal.

6 cups water
¼ teaspoon salt - optional
3 cups old fashioned oats
1 teaspoon almond extract

1 (21-ounce) can lite cherry pie filling (Thank You brand)
*¾ cup Domino strawberry-flavored powdered sugar

♥ Bring water and salt to a boil on high heat in a large pan (Dutch oven). Add oats. Reduce heat to medium, but keep the oatmeal boiling for 5 minutes, stirring occasionally.

♥ After 5 minutes, remove from heat. Add almond extract, cherry pie filling and strawberry flavored powdered sugar*. Stir until well mixed. Cover. Let sit for 2 minutes longer. Serve immediately while hot.

♥ (Some people may like theirs sweeter. I set sugar on the table so each person can sweeten their own oatmeal as desired.)

Yield: 7 (1-cup) servings

Calories: 253   Total fat: 2.9 grams (10% fat)
Cholesterol: 0 mg   Sodium: 9 mg

Total time: 10 minutes or less.

Menu ideas: Tea, coffee, or skim milk.

If you don't have strawberry-flavored powdered sugar, regular powdered sugar will be fine.

COCONUT CREAM OATMEAL

Budget
Friendly

Recipe

*This hearty, stick to your bones, breakfast
is a special treat with it's creamy toasted coconut flavor.
It's a great way to start a cold day!*

2 tablespoons coconut - flaked
(found in baking section of
store)
¼ teaspoon lite salt - optional
4 cups water
2 cups quick cooking oats

½ cup fat-free sweetened
condensed skim milk
(I use Eagle Brand)
1 teaspoon coconut extract
(found in spice section of store)

♥ Broil coconut on a cookie sheet for 15 seconds or until toasty brown. Set aside.

♥ Bring salt and water to a boil in a medium-size pan. Add oats. Cook for 1 minute, stirring occasionally.

♥ Remove from heat. Stir in sweetened condensed milk, coconut extract and toasted coconut. Stir until all ingredients are well blended.

♥ Cover. Let sit for 2 to 3 minutes. Oatmeal will thicken as it sits, yet it will have a creamy consistency to it.

♥ Serve warm.

Yield: 4 (1-cup) servings

Calories: 277   Total fat: 4.0 grams (13% fat)
Cholesterol: 2 mg   Sodium: 52 mg

Total time: 7 minutes or less.

Menu ideas: ½ of a grapefruit, skim milk, tea or coffee.

PEACHES & CREAM OATMEAL

Budget
Friendly

Recipe

The slight tartness and gentle texture of the peaches combined with the sweet creamy oatmeal gives this a unique and tasty flavor.

4 cups water
dash of lite salt - optional
½ cup finely chopped dried
   peaches (I use Sunsweet)
2 cups quick-cooking oats

½ cup fat-free sweetened
   condensed skim milk (I use
   Eagle Brand)
1 teaspoon vanilla

♥ In a medium-size pan on high heat, bring water and salt to a boil.

♥ Reduce heat to low. Stir in peaches and oats. Let cook one minute.

♥ Turn off heat. Stir in sweetened condensed milk and vanilla. Cover. Let sit for 3 minutes.

Yield: 5 (1-cup) servings

Calories: 253   Total fat: 2.2 grams (8% fat)
Cholesterol: 2 mg   Sodium: 35 mg

Total time: 7 minutes or less.

Menu ideas: Fresh sliced peaches or oranges on the side, skim milk, tea or coffee.

CRAN-APPLE OATMEAL

Budget Friendly Recipe

This will wake up your taste buds!!
The sweet tartness adds a zesty touch to an
old time breakfast favorite.

2½ cups apple cider
1½ cups quick cooking oats

⅓ cup sweetened dried
cranberries (by Ocean Spray)

♥ In a medium-size pan bring apple cider to a boil.

♥ Add the oats and dried cranberries. Let cook for one minute. Turn off heat.

♥ Cover. Let sit for 3 minutes.

Yield: 3 servings

Calories: 296   Total fat: 2.9 grams (9% fat)
Cholesterol: 0 mg   Sodium: 8 mg

Total time: 7 minutes or less.

Menu ideas: Skim milk, tea or coffee.

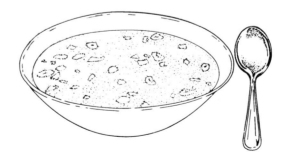

BANANA CREAM OATMEAL

Budget
Friendly

Recipe

*If you like Banana Cream Pie, you'll love this!
It's my daughter Ashley's favorite of all my
different flavored oatmeals.*

4 cups water
2 cups quick cooking oats (get a brand of oats that cook in one minute)

2 medium bananas - sliced thinly into 1/8- to 1/4-inch pieces
1/2 cup fat-free Eagle Brand sweetened condensed skim milk (2/5th's of a can)

♥ In medium-size saucepan bring water to a boil over high heat.

♥ Once boiling, reduce heat to medium. Add quick oats and cook for 1 minute, stirring occasionally.

♥ Remove from heat. Add banana slices and sweetened condensed skim milk.

♥ Cover and let sit for 2 to 3 minutes. Oatmeal will thicken as it sits.

♥ Serve warm.

Yield: 4 (1½-cup) servings

Calories: 320   Total fat: 2.8 grams (8% fat)
Cholesterol: 2 mg   Sodium: 42 mg

Total time: 7 minutes or less.

Menu ideas: Skim milk, tea or coffee.

44

CINNAMON DROPS

Budget
Friendly

Recipe

Move over traditional fatty cinnamon rolls,
Cinnamon Drops are here!

½ cup sugar

2 tablespoons ground cinnamon

2 (7.5-ounce) cans Pillsbury
buttermilk biscuits (10 per roll -
found in refrigerator section)

¼ cup Fleischmann's Fat-Free
Buttery Spread

2 tablespoons low-fat frosting
(Betty Crocker Creamy Deluxe)
- optional

♥ Preheat oven to 350 degrees.

♥ Spray a 9 x 13-inch pan with non-fat cooking spray.

♥ Mix sugar and cinnamon together in a cereal bowl. Set aside.

♥ Cut each biscuit into quarters.

♥ Put a little dab of buttery spread on each biscuit piece. Coat with
cinnamon-sugar mixture.

♥ Set coated dough pieces in prepared pan with pieces touching each
other. Some overlapping will occur. If there is any leftover cinnamon-
sugar, sprinkle it over dough in pan.

♥ Bake at 350 degrees for 15 minutes.

♥ Optional - Microwave frosting a few seconds, just long enough to melt
frosting into a glaze. Drizzle glaze over cinnamon drops. Let cool a
couple of minutes before eating.

Yield: 7 breakfast entrée servings

Calories: 236   Total fat: 2.8 grams (10% fat)
Cholesterol: 0 mg   Sodium: 525 mg

16 side dish servings

Calories: 103   Total fat: 1.2 grams (10% fat)
Cholesterol: 0 mg   Sodium: 230 mg

Total time: 20 minutes or less.

Menu ideas: Terrific for brunch buffets,
or on the side for a special breakfast instead of toast.

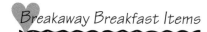
Mm! (Possibly the world's shortest published recipe title)

Budget Friendly Recipe

This scrumptious crumb cake makes an excellent breakfast cake, coffee cake, snack cake or dessert!

1 (18.25-ounce) box Betty Crocker Reduced Fat Sweet Rewards yellow cake mix, dry (do not make as directed on box) - divided

1 (10-ounce) package frozen strawberries - thawed
1 (8-ounce) package fat-free cream cheese - softened (I used Healthy Choice)

♥ Preheat oven to 350 degrees.

♥ Set aside 1 cup of dry cake mix.

♥ Line a 9x13-inch pan with foil. (For easier clean-up). Spray lined pan with non-fat cooking spray.

♥ With mixer on low speed, beat together strawberries and cream cheese for 1 minute.

♥ Add ½ of the remaining cake mix to cream mixture and continue beating until well mixed, then add remaining cake mix. (Do not use the 1 cup reserved!) Beat for 2 minutes on medium speed.

♥ Spread into prepared pan. Sprinkle the 1 cup reserved cake mix on top of batter.

♥ Bake at 350 degrees for 30 minutes or until a knife inserted in center comes out clean.

Yield: 15 servings

Calories: 160   Total fat: 1.9 grams (11% fat)
Cholesterol: 1 mg   Sodium: 282 mg

 Preparation time: 10 minutes or less.

Baking time: 30 minutes.

Total time: 40 minutes or less.

Menu ideas: Tea, coffee, skim milk and a piece of fruit.

MAN-HANDLER BREAKFAST BAKE

Budget
Friendly

Recipe

*This is an excellent "whip it up fast" entrée that
is perfect for a hearty breakfast or brunch,
without numerous pans and skillets!*

3 (8-ounce) cartons Egg Beaters (I use Kroger Break-Free)
1 (8-ounce) package Kroger Healthy Indulgence fat-free shredded pizza cheese (a blend of non-fat mozzarella and non-fat cheddar cheese)

$\frac{1}{2}$ pound Canadian bacon, thinly sliced and cut into bite-size pieces. (Oscar Mayer 93% Fat-Free)
1 (7.5-ounce) can Pillsbury buttermilk biscuits (10 biscuits per roll)

♥ Preheat oven to 350 degrees.

♥ Spray a 9x13-inch pan with non-fat cooking spray.

♥ In a bowl, mix Egg Beaters, cheese and Canadian bacon. Set aside.

♥ Arrange biscuits on bottom of prepared pan.

♥ Pour egg mixture over biscuits. (You may need to press the biscuits down so they are covered with the egg, cheese and Canadian bacon mixture.)

♥ Bake at 350 degrees for 30 minutes or until knife inserted in center comes out clean.

♥ Serve hot.

♥ If desired, sprinkle sparingly with lite salt.

Yield: 6 large servings

Calories: 243   Total fat: 2.5 grams (10% fat)
Cholesterol: 24 mg   Sodium: 1310 mg

Preparation time: 5 minutes or less.

Baking time: 30 minutes.

Total time: 35 minutes or less.

Menu ideas: Fruit cup, skim milk, coffee or tea.

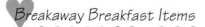

BROCCOLI, HAM & CHEESE FRITTATA

This hearty frittata is good for breakfast, lunch or dinner!

Budget Friendly Recipe

¼ cup finely chopped red onion
  (or ¼ cup frozen chopped onion)
½ pound turkey ham, chopped
¾ (12 to 16-ounce) bag frozen
  broccoli

9 egg whites
2 drops yellow food coloring
½ cup fat-free fancy shredded
  cheddar cheese (I use Healthy
  Choice)

♥ Dash of Lawry's seasoned salt - optional

♥ Preheat oven to 350 degrees.

♥ Spray a large skillet with non-fat cooking spray. (A Teflon non-stick skillet works best but is not necessary).

♥ Cook onion and ham 2 to 3 minutes over medium heat. Microwave broccoli 3 minutes. Beat egg whites and yellow food coloring about 100 strokes. Put broccoli into pan with ham and onion. Pour eggs over mixture in pan. Cook on low heat for 3 minutes.

♥ Sprinkle with cheese. Spray non-fat cooking spray over cheese. (It helps the cheese to not get tough or chewy and makes it melt better.)

♥ Bake at 350 degrees about 5 to 8 minutes or until eggs are fully cooked. Sprinkle with Lawry's seasoned salt if desired. Serve hot. Cut frittata into thirds.

Yield: 3 servings

Calories: 193   Total fat: 3.4 grams (16% fat)
Cholesterol: 57 mg   Sodium: 1168 mg

Preparation time: 6 minutes.

Cooking time: 14 minutes or less.

Total time: 20 minutes or less.

Menu ideas: Great for breakfast, brunch or lunch. Serve with fat-free toast, jam and fresh melon; Cucumber Dill Salad (page 108) or Blueberry Crumb Cake (page 53).

BLUEBERRY CUSTARD BAKE

Budget Friendly

Recipe

*Serve as an elegant entrée
for a special breakfast or brunch.*

1 (3.4-ounce) package instant
  vanilla pudding mix
  (I use Jell-O brand)
16 egg whites
  (or 2 cups Egg Beaters)

1 cup blueberries
½ (10-ounce) jar blueberry
  spreadable fruit
  (I use Smuckers Simply Fruit)

♥ Preheat oven to 350 degrees.

♥ Spray a 9x13-inch casserole dish with non-fat cooking spray. Set aside.

♥ Beat pudding mix with egg whites for 5 minutes on high with mixer. Pour into prepared casserole dish.

♥ Bake at 350 degrees for 30 minutes.

♥ In the meantime, heat blueberries and blueberry preserves in a saucepan over low heat.

♥ Let dessert cool 2 minutes before cutting. Cut into 8 squares. Serve hot with a few hot tablespoonfuls of blueberry sauce served on top. Allow the sauce to flow over the top and down the sides of each serving.

Yield: 8 entrée servings

Calories: 119 Total fat: 0 grams   (0% fat)
Cholesterol: 0 mg Sodium: 292 mg

15 side dish servings

Calories: 63 Total fat: 0 grams (0% fat)
Cholesterol: 0 mg Sodium: 156 mg

Preparation time: 8 minutes or less.

Baking time: 30 minutes.

Total time: 38 minutes or less.

*Menu ideas: Cinnamon Rolls (page 50),
fruit cup, skim milk, coffee or tea.*

CINNAMON ROLLS (MINI SIZE)

Budget
Friendly

These cinnamon rolls aren't too sweet, they're just right!

Recipe

1 (10-ounce) can Pillsbury Pizza Crust (found in refrigerator section - just unroll)

2 tablespoons 70% Low-Fat Promise margarine (3 grams fat per tablespoon, not the Fat-Free Ultra Promise)

⅓ cup sugar

2 teaspoons ground cinnamon

1 tablespoon low-fat vanilla frosting (I use Betty Crocker)

♥ Preheat oven to 375 degrees.

♥ Spray a jelly roll pan (17x 11-inch cookie sheet with 1-inch edge) with non-fat cooking spray.

♥ Roll dough out in jelly roll pan. Press dough out with hands until dough touches edges of pan.

♥ Microwave margarine until melted.

♥ Drizzle melted margarine over dough. With fingertips spread melted margarine over dough evenly.

♥ Mix sugar and cinnamon together and sprinkle ⅔ of the sugar-cinnamon mixture over melted margarine.

♥ Roll up dough, (jelly roll style) beginning from the longest side.

♥ With fingers, pinch the seam of the dough to seal.

♥ Cut into 12 pieces. This is easy to do with a scissors.

♥ Spray 12 mini muffin tins with non-fat cooking spray. (Regular size muffin tins work fine also).

♥ Place one mini roll into each muffin tin.

♥ Sprinkle remaining sugar-cinnamon mixture evenly on tops.

♥ Bake at 375 degrees for 15 minutes.

♥ Microwave frosting for a few seconds and immediately drizzle frosting lightly on top of cinnamon rolls.

♥ Let cool one to two minutes before eating.

Yield: 12 servings

Calories: 99   Total fat: 2.8 grams (25% fat)
Cholesterol: 0 mg   Sodium: 148 mg

(Cinnamon Rolls continued)

Preparation time: 10 minutes or less.

Baking time: 15 minutes or less.

Total time: 25 minutes or less.

Menu ideas: Brunch, breakfast buffets, showers, or special holidays.

BREAKFAST BURRITO

Budget
Friendly

Recipe

*Move over McDonalds! I've created my own breakfast
burrito that's fast and easy to prepare. It's delicious and a
lot lower in fat and calories than yours. (These can be made in
advance, refrigerated, and rewarmed in the microwave when needed.)*

½ pound Healthy Choice kielbasa
 - diced into tiny pieces
8 egg whites
¼ cup chunky salsa

½ cup fat-free fancy shredded
  cheddar cheese (I use Healthy
  Choice)
10 fat-free soft flour tortillas (I use
  Buena Vida)

♥ In a large non-stick skillet, heat diced kielbasa 3 to 4 minutes over medium-high heat.

♥ Beat egg whites and chunky salsa together. Cook egg-salsa mixture with kielbasa as you would scrambled eggs, stirring every 30 seconds. When eggs are completely cooked, yet still slightly damp, stir in cheddar cheese. Cook about 30 seconds more to melt cheese.

♥ Microwave tortillas 10 to 30 seconds or until soft and warm.

♥ Fill the middle of each tortilla with the prepared egg mixture. Fold as you would a burrito. Presto! You're done!

Yield: 10 servings

Calories: 163   Total fat: 0.6 grams (3% fat)
Cholesterol: 9 mg   Sodium: 649 mg

Total time: 10 minutes or less.

Menu ideas: Orange, coffee or tea.

CHERRY PIZZA

Budget
Friendly

Recipe

*Delicious fresh out of the oven or served
at room temperature. The perfect ringer for those who like
to eat pizza for breakfast! (Great for dessert, too!)*

1 (10-ounce) can Pillsbury pizza crust (found in refrigerator section - just unroll)
1 (21-ounce) can cherry pie filling
¼ cup "I Can't Believe It's Not Butter" non-fat spread

1 (20-ounce) package cherry-oatmeal crunch mix - (I use Calhoun Bend Mill brand - found in baking supplies section)
¼ cup low-fat Betty Crocker Creamy Deluxe vanilla frosting

- ♥ Preheat oven to 425 degrees.
- ♥ Spray a jelly roll pan (17x 11-inch cookie sheet with 1-inch edge) with non-fat cooking spray.
- ♥ With hands, press pizza crust evenly to cover entire pan.
- ♥ Spread cherry pie filling evenly over crust.
- ♥ With a knife, cut non-fat spread into cherry oatmeal crunch mix until mixture has a crumbly consistency with no pieces being larger than pea size.
- ♥ Sprinkle crumb mixture evenly over pie filling.
- ♥ Bake at 425 degrees for 12 minutes or until crust is golden brown and top is slightly crunchy.
- ♥ Microwave frosting for a few seconds or until just melted.
- ♥ Drizzle frosting over Cherry Pizza. Let cool a few minutes before serving.

Yield: 15 servings

Calories: 244   Total fat: 2.1 grams (15% fat)
Cholesterol: 0 mg   Sodium: 248 mg

Preparation time: 10 minutes or less.

Baking time: 12 minutes or less.

Total time: 22 minutes or less.

Blueberry Pizza: Follow directions exactly but substitute blueberry pie filling instead of cherry pie filling.

Menu ideas: Skim milk, tea or coffee. Scrambled no-fat eggs (see "Back to Basics" Section.) Good for breakfast buffets, brunches or luncheons.

BLUEBERRY CRUMB CAKE

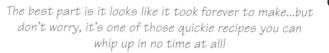

Budget Friendly

Recipe

The best part is it looks like it took forever to make...but don't worry, it's one of those quickie recipes you can whip up in no time at all!

1 (18.25-ounce) package Betty Crocker Reduced Fat Sweet Rewards yellow cake mix - dry - divided

4 egg whites

1 (21-ounce) can blueberry pie filling - divided

♥ Preheat oven to 350 degrees.

♥ Spray two (8-inch) round cake pans with non-fat cooking spray.

♥ Set aside ½ cup of dry cake mix to use later.

♥ Beat egg whites with mixer on low speed for 30 seconds.

♥ Add 1¼ cups blueberry pie filling and cake mix (except for the ½ cup you set aside earlier) to egg whites and beat on medium speed for 2 minutes.

♥ Spread batter into prepared pans.

♥ Sprinkle remaining dry cake mix evenly on top of batter in both pans.

♥ Bake at 350 degrees for 28 minutes or until a knife inserted in center comes out clean.

♥ When eating as a dessert (if desired), put a dab of remaining blueberry pie filling on top of each serving.

Yield: 16 servings

Calories: 174   Total fat: 1.9 grams (10% fat)
Cholesterol: 0 mg   Sodium: 219 mg

Preparation time: 7 minutes.

Baking time: 28 minutes.

Total time: 35 minutes.

Menu ideas: This festive crumb cake is terrific for breakfast in the morning, or light enough for a dessert after a heavy meal.

TINY TURNOVERS

Budget Friendly Recipe

Once thought of as a "dieters nightmare", these crispy pastries will satisfy anybody's light and flaky sweet tooth! Although these are extremely easy to make, please note this recipe makes a lot. Making so many is time consuming. You may prefer to make only a dozen at a time, or only half the recipe.

1 (16-ounce) package filo dough pastry sheets (I use Athens Food brand - found in freezer section)
1 (8-ounce) bottle "I Can't Believe It's Not Butter" spray

1 (21-ounce) can blueberry pie filling (or cherry or strawberry)
Sugar

♥ Allow filo to thaw in package in refrigerator.

♥ Preheat oven to 350 degrees.

♥ Carefully unroll filo sheets onto a smooth, dry surface.

♥ Cut filo sheets into 4 strips.

♥ Preparing only one strip at a time, spray strip with 3 sprays of "I Can't Believe It's Not Butter" spray.

♥ Continue using only one filo sheet strip at a time; put half of a heaping teaspoon (to 1 level teaspoon) of pie filling about one inch from the bottom of the strip.

♥ Carefully fold corner of filo diagonally across and over the pie filling to opposite edge to form a triangle.

♥ Continue to fold triangle onto itself until completely folded into a triangle.

♥ Spray one spray of "I Can't Believe It's Not Butter" on outside of both sides of the turnover.

♥ Sprinkle sugar over turnover to cover. Gently shake off any extra sugar.

♥ Place turnover, seam-side down, on an ungreased cookie sheet.

♥ Bake at 350 degrees for 10 to 12 minutes or until edges are crispy golden brown.

♥ Let cool before serving. (Piping hot filling will burn your mouth!)

Yield: 80 turnovers

Calories: 25   Total fat: 0.4 grams (13% fat)
Cholesterol: 0 mg   Sodium: 29 mg

(Tiny Turnovers continued)

Preparation time: 10 minutes per dozen.

Baking time: 10-12 minutes per dozen.

Total time: 22 minutes or less.

Menu ideas: Not only are they terrific for brunch, breakfast or dessert, they're also pretty and fancy enough for special celebrations such as showers, holidays and candlelight dinners.

Note - I once was afraid of filo because I had never used it before and thought it would be difficult and time consuming to use. But it is not. Actually, it is quite easy. If you've never baked with it before, I strongly encourage you to. I think you'll agree... once you've tried it, you'll like it!

Don't be discouraged about what you can not do to make our world better. Instead, enjoy doing what you can do to make a positive difference.

Breakfast Fruit-Filled Pockets

Budget
Friendly

Recipe

In my first low-fat cookbook, "Down Home Cookin' Without the Down Home Fat", I created delicious entrée pockets such as "Pizza Pockets", "Ham & Cheese Pockets", etc...When preparing them for a T.V. show I came up with these creative and tasty babies. I think you'll agree, they are every bit as good as the ones in my first book.

1 (7.5-ounce) can buttermilk biscuits (found in refrigerator section - I use Pillsbury)
1 (21-ounce) can cherry pie filling (or blueberry or strawberry)

1 egg white - beaten
1 teaspoon ground cinnamon
2 tablespoons sugar
3 tablespoons low-fat vanilla frosting (I use Betty Crocker)

♥ Preheat oven to 425 degrees.

♥ Spray a cookie sheet with non-fat cooking spray. Set aside.

♥ Spray hands with non-fat cooking spray. With hands, flatten each biscuit (dough) into about a 3-inch circle.

♥ Put a rounded teaspoonful of pie filling into center of each circle.

♥ Brush a little beaten egg white on outer ¼-inch rim of dough. (This will act as the glue to hold it together.)

♥ Fold dough over into the shape of a half-moon.

♥ With a fork, press dough edges together to seal.

♥ Mix ground cinnamon and sugar together. Sprinkle on top of each pocket.

♥ Bake at 350 degrees for 10 minutes or until golden brown.

♥ Once pockets are done baking, microwave frosting for a few seconds or until just melted.

♥ Drizzle frosting over top of pockets.

♥ Let cool a few minutes before eating. (Piping hot filling will burn your mouth.)

Yield: 10 servings

Calories: 153   Total fat: 1.4 grams (8% fat)
Cholesterol: 0 mg   Sodium: 187 mg

Preparation time: 15 minutes or less.

Cooking time: 10 minutes.

Total time: 25 minutes or less.

Menu ideas: Great for breakfast, brunch buffets or snacks. Also warm and delicious for a quick on the run breakfast.

56

Refreshing Refreshments

ORANGE LEMONADE

Budget Friendly Recipe

*My husband created this and we really like it.
It's not too sweet or too tart - but like Goldilocks
would say, "it's just right"!*

Juice of 4 lemons
Juice of 2 oranges

½ cup sugar (or ½ cup Equal Spoonful)
2 quarts cold water

♥ Mix together. Serve chilled on ice.

Yield: 8 servings

With sugar:
Calories: 63   Total Fat: 0 grams (0% fat)
Cholesterol: 0 mg   Sodium: 1 mg

With Equal:
Calories: 21   Total Fat: 0 grams (0% fat)
Cholesterol: 0 mg   Sodium: 1 mg

Preparation time: 5 minutes or less.

Menu ideas: Great for hot summer days, near the pool, picnics or cookouts.

FRUITY FREEZE DRINK

Budget Friendly Recipe

An invigorating drink for summer festivities.

1 cup Fat-Free frozen yogurt -
your favorite flavor

1 cup Diet Sprite - chilled
7 ice cubes

♥ Put all ingredients in a blender on high for 45 seconds or until ice cubes are crushed.

Yield: 2 drinks

Calories: 97   Total Fat: 0 grams (0% fat)
Cholesterol: 2 mg   Sodium: 67 mg

Preparation time: 5 minutes or less.

Menu ideas: Refreshing on hot summer days, after a good workout or for a snack. Multiplied, this recipe is also great for bridal or baby showers.

58

SHERBET BREEZE

Budget
Friendly

Recipe

A refreshing refreshment for those lazy summer days.

1 cup frozen sherbet - your
favorite flavor

1 cup Diet Sprite - chilled
7 ice cubes

♥ Put all ingredients in a blender on high for 45 seconds or until ice
cubes are crushed.

Yield: 2 drinks

Calories: 138   Total Fat: 2 grams (12% fat)
Cholesterol: 5 mg   Sodium: 49 mg

 Preparation time: 5 minutes or less.

Menu ideas: As a snack, or cool "pick-me-up" after a long hot day.

BERRY FRUIT FREEZE DRINK

Budget
Friendly

Recipe

Cool and refreshing for those hot summer days!

2 cups Diet Sprite (or Diet 7-Up)
10 ice cubes
1 cup raspberry sherbet

½ cup blackberries (or
blueberries)

♥ Put all ingredients in a blender on high speed for 10 to 15 seconds.
Turn off. Repeat.
♥ Pour into glasses.
♥ Serve immediately.

Yield: 4 (1-cup) servings

Calories: 79   Total Fat: 1.1 grams (12% fat)
Cholesterol: 3 mg   Sodium: 26 mg

Preparation time: 5 minutes or less.

*Menu ideas: Great for picnics, cookouts or
a snack on a sizzling, scorcher day!*

Budget
Friendly

Recipe

TROPICAL FIZZ (SLUSHY)

I love virgin frozen Piña Coladas, but they're so
fattening that I decided to give it a try. My version is
delicious! And a fraction of the cost of those expensive restaurants!

3 to 3½ cups ice
2 (12-ounce) cans Diet Sprite

1½ cups Mr. & Mrs. T. Piña
    Colada mix (this does not have
    alcohol in it)

♥ Put all ingredients in a blender. (Ingredients will come about ½" - ¾"
from the top of a 5-cup blender.) Put on high speed, (ice crush speed)
for about 30 seconds. Ice will be completely crushed and drink will be
slushy when ready.

♥ Pour into tall 12-ounce glasses. Garnish with a fresh slice of pineapple
if desired.

Yield: 4 (12-ounce) servings

Calories: 97   Total Fat: 1.7 grams (16% fat)
Cholesterol: 0 mg   Sodium: 11 mg

Preparation time: 5 minutes or less.

Menu ideas: Fancy summer luncheons, or a special cookout.

60

 Kids Cookin'

FRUITY FROTHY

 Budget Friendly Recipe

This smooth, frothy drink
is as refreshing as it is easy to make!

20 ice cubes
3½ cups Tropicana Pure Tropics
  100% juice - combination
  flavor of orange, strawberry and
  banana

1 cup Mr. T. Piña Colada mix (or
  a virgin mix - no alcohol)

♥ Put all ingredients in a blender on high for 30 to 60 seconds or until
  ice is crushed and drink is smooth.

♥ Serve immediately.

Yield: 4 (10-ounce) servings

Calories: 161   Total Fat: 1.6 grams (9% fat)
Cholesterol: 0 mg   Sodium: 6 mg

Total preparation time: 5 minutes or less.

Menu ideas: Great to serve on hot summer days and at cookouts.
Also a delicious and satisfying compliment to main dish salad
meals such as: Tangy Tossed Salad (page 113) or
Mother-Daughter Salad (page 114).

TOOTIE-FRUITY FROZEN DRINK

Budget Friendly

Recipe

The fruity texture of the pineapple gives this otherwise creamy-smooth drinka unique texture and flavor.

4 cups low-fat frozen peach yogurt (Kroger's brand is good)

1 cup orange juice

1 cup canned crushed pineapple in its own juice

1 small orange - cut into 6 slices - optional

♥ Put all ingredients except orange in a blender. For short periods of time (5 seconds) turn blender on and off. You may need to assist by rearranging ingredients in blender with a long spoon when blender is off to assure that all ingredients are well blended. Repeat 4 or 5 times.

♥ Pour into pretty cups. If desired, put a slit into the rind of each orange slice. Sit orange slice on rim of glass for an eye appealing effect.

Yield: 6 (1-cup) servings

Calories: 179   Total Fat: 1.9 grams (9% fat)

Cholesterol: 7 mg   Sodium: 80 mg

Total preparation time: 5 minutes or less.

Menu ideas: Perfect for a hot summer day's mid-afternoon or evening snack. Or for showers that are only serving refreshments and not a meal.

62

SPICED TEA

Budget
Friendly

Recipe

This is wonderful to drink warm or chilled over ice.
A terrific drink for all seasons!

1 gallon hot water
8 tea bags
2 tablespoons cinnamon red hots

½ cup brown sugar
2 teaspoons ground cinnamon
½ teaspoon ground allspice

♥ Put everything into a large kettle. (Or a soup pot).

♥ Stir until seasonings are dissolved.

♥ Bring to a boil.

♥ Turn off heat. Stir again.

♥ Remove tea bags. Ready to drink as is or served over ice.

Yield: 16 (1-cup) servings

Calories: 34   Total Fat: 0 grams (0% fat)
Cholesterol: 0 mg   Sodium: 3 mg

Total time: 5 minutes or less.

Menu ideas: Anytime, anyplace!
You can't go wrong with this drink!

CHRISTMAS PUNCH

*The deep redness of this full-bodied
punch gives this special holiday drink its name.*

Budget
Friendly

Recipe

1 gallon apple juice
1 (2-liter) bottle Diet Mountain
  Dew

½ cup cinnamon red hots
⅓ cup lemon juice (bottled from
  concentrate is fine)

♥ In a large pot, bring apple juice, Mountain Dew, and red hots to a boil.
Reduce heat. Keep stirring until all red hots are dissolved.

♥ Add lemon juice. Stir well.

♥ Serve warm or chilled.

Yield: 24 (1-cup) servings

Calories: 99   Total Fat: 0.2 grams (2% fat)
Cholesterol: 0 mg   Sodium: 13 mg

 Total preparation time: 10 minutes or less.

*Menu ideas: Serve with your favorite Christmas meal! It's
also delicious served at showers, birthday parties and graduations.*

Great Beginnings

HAM AND CHEESE SPREAD

Budget Friendly Recipe

*For years I've had to stay away from the deli's ham
and cheese spread. It was one of my favorite high fat foods
that I did miss. But no more! Mine is absolutely, positively delicious!
On a scale of 1 to 10, with 10 being the best, I think mine's a 12!*

¼ cup Kraft Free Miracle Whip
3 tablespoons Kraft fat-free
   Thousand Island Salad Dressing
1 tablespoon mustard

¾ pound extra lean ham (2 ounces
   of ham = 2 grams of fat)
1 cup Healthy Choice fat-free
   fancy shredded cheddar cheese

♥ In a small bowl, using a fork, mix the first three ingredients together until creamy and well mixed. Set aside.

♥ Cut ham into tiny ¼-inch or smaller pieces and put into a blender or food processor. With setting on grind, press the "pulse" button for a few seconds to turn appliance on and off quickly. You may need to use a spatula to rearrange pieces that are not getting ground. Continue turning on for 3 to 5 second intervals until all ham pieces are ground.

♥ Add ground ham and cheddar cheese to cream mixture. Stir until well mixed. Serve as is or cover and keep chilled until ready to use. You may keep refrigerated and use up to 5 days.

Yield: 6 (¼-cup) servings

Calories: 125   Total fat: 2.9 grams (23% fat)
Cholesterol: 28 mg   Sodium: 1146 mg

Total preparation time: 10 minutes or less (most of the time derived from cutting and grinding ham.)

*Menu ideas: As an appetizer use as a filling to stuff
cherry tomatoes or serve with fat-free crackers. It's also great
on fat-free bread as a sandwich with lettuce.*

Chicken and Onion Cheese Spread

 Budget Friendly

Recipe

This multiple use spread is scrumptious no matter how it's used.

1 (10-ounce) can premium chunk white chicken in water - do not drain - (I used Swanson brand)
2 (8-ounce) packages Healthy Choice fat-free cream cheese - softened

½ cup fat-free sour cream
1 envelope dry onion soup mix - (I use Lipton Brand. There are 2 envelopes in a box.)
¼ cup green or red pepper - chopped - optional

♥ Mix all ingredients with a hand mixer on low speed for about 1 to 2 minutes or until well mixed. (Also add the water that is in the can with the chicken.)

♥ Serve with crackers. (Or menu idea listed below.)

Yield: 30 (2-tablespoon) servings

Calories: 30   Total fat: 0.2 grams (7% fat)
Cholesterol: 5 mg   Sodium: 198 mg

Preparation time: 6 minutes or less.

Menu ideas: Use as a vegetable dip or stuff in celery sticks. Spread on soft flour tortillas, top with lettuce and tomatoes and roll up. Or spread on one piece of toast for an open faced sandwich. (If desired top with a fresh green pepper ring.)

DEVILED EGGS -
(NO-FAT, NO CHOLESTEROL)

Budget
Friendly

Recipe

Sharon Swick, from Delta, Ohio sent me this one.

5 hard boiled eggs - chilled
1 cup Egg Beaters
3 tablespoons fat-free Miracle
  Whip
¼ teaspoon horseradish

½ teaspoon Grey Poupon
  mustard
½ teaspoon vinegar
½ teaspoon salt - optional
Black pepper and paprika -
  optional

- ♥ (If you prefer a sweeter taste, use less mustard and add 1 to 2 tablespoons sweet relish).
- ♥ Cut boiled eggs in half and discard yolks. Set aside.
- ♥ Spray a skillet with non-fat cooking spray. Add Egg Beaters and cook and stir over medium heat until done. Cool.
- ♥ Combine cooled Egg Beaters and all remaining ingredients except paprika in a food processor until smooth.
- ♥ Fill mixture into egg halves and sprinkle with paprika.

Yield: 10

Calories: 25   Total fat: 0 grams (0% fat)
Cholesterol: 0 mg   Sodium: 109 mg

Preparation time: 10 minutes.

Total time: 20 minutes.

Menu ideas: Serve as an appetizer and also great for picnics.

68

SWEET AND SOUR TEENIE - WEENIES

This is a simple hors d'oeuvre that is good to take to potluck parties.
This tends to be especially popular with children.

1 (14-ounce) package fat-free hot   ¼ cup grape jelly
   dogs (I use Oscar Mayer)   2 tablespoons mustard

- ♥ Slice each hot dog diagonally into 5 pieces. Set aside.
- ♥ In a medium serving bowl, mix jelly and mustard together until well mixed. Heat on high in microwave for 15 seconds.
- ♥ Add hot dogs to bowl and coat with sauce. Cook in microwave 3 to 5 minutes or until completely warmed. Stir while cooking at one minute intervals to coat hot dogs.
- ♥ Serve with toothpicks.
- ♥ This recipe can be tripled and kept warm on low in a crockpot for up to 4 hours.

Yield: 16 servings

Calories: 31   Total fat: 0 grams (0% fat)
Cholesterol: 7 mg   Sodium: 270 mg

Preparation time: 4 minutes or less

Microwave time: 6 minutes or less.

Total time: 10 minutes or less.

Menu ideas: Great as an appetizer or serve as an hors d'oeuvre.

CHICKEN ONION DIP

A friend of mine (Mable) introduced me to a high-fat version of this recipe. I modified it to low-fat. It's now a family favorite!

2 (8-ounce) package fat-free Healthy Choice cream cheese - softened

1 (10-ounce) can premium chunk chicken in water (Swanson) - do not drain

²⁄₃ cup chopped sweet onion (¹⁄₂ medium onion) (I like Vidalia onions)

1 teaspoon mustard

♥ Put all ingredients in medium bowl. Mix well with fork until well blended.

♥ Keep chilled until ready to serve.

Yield: 15 (3-tablespoon) servings

Calories: 50   Total fat: 0.3 grams (23% fat)
Cholesterol: 10 mg   Sodium: 225 mg

Total preparation time: 5-6 minutes.

Menu ideas: Dip - With fat-free crackers as a spread

Dip - Serve with Baked Tostitos tortilla chips

Salad - On a bed of leafy greens as a salad (top with croutons)

Appetizer - Cut cherry tomatoes in half. Take out inside of tomatoes. Stuff with chicken onion dip. Sprinkle with paprika for a prettier color.

Sandwich - Spread on toast. Top with slice of tomato and lettuce.

Warm Dip - Microwave on high for a few minutes, until hot and bubbly. Stir. Serve with crackers or Baked Tostitos Tortilla Chips as a warm appetizer.

PARTY POPPERS

Budget
Friendly

Recipe

These spicy sausage slices are a perfect warm
appetizer to serve for any occasion. Please note: they are spicy!

¼ cup White Zinfandel Wine by
Ernest & Julio Gallo
½ cup Heinz 57 sauce

1 (14-ounce) package Healthy
Choice smoked sausage

♥ In a small bowl, stir wine and Heinz 57 Sauce together. Set aside.

♥ Cut sausage into about ⅓-inch thick slices.

♥ Dip sausage slices into sauce. Grill on an electric non-stick griddle or pan at 250 degrees for 1 to 2 minutes. Turn over. With a teaspoon give each sausage slice a dab more sauce. Heat for 1-2 minutes longer.

♥ Insert a toothpick into each slice.

♥ Reduce heat to very low - just enough to keep these tasty and spicy delectables warm until ready to serve.

Yield: 14 (1-ounce) servings

Calories: 47   Total fat: 0.9 grams (18% fat)
Cholesterol: 10 mg   Sodium: 395 mg

 Total time: 10 minutes or less including cooking.

Menu ideas: Any party, New Year's Eve celebration or
appetizer for a fancy quiet candlelight dinner.

Age is matter of mind and if you don't mind it doesn't matter.

VEGETABLE DIP

Budget Friendly

Recipe

This was given to me by Vickie Barber of Swanton, Ohio.

2 cups Hellmans low-fat
mayonnaise
1 (8-ounce) container fat-free
sour cream

½ teaspoon onion powder
½ teaspoon garlic powder
1 teaspoon dill weed
1 teaspoon parsley flakes

♥ Mix all ingredients together. Chill and serve.

Yield: about 3 cups, 24 (2-tablespoon) servings

Calories: 44   Total fat: 1.3 grams (28% fat)
Cholesterol: 0 mg   Sodium: 194 mg

 Preparation time: 6 minutes or less.

*Menu ideas: Serve with your favorite vegetables,
low-fat crackers, or Baked Lays Potato Crisp.*

RUBY RASPBERRY (FRUIT DIP)

Budget Friendly

Recipe

*My daughter Whitney and I created this sweet,
smooth and creamy dip to use with fresh fruit. We both
loved it! It also tastes good as a dip for pretzels. (If you like a
sweet and salty combination, you'll like it with pretzels.)*

1 cup marshmallow creme

¼ cup fat-free raspberry salad
dressing (I use T. Marzettis')

♥ Mix ingredients together and serve. This is excellent served at room
temperature.

Yield: 10 (2-tablespoon) servings

Calories: 104   Total fat: 0 grams (0% fat)
Cholesterol: 0 mg   Sodium: 58 mg

Preparation time: 2-5 minutes.

Total time: 5 minutes.

Menu ideas: Serve with Brunch, or serve as a delectable treat.

 # BUTTERMILK RANCH DRESSING

Budget Friendly

Recipe

I created this for all those who can't stand fat-free dressing!
This is a real fooler! Don't tell them and they won't know!

1½ cups low-fat buttermilk
1 tablespoon light Miracle Whip
¾ cup fat-free sour cream
1 cup skim milk

1 (2-ounce) package low-fat
Original Hidden Valley Ranch
salad dressing mix

♥ With a whisk, beat all ingredients together for about 2 minutes. Refrigerate until chilled. Serve.

Yield: 26 (2-tablespoon) servings

Calories: 23   Total fat: 0.3 grams (11% fat)
Cholesterol: 1 mg   Sodium: 182 mg

 Preparation time: 5 minutes or less.

Menu ideas: Serve over your favorite salad, or
as a dip with your favorite vegetables.

Budget Friendly

Recipe

MILD MUSTARD/DILL DIPPING SAUCE

Just the right ZIP for your dip!

1 tablespoon mustard
⅓ cup fat-free sour cream

⅛ teaspoon dried dill weed

♥ Mix above ingredients together until well blended.

Yield: 6 servings

Calories: 16   Total fat: 0.1 grams (7% fat)
Cholesterol: 0 mg   Sodium: 43 mg

Preparation time: 3 minutes.

Menu ideas: Serve with Breaded Pork
Tenderloins (page 190) or even as a vegetable dip!

73

MEXICAN CHEESE MOONS

Budget
Friendly

Recipe

*These tasty delectables make wonderful appetizers
or hors d'oeuvres. Their unique half-moon shape and golden
brown crust with colorful seasonings on top make them appealing
to everyone. (Children like the special surprise of creamy filling inside!)*

3 teaspoons taco seasoning mix
(use your favorite brand) -
divided
1/2 cup fat-free cream cheese
(I used Kraft Philadelphia Free)

1/2 cup your favorite salsa
(I use Chi-Chi's)
1/2 cup Healthy Choice fat-free
fancy shredded cheddar cheese
2 (7.5-ounce) cans Pillsbury
buttermilk biscuits

♥ Preheat oven to 400 degrees.

♥ For easier clean-up, line two cookie sheets with foil. Spray foil with non-fat cooking spray.

♥ Mix 1 teaspoon taco seasoning mix, cream cheese, salsa, and cheddar cheese together with blender until well mixed. (Set remaining 2 teaspoons of taco seasoning aside for future use.)

♥ Press 1 biscuit at a time between palms of hands to flatten dough into about a 3 1/2- - 4-inch oval. (You may want to spray your hands with non-fat cooking spray so biscuits won't stick to you.)

♥ With a measuring spoon, put one level tablespoon of prepared filling inside flattened dough. Fold dough in half and pinch edges together firmly to secure seal. Once folded, the biscuit will have a half moon shape.

♥ Set half-moon biscuit on prepared cookie sheet. Continue making half-moons filled with mixture one at a time. (There will be 5 biscuits left over.)

♥ Lightly sprinkle the tops of the half-moons with remaining 2 teaspoons taco seasoning mix.

♥ Bake at 400 degrees for 8 minutes or until tops and bottoms are golden brown. Let cool a couple of minutes before serving. Best served warm.

Yield: 15 servings

(Mexican Cheese Moons continued)

Calories: 86   Total fat: 1.0 gram (11% fat)
Cholesterol: 1 mg   Sodium: 385 mg

Preparation time: 5-10 minutes.

Baking time: 8 minutes

Total time: 18 minutes or less.

Menu ideas: If desired serve with taco sauce for dipping.

ITALIAN DUNKERS

Budget
Friendly

Recipe

Created by our daughters Whitney and Ashley.
If you like pizza you'll like this!!

4 hot dog buns (I like Aunt Millie)   1 (14-ounce) jar your favorite
Italian seasonings   pizza sauce
4 fat-free cheddar cheese slices -
   cut in half

♥ Cut hot dog bun in half, lengthwise.
♥ Sprinkle bun with Italian seasoning.
♥ Lay cheese on top of bun.
♥ Microwave until cheese softens.
♥ Microwave sauce until warmed.
♥ Dip cheesie bread into sauce. Presto! You're done!

Yield: 8 servings

Calories: 82   Total fat: 0.8 grams (9% fat)
Cholesterol: 0 mg   Sodium: 295 mg

Preparation time: 4-5 minutes.

Microwave time: 5-10 seconds for dunkers, 45 seconds for sauce.

Total time: 5 minutes or less.

Menu ideas: Great as a snack or lunch.

DIJON MAYO SPREAD FOR SANDWICHES

Budget Friendly
Recipe

This is from Sharon Swick of Delta, OH and she really enjoys this one!

1 cup fat-free mayonnaise
1 tablespoon Dijon mustard

Dash of garlic salt
Dash of pepper

♥ Mix all ingredients by hand.

♥ Chill and use as needed.

Yield: 8 (2-tablespoon) servings

Calories: 22   Total fat: 0.2 grams (8% fat)
Cholesterol: 0 mg   Sodium: 257 mg

Preparation time: 5 minutes or less.

Menu ideas: Enjoy this tasty spread on your favorite sandwich!

CUCUMBER SANDWICHES

Budget Friendly
Recipe

This was given to me by Vickie Barber, from Swanton, Ohio.

2 (8-ounce) packages fat-free
cream cheese - softened
1 (0.7-ounce) package Italian
salad dressing mix - dry

1 (16-ounce) package pita bread -
each bread cut into quarters
1-2 cucumbers - peeled and
sliced thin

♥ Blend cream cheese and salad dressing mix together until well mixed.

♥ Spread into pita bread and fill with slices of cucumber.

Yield: 16 servings

Calories: 109   Total fat: 0.4 grams (3% fat)
Cholesterol: 2 mg   Sodium: 450 mg

Preparation time: 5 minutes or less.

*Menu ideas: Great as a finger food type
sandwich for lunch along with a fresh vegetable tray
and fat-free dip. Also good as an appetizer.*

TOMATO BISCUITS

Budget Friendly Recipe

No ho-hum biscuit when you pop this baby in your mouth!

1 (7½-ounce) can Pillsbury buttermilk biscuits
⅓ cup Kraft Free non-fat grated topping

½ medium ripe tomato - cut into ¼-inch quartered slices (10 pieces total)
¼ cup grated Parmesan cheese
Garlic salt - optional

♥ Preheat oven to 425 degrees.

♥ Line cookie sheet with aluminum foil.

♥ Spray foil with non-fat cooking spray. Set aside.

♥ Cut tomato into 3 (¼-inch thick) slices. Cut each slice into pie-shaped quarters. Set aside. (There will be 2 quartered slices remaining, discard these.)

♥ Press each biscuit individually into the Kraft non-fat grated topping and place on prepared cookie sheet.

♥ Arrange 1 quartered tomato slice on each biscuit.

♥ Sprinkle grated Parmesan cheese evenly over all tomato biscuits.

♥ Sprinkle lightly with garlic salt if desired.

♥ Bake at 425 degrees for 10 to 13 minutes or until golden brown.

♥ Serve immediately.

Yield: 10 biscuits

Calories: 72   Total fat: 1.6 grams (19% fat)
Cholesterol: 5 mg   Sodium: 236 mg

Preparation time: 10 minutes.

Baking time: 10 minutes.

Total time: 20 minutes or less.

Menu ideas: These would taste great with Spicy, Thick Vegetarian Chili (page 92), or any Italian entrée.

SWEET CORN BREAD

*This is from Sharon Swick of Delta, OH and it is
one of her husband Bob's favorites.*

¹/₃ cup Egg Beaters
1 cup evaporated skim milk
¹/₂ cup brown sugar
2 teaspoons dry Molly McButter

1 teaspoon salt - optional
1 ¹/₄ cup reduced-fat Bisquick
  baking mix
³/₄ cup cornmeal

♥ Preheat oven to 400 degrees.

♥ Spray a 9-inch square baking dish with non-fat cooking spray.

♥ In a large bowl, combine Egg Beaters, evaporated skim milk and sugar.
Add Molly McButter and salt. Mix thoroughly. Add biscuit mix and
cornmeal and stir until well mixed.

♥ Bake in prepared dish at 400 degrees for 20 to 25 minutes or until
golden brown.

Yield: 9 servings

Calories: 179   Total fat: 1.3 grams (7% fat)
Cholesterol: 1 mg   Sodium: 251 mg

Preparation time: 10 minutes or less.

Baking time: 25 minutes or less.

Total time: 35 minutes or less.

*Menu ideas: Have on the side with one of your favorite soups, or
with your main entrée instead of regular bread. Also good with
Mexican-based and pork-based entrées.*

GARLIC TOAST

Perfect for fast and easy meals that aren't fancy.

Budget
Friendly

Recipe

1 slice fat-free wheat, white,
  potato or sourdough bread
  (Aunt Millie or Wonder)

5 sprays "I Can't Believe It's Not
  Butter" spray
Garlic salt
Dried parsley - optional

♥ Toast slice of bread to desired darkness in toaster.

♥ Spray one side of toast with 5 sprays of "I Can't Believe It's Not Butter".

♥ Sprinkle lightly with garlic salt, then with dried parsley if desired.

Yield: 1 serving

Calories: 71   Total fat: 0 grams (0% fat)
Cholesterol: 0 mg   Sodium: 161 mg

 Preparation time: 3 minutes or less

Menu ideas: Great with any Italian entrée.

Don't put God in a box. You'll smother His abilities to work through you!

--Tracy Hall

SOUTHWESTERN CORN MUFFINS

Budget Friendly

Recipe

*The slight zest of these unique corn muffins goes
perfectly with chili! I especially like them with my Spicy,
Thick Vegetarian Chili!! Now we're talkin' some good 'ol fashioned eatin'!*

⅓ cup plus 1 tablespoon your
favorite chunky salsa
2 tablespoons cinnamon-flavored
applesauce

2 egg whites
1 (6½-ounce) Gold Medal Smart
Size Golden Corn Bread and
Muffin Mix

- ♥ Preheat oven to 400 degrees.
- ♥ Spray 6 medium muffin cups with non-fat cooking spray, or line muffin tin with cupcake liners.
- ♥ Mix together salsa, applesauce, and egg whites until well mixed.
- ♥ Add corn bread mix, stir until blended but still lumpy.
- ♥ Spoon batter evenly into cups.
- ♥ Bake at 400 degrees for 15 minutes or until tops are lightly browned.
- ♥ Remove muffins immediately.
- ♥ Note: These muffins can be made ahead of time and quickly reheated in the microwave for toasty, warm muffins anytime!

Yield: 6 servings

Calories: 137   Total fat: 3.1 grams (21% fat)
Cholesterol: 7 mg   Sodium: 347 mg

Preparation time: 4-5 minutes.

Baking time: 15 minutes.

Total time: 20 minutes or less.

*Menu ideas: Serve with chili as I suggested,
or with your favorite soup or Mexican entrée.*

CHEESE BISCUITS

Budget
Friendly

Recipe

*I got this recipe idea from a favorite seafood restaurant.
Betcha' don't have the slightest idea what restaurant that
could be, do you? These are not half as fattening, but don't let that
fool you . . . these babies are delicious!*

2 cups skim milk
1 (8-ounce) package Healthy
 Choice fat-free fancy shredded
 cheddar cheese
2 tablespoons dry Butter Buds
 Sprinkles

2 teaspoons garlic salt
5 cups reduced-fat Bisquick
 baking mix
48 sprays "I Can't Believe It's Not
 Butter" spray

♥ Preheat oven to 350 degrees.

♥ Spray 2 cookie sheets with non-fat cooking spray. Set aside.

♥ In a large mixing bowl, pour milk over cheese and let sit for 3 minutes.

♥ Add Butter Buds and garlic salt to milk, stirring until they are dissolved.

♥ Stir in Bisquick. Dough will become very stiff. At the end of stirring
 you may find it easier to finish mixing with your hands. Keep mixing
 until there is no Bisquick on bottom or sides of bowl.

♥ Drop by rounded tablespoonfuls onto prepared cookie sheets. (This is
 easiest to do with two spoons. Using a measuring tablespoon get a
 rounded tablespoon of dough. Push dough off spoon with second
 spoon.)

♥ Bake at 350 degrees for 15 to 17 minutes or until tops are golden
 brown. Spray each biscuit with 2 sprays of "I Can't Believe It's Not
 Butter" before serving.

Yield: 24 (1-biscuit) servings

Calories: 117   Total fat: 1.6 grams (13% fat)
Cholesterol: 1 mg   Sodium: 531 mg

Preparation time: 5 minutes.

Baking time: 15-17 minutes.

Total time: 22 minutes or less.

*Menu ideas: Here's another recipe that would
be wonderful with chili or soup.*

81

PINWHEEL DINNER ROLLS

As visually pretty as they are delicious!

1 (10 ounce) can Pillsbury pizza crust dough
52 sprays "I Can't Believe It's Not Butter" spray
1 teaspoon garlic salt
1 tablespoon dried parsley - crushed

♥ Preheat oven to 425 degrees.

♥ Spray a cookie sheet with non-fat cooking spray.

♥ Unroll dough and press out to ¼-inch thickness onto cookie sheet.

♥ Spray 40 sprays of "I Can't Believe It's Not Butter" evenly over dough.

♥ Sprinkle garlic salt and parsley evenly on top.

♥ Roll dough up (jelly roll style) starting from the long side of the dough.

♥ Pinch seam of dough once completely rolled to seal.

♥ Cut into 12 pieces, making 12 pinwheels.

♥ Set each pinwheel so that you can see the pinwheel on top of the prepared cookie sheet.

♥ Bake at 425 degrees for 8 - 10 minutes or until golden brown.

♥ Spray tops of each roll with one spray of "I Can't Believe It's Not Butter" before serving.

Yield: 12 rolls

Calories: 54   Total fat: 0.7 grams (12% fat)
Cholesterol: 0 mg   Sodium: 271 mg

Preparation time: 5 minutes or less.

Cooking time: 10 minutes or less.

Total time: 15 minutes or less.

Menu ideas: Serve with your favorite main entrée.

Super Easy Soups & Salads

STEAK & POTATO CATTLEMEN'S SOUP

Budget
Friendly

Recipe

A terrific way to use leftover steak and potatoes!
(Or a eye of round roast and potatoes.)

2½ cups (1 pound) leftover lean cooked eye of round steak - cut into bite-size chunks
2½ cups (2 large potatoes) leftover fully cooked potatoes (with skins on) - cut into bite-size chunks
4 ounces fresh sliced mushrooms

½ cup your favorite barbecue sauce (I use Bullseye)
½ cup chopped onions (frozen onions work well)
1 (1.25-ounce) envelope dry onion soup mix
4 cups water

♥ Crockpot method: Spray a crockpot with non-fat cooking spray. Mix all ingredients together until well mixed. Cover. Cook on low for 4 hours.

♥ Stovetop method: Spray a Dutch oven (large saucepan) with non-fat cooking spray. Mix all ingredients over medium-low heat for 5 to 10 minutes or until fully heated.

♥ Microwave method: Spray microwavable covered dish with non-fat cooking spray. Mix all ingredients well. Cover. Cook on high power in carousal microwave for 8 minutes. Stir. If needed, cook an additional 2 to 3 minutes.

Yield: 6 servings

Calories: 235   Total Fat: 4.4 grams (17% fat)
Cholesterol: 53 mg   Sodium: 752 mg

Preparation time: 15 minutes or less.

Cooking time: As little as 5 minutes.

Total time: As little as 20 minutes or less.

Menu ideas: This hearty soup is a meal in itself.
Serve with sourdough bread, (Aunt Millie fat-free brand
is delicious!) and a tossed salad.

CALIFORNIA MEDLEY SOUP

Budget Friendly Recipe

*This is a "make me feel good soup." It smells good,
it tastes good and it makes you feel warm and cozy inside.
A great soup for anyone trying to lose weight.*

1 gallon water
12 chicken bouillon cubes
2 tablespoons Village Saucerie
  Brand Garden Herb Sauce and
  Recipe Mix - (found in same
  aisle as "Shake n' Bake")

1 pound boneless, skinless
  chicken breast - cut into bite-
  size pieces
2 pounds frozen California blend
  vegetables (broccoli,
  cauliflower and carrots)

♥ In a large soup pan, bring water, bouillon cubes and Village Saucerie Sauce Mix to a boil over high heat.

♥ Add chicken and vegetables. Bring to a boil once again. Reduce heat. Cover. Let simmer 6 minutes.

♥ Remove about 2 cups of the vegetables with a strainer-type ladle. Put vegetables on a plate and mash with a potato masher. Return back to soup.

Yield: 18 (1-cup) servings

Calories: 50   Total Fat: 0.6 grams (10% fat)
Cholesterol: 15 mg   Sodium: 822 mg

Preparation time: 10 minutes or less.

Cooking time: 20 minutes.

Total time: 30 minutes or less.

*Menu ideas: fat-free crackers and tossed salad, fat-free
cottage cheese with canned tropical fruit (by Dole.)*

Make sure your attitude is one on a high latitude of gratitude.

SMOKEY BEAN SOUP

Nothing like comin' home to the wonderful
aroma of this mouth-watering soup awaiting you!
So hearty, you could almost call it a stew!

1 (48-ounce) jar deluxe mixed
  beans (I use Randall's fully
  cooked and ready to eat brand)
48 ounces water
3/4 pound smoked lean ham
  lunchmeat or turkey ham -
  chopped
1 teaspoon liquid smoke (found
  in Barbecue Sauce aisle of
  grocery store)

1 (1½-ounce) envelope dry onion
  soup mix (I use Mrs. Grass)
3/4 teaspoon dried thyme -
  optional
1 (16-ounce) bag frozen
  vegetables for stew (I use
  Freshlike) - remove the peas
  yourself

♥ This soup can be made quickly by mashing the beans with a potato masher or slotted spoon in the bottom of a large soup pan until one-third of the beans are mashed. Add all other ingredients. Bring to a boil, reduce heat to low, simmer for 12 minutes and its ready to eat. However, I prefer to prepare this soup the other "fast and easy" way . . . using a crockpot. (Also known as a slow cooker.)

♥ I like to put all of my ingredients in the crockpot on low heat before leaving for work. When I come home 9 to 10 hours later, the wonderful smoky fragrance of this hearty homestyle soup soothes the soul and tantalizes my taste buds! I can't wait to dig in! The nice thing about preparing it in advance is when I get home from a long, hard day's work I don't have to "wait!" It's already for our family to dig into! That's exactly what we like to do!

♥ Put beans into crockpot. With a potato masher, mash beans until at least ⅓ of the beans are mashed. Fill the bean jar you just emptied with 48 ounces of water and add to crockpot. Add all remaining ingredients. Be sure to remove the peas from the frozen vegetables before combining with other ingredients. Stir until well mixed and until the onion soup mix is completely dissolved. Cover with lid. Turn crockpot on low. Let simmer all day, about 8 to 10 hours or until ready to eat.

♥ Before serving, if you want the broth thicker, simply mash with potato masher again. Stir. Serve hot!

(Smokey Bean Soup continued)

♥ Note: Except for the frozen vegetables, all of the ingredients in this soup have been previously full cooked. We're simply combining these ingredients into a unique ensemble for a fast and easy delicious homestyle meal.

♥ The soup actually only needs 5 hours on low in the crockpot before it's ready to eat. It's hard to overcook this soup, so don't worry if it's in the crockpot for longer than 10 hours.

♥ Also, as stated earlier, if desired you can use a pan and have it completely cooked in 20 to 25 minutes from start to finish.

Yield: 15 (1-cup) servings

Calories: 161   Total Fat: 2.0 grams (11% fat)
Cholesterol: 11 mg   Sodium: 1002 mg

Preparation time: 10 minutes or less.

Cooking time: Varies depending on you cooking method.

Menu ideas: Corn bread and a pot of greens on the side.

SOUTHWESTERN CHICKEN SOUP

Budget
Friendly

Recipe

*This soup has a slight "bite" to it, which
gives it a unique flavor. It's a good alternative
to traditional chicken noodle soup.*

2 pounds boneless, skinless
   chicken breast - cut into
   bite-size pieces
3 quarts water
12 chicken bouillon cubes

2 cups salsa (use your favorite
   brand)
1 (6.8-ounce) box Spanish Rice
   Flavored Rice-a-Roni

♥ Put everything into a large pot. Bring to a boil. Boil 3 to 4 minutes.
  Reduce heat. Let simmer 10 minutes. Serve hot.

Yield: 18 (1-cup) servings

Calories: 110   Total Fat: 1.0 gram (9% fat)
Cholesterol: 30 mg   Sodium: 1088 mg

Preparation time: 10 minutes or less.

Cooking time: 20 minutes.

Total time: 30 minutes or less.

*Menu ideas: Very tasty with a grilled cheese sandwich
(see Back to Basics Section) or cornbread on the side.*

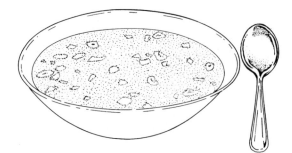

TACO VEGETABLE SOUP

*My family thinks this flavorful, zesty soup
is delicious served with crushed Baked Tostitos Tortilla
Chips sprinkled on top of each serving.*

1 pound lean ground turkey
breast
1 (2-pound) package frozen
Freshlike vegetables for soup
1 (1½-ounce) package taco
seasoning mix (your favorite
brand)

1 (49½-ounce) can Swanson
chicken broth - visible fat
removed
1 (16-ounce) jar your favorite
salsa

♥ Put all ingredients in a large soup pan. Bring to a boil. Reduce heat to
low. Cover. Let simmer for 13 minutes.

♥ If desired, served with crushed Baked Tostitos Tortilla Chips sprinkled
on top of each serving.

♥ If you like a spicier soup, add a few drops of Tabasco sauce.

Yield: 12 (1-cup) servings

Calories: 115   Total Fat: 0.4 grams (3% fat)
Cholesterol: 26 mg   Sodium: 1063 mg

Preparation time: 5 minutes or less.

Cooking time: 13 minutes or less.

Total time: 18 minutes or less.

*Menu ideas: Mexican Chicken Salad (page 99),
and Southwestern Corn Muffins (page 80).*

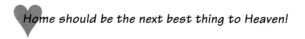

Home should be the next best thing to Heaven!

SOUTHWESTERN VEGETARIAN SOUP

Budget
Friendly

Recipe

Great on a cold winter day!

6 cups chicken broth
(or 6 bouillon cubes with
6 cups water)
2 cups your favorite salsa
1 (1½-ounce) package taco
seasoning mix (use your
favorite brand)

1 (1-pound) package frozen
vegetables for soup (Freshlike)
1 (31-ounce) can fat-free refried
beans (Old El Paso)

♥ Stir all ingredients in a large soup pan until beans are dissolved. Bring
to a boil, reduce heat to low. Cook, covered, for 12 minutes.

♥ Crockpot method: Cook in a crockpot on low for 8 hours or on high for
4 hours.

*If desired, sprinkle crushed Baked Tostitos Tortilla Chips on
individual servings of soup before eating. For a spicier soup, add a
few drops Tabasco sauce.*

Yield: 12 (1-cup) servings

Calories: 117   Total Fat: 0 grams (0% fat)
Cholesterol: 0 mg   Sodium: 1393 mg

Preparation time: 5 minutes or less.

Cooking time: As little as 15 minutes or less.

Total time: 20 minutes or less.

*Menu ideas: Mexican Chicken Salad (page 99),
and Southwestern Corn Muffins (page 80).*

*There's a big difference between "testing" the Lord and "trusting"
the Lord.*

CORN CHOWDER

Budget Friendly

Recipe

This soup makes a great accompaniment to any sandwich.
(Actually, half of a sandwich with a 1-cup serving of
corn chowder is very filling for me.)

²/₃ cups Healthy Choice fat-free
  Shredded cheddar cheese
1 teaspoon onion salt
1 (11-ounce) can Freshlike sweet
  corn and diced peppers

2 (15-ounce) cans cream style
  corn
1 (14.5-ounce) can chicken broth
¼ teaspoon ground pepper -
  optional

♥ In a Dutch oven (large sauce pan) bring all ingredients to a boil over medium-high heat, stirring constantly. (About 3-4 minutes.)

♥ Remove from heat. Let sit 3 to 4 minutes to cool a little before serving.

Yield: 6 (1-cup) servings

Calories: 170   Total Fat: 1.8 grams (8% fat)
Cholesterol: 1 mg   Sodium: 1297 mg

Preparation time: 6 minutes or less.

Cooking time: 5 minutes.

Total time: 11 minutes or less.

Menu ideas: Half of a sandwich or a tossed salad.

CHICKEN CORN CHOWDER:
For a more complete meal, add 1 cup cooked diced chicken breast.

Yield: 7 servings

Calories: 181   Total Fat: 2.4 grams (11% fat)
Cholesterol: 18 mg   Sodium: 1127 mg

Preparation time: 6 minutes or less.

Cooking time: 5 minutes.

Total time: 11 minutes or less.

Menu ideas: Tossed salad, crackers,
or Mint Mousse (page 223).

SPICY THICK VEGETARIAN CHILI

Budget Friendly

Recipe

*This thick, hearty, stick to your bones (but not your thighs!)
chili is power packed with protein and fiber.*

2 (15-ounce) cans Mexican style
hot chili beans
1 (16-ounce) can vegetarian
refried beans (I use Old El Paso)

1 (15-ounce) can black beans
(I use Progresso ready to serve
brand)
2 cups chunky salsa
(I use Chi-Chi's)
1 (6-ounce) can tomato paste

♥ Stir all ingredients together in a 3-quart or larger non-stick saucepan over medium heat until thoroughly heated and well mixed. Presto! You're done! Now enjoy!

Yield: 9 (1-cup) servings

Calories: 178   Total Fat: 1.7 grams (8% fat)
Cholesterol: 0 mg   Sodium: 1137 mg

Additional ideas: - optional

- for spicier chili add Tabasco Sauce

- for an eye appealing garnish sprinkle bowl of chili with Healthy Choice fancy shredded cheddar cheese

- for a chili not as thick add water or tomato juice - 1 cup at a time until desired consistency.

 Total preparation and cooking time: 10 minutes or less.

Menu ideas: Southwestern Corn Muffins (page 80).

 Many times if someone has a chip on their shoulder it's in their head!

HEARTY VEGETABLE SOUP SUPREME

Budget Friendly Recipe

This has almost every vegetable you can think of in it!

1 gallon water
4 (1-pound) packages frozen
  stir-fry vegetables
3 (1.5-ounce) envelopes dry
  onion soup mix (I use Mrs.
  Grass or Campbell's)
1 (16-ounce) bag frozen
  vegetables for soup (Freshlike)

1 (18-ounce) can tomato paste
6 tablespoons Village Saucerie
  Garden Herb Flavor (usually
  found in aisle with Shake 'n
  Bake)
3 bay leaves - optional

♥ In a large soup pan, bring all ingredients to a boil. Cover. Reduce heat
  and cook for 15 minutes. Stir occasionally. Serve promptly. Remove
  bay leaves before serving.

♥ Season with garlic salt if desired.

♥ This soup can be frozen.

Yield: 28 (1-cup) servings

Calories: 66   Total Fat: 0.5 grams (6% fat)
Cholesterol: 0 mg   Sodium: 766 mg

 Preparation time: 10 minutes or less.

Cooking time: 25 minutes.

Total time: 35 minutes or less.

*Menu ideas: Serve this Hearty soup with
Sweet Corn Bread (page 78) or Cheese Biscuits (page 81).*

Wise people are the ones who "know they don't know everything".

ORIENTAL CHICKEN SOUP

*This flavorful oriental soup is delicious on cold days.
It's loaded with colorful vegetables and is as
eye appealing as it is delicious.*

6 Mesquite flavor chicken breasts
 - (I use Tyson)
4 (1-pound) packages frozen stir
 fry vegetables (I use Flav-R Pac,
 it has broccoli, carrots, water
 chestnuts, Chinese pea pods,
 mushrooms, red peppers and
 bamboo shoots)
1 (12-ounce) bottle Teriyaki Baste
 and Glaze (I use Kikkoman brand)

2 tablespoons garlic salt
18 cups chicken broth
 (Make your own with chicken
 bouillon - 1 chicken bouillon
 cube per cup of water. Or use
 canned chicken broth, but
 remove any visible fat with a
 napkin.)

♥ Put everything into a large soup pot. Bring to a boil. Reduce heat to
low. Remove chicken breast and cut into tiny ½-inch pieces.

♥ Add cut up chicken pieces back into soup. Let the soup simmer a
couple of minutes to reheat chicken pieces.

Yield: 29 (1-cup) servings

Calories: 102   Total Fat: 0.9 grams (8% fat)
Cholesterol: 29 mg   Sodium: 1570 mg

Preparation time: 10 minutes or less.

Cooking time: 10 minutes.

Total time: 20 minutes or less.

*Menu ideas: Since this has your meat already in it, it would be
great as a main entrée with your choice of bread on the side.*

*You know you're operating within a narrow margin when having to stop at
a red light throws your whole day off schedule.*

FRENCH ONION SOUP

Onion lovers rejoice! A low-fat version of a very popular soup!

2 quarts water
2 tablespoons sugar
¼ cup flour
2 packets dry Butter Buds
  (or 2 tablespoons Butter Bud
  Sprinkles)
*6 cups onions - sliced very
  thinly (about 3 medium onions)

8 beef bouillon cubes
2 teaspoons pure sherry extract
  (found next to vanilla flavoring
  in baking section)
½ cup Kraft Free non-fat grated
  topping (Parmesan cheese) -
  optional

♥ In a crockpot using a whisk, briskly stir together water, sugar, flour and Butter Buds until flour is dissolved. Add onions and bouillon cubes. Cover. Cook on low for 9 to 10 hours.

♥ After 9 to 10 hours cooking on low, add sherry extract and non-fat grated topping.

♥ Put soup into individual bowls. Sprinkle with fat-free croutons or cubed rye bread.

♥ If desired top each serving with 1 teaspoon fat-free Parmesan cheese. With spoon gently press the cheese into the soup. Let set for about 30 seconds to melt the cheese.

♥ *The fastest way to cut onions without crying is with a food processor.

Yield: 8 servings

Calories: 73   Total Fat: 0.3 grams (4% fat)
Cholesterol: 0 mg   Sodium: 882 mg

Preparation time: 20 minutes or less.

Cooking time: 9 hours.

Total time: 9 hours plus 20 minutes.

Menu ideas: Serve with Tangy Tossed Salad (page 113).

Never give up your kids! Our Heavenly Father never gives up on us.

PEACHES & CREAM GELATIN SALAD

Sharon Swick from Delta, Ohio sent me this "Peachy Treat".

1 (29-ounce) can peaches in own juice - drained with juice reserved
½ cup fat-free cream cheese
⅓ cup fat-free sour cream

¼ cup sugar (or ¼ cup Equal Spoonful)
1 (3-ounce) package peach flavored gelatin - dry

♥ In a food processor, combine ½ can drained peaches, cream cheese, sour cream and sugar. Blend until smooth. Add the other ½ can of peaches (saving out 4 or 5 slices to garnish the top of the salad.) Blend until smooth.

♥ Heat 1 cup of reserved peach juice over medium heat until almost boiling. Remove from heat and stir in gelatin until dissolved.

♥ Cool slightly and combine with cream cheese mixture.

♥ Cover and refrigerate about 3 hours or until chilled.

Yield: 6 servings

With sugar:
Calories: 178   Total Fat: 0 grams (0% fat)
Cholesterol: 2 mg   Sodium: 154 mg

With Equal Spoonful:
Calories: 149   Total Fat: 0 grams (0% fat)
Cholesterol: 2 mg   Sodium: 154 mg

Preparation time: 12 minutes or less.

Cooking time: 5 minutes.

Total time: 17 minutes or less.

Menu ideas: This would be wonderful after dining on Herbed Eye of Round with Seasoned Potatoes and Buttered Mushrooms (page 204).

POLYNESIAN FRUIT SALAD

Budget Friendly

Recipe

A nutritious and delicious way to get calcium.

1 (20-ounce) can crushed
  pineapple in its own juice
7 ice cubes
1 (1-ounce) box sugar free fat-free
  instant vanilla pudding - dry
  (I use Jell-O)

2 cups fat-free cottage cheese
1 cup Cool Whip Free
2 medium bananas - sliced

♥ Squeeze out as much pineapple juice as possible into a measuring cup. Add up to 7 ice cubes to pineapple juice to equal 2 cups of liquid.

♥ Pour juice and ice cubes into a medium mixing bowl. Add pudding mix and stir briskly for 2 minutes. Remove any ice cubes that have not dissolved. Add drained pineapple to pudding mixture. Stir until well mixed.

♥ Stir cottage cheese and Cool Whip Free into pudding mixture until well mixed.

♥ Gently stir in bananas.

♥ Serve as is or keep chilled until ready to serve.

Yield: 13 (½-cup) servings

Calories: 84   Total Fat: 0 grams (0% fat)
Cholesterol: 3 mg   Sodium: 229 mg

Total preparation time: 7 minutes or less.

*Menu ideas: Great served for lunch as a main course
stuffed in half of a cantaloupe or honeydew. Delicious as a
nutritious combination side dish and dessert with any dinner.*

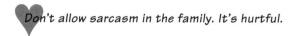
Don't allow sarcasm in the family. It's hurtful.

VERY BERRY FRUIT SALAD

Budget Friendly

Recipe

Not only is this delicious it's also nutritious.

1 (1.7-ounce) box fat-free sugar free instant vanilla pudding - dry (I use Jell-O brand)
2 cups skim milk

1 quart fresh blackberries or blueberries
2 medium bananas

♥ With a whisk, beat fat-free pudding and skim milk in a bowl for 2 minutes.

♥ Gently stir in berries until well mixed.

♥ Keep chilled until ready to serve.

♥ Stir in bananas when ready to serve.

Yield: 8 (½-cup) servings

With blackberries:
Calories: 105   Total Fat: 0.5 grams (4% fat)
Cholesterol: 1 mg   Sodium: 280 mg

With blueberries:
Calories: 108   Total Fat: 0.5 grams (4% fat)
Cholesterol: 1 mg   Sodium: 285 mg

Preparation time: 5 minutes or less.

Menu ideas: The perfect ending to any heavy meal.
Also great for brunch or buffets.

Reading a book on a subject does not make you an authority on the subject.

Mexican Chicken Salad

Budget Friendly Recipe

The perfect flavor combination for a delicious lunch!

½ cup chunky salsa
⅓ cup Ranch fat-free salad dressing (I used Seven Seas)
⅓ cup Western fat-free salad dressing
⅓ cup Healthy Choice fancy shredded cheddar cheese

½ pound cooked chicken breast (or chicken breast lunchmeat) - cut into bite-size pieces
1 large head Iceberg lettuce - shredded (or 2 (1-pound) packages prepared salad mix)
1 fat-free tortilla - cut into ¼-inch strips and the strips cut into 1-inch lengths

♥ Mix salsa, Ranch dressing, Western dressing, cheese and chicken until well mixed. Keep refrigerated until ready to serve.

♥ When ready to serve, toss shredded lettuce with chicken mixture and tortilla strips. Do not toss beforehand or salad will become soggy.

Yield: 4 luncheon entrée salad servings

Calories: 227   Total Fat: 2.8 grams (11% fat)
Cholesterol: 49 mg   Sodium: 782 mg

8 side salad servings

Calories: 113   Total Fat: 1.4 grams (11% fat)
Cholesterol: 25 mg   Sodium: 391 mg

 Preparation time: 10 minutes or less.

Menu ideas: Perfect as a main entrée for lunch or a light dinner. As a side salad for any fish, chicken, or Mexican entrée.

I want to make more than just a living . . . I want to make a difference!

SOUTHWESTERN THREE BEAN SALAD

The zip in this salad will add zest to any meal.

1 (19-ounce) can Progresso black bean soup - drained
½ cup Kraft red wine vinegar fat-free salad dressing
1 (15.5-ounce) can light red kidney beans - drained

1 (16-ounce) jar your favorite thick and chunky salsa (I use Tostitos)
1 (15.5-ounce) can Navy beans - drained

♥ Mix all ingredients together. If you like spicy food, add a few drops of Tabasco sauce.

Yield: 12 (½-cup) servings

Calories: 91   Total Fat: 0.4 grams (4% fat)
Cholesterol: 0 mg   Sodium: 575 mg

Preparation time: 5 minutes or less. The time consuming and hardest part of this recipe is opening the cans! Pretty nice - huh?

Menu ideas: A great side salad for a Mexican meal.
Also a terrific dip with fat-free Baked Tostitos Chips.

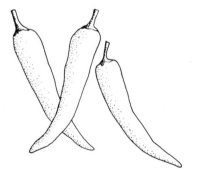

 # CRUNCHY CUCUMBERS WITH CREAM

Budget Friendly Recipe

They're crisp, crunchy and seasoned just right!

1 (1-ounce) envelope dry Hidden Valley Original Ranch Salad Dressing mix

1 (16-ounce) container fat-free sour cream (I use Land O Lakes)

5 medium cucumbers - peeled and sliced

1 medium onion - sliced into ½-inch rings and separated

♥ In a large bowl, stir together dressing mix and sour cream until well mixed.

♥ Stir in cucumbers and onions until all vegetables are coated with cream.

♥ Keep chilled until ready to eat.

Yield: 20 (½-cup) servings

Calories: 40   Total Fat: 0 grams (0% fat)
Cholesterol: 0 mg   Sodium: 119 mg

Total preparation time: 15 minutes or less (most of the time derives from peeling and slicing vegetables.) To prepare faster, you could purchase 4 cups peeled and sliced cucumbers and 1 cup sliced onion from the salad bar at a grocery store. However, this would be extremely expensive and I would not advise doing so.

Menu ideas: These are scrumptious for any barbecue or cookout. They compliment all types of grilled meats such as chicken, pork or beef.

Please note after a few days the cucumbers become less crunchy. I prefer them crunchy.

Contrary to what many believe - the most important thing in living is not making a living!

SWEET & SOUR
FRESH VEGETABLE GARDEN SALAD

Budget
Friendly

Recipe

This crunchy, sweet and sour salad puts zing into any meal.

2 small unpeeled cucumbers - cut
  into ¼-inch slices (3½ cups)
2 small green peppers - cut into
  ¼-inch slices (1½ cups)
4 ears uncooked fresh white
  sweet corn - cut corn from the
  cob with knife (3½ cups packed.)

1 (4-ounce) jar pimento - do not
  drain
¾ cup brown sugar
⅔ cup apple cider vinegar
4 ice cubes

♥ Put first 4 ingredients in a medium size serving bowl. Set aside.

♥ Stir brown sugar and apple cider vinegar in a microwavable container.
  Microwave on high for 2 minutes.

♥ Stir ice cubes into hot vinegar. Keep stirring for about 30 seconds or
  until ice cubes are completely dissolved.

♥ Pour vinegar mixture over vegetables. Stir until all vegetables are
  coated.

♥ Serve immediately or keep chilled until ready to eat.

Yield: 17 (½-cup) servings

Calories: 72   Total Fat: 0.4 grams (5% fat)
Cholesterol: 0 mg   Sodium: 10 mg

**Preparation time: 25 minutes (Time derives mostly from cutting
fresh vegetables.)**

Cooking time: 2 minutes (plus 2 minutes cooling time).

Total time: 30 minutes or less.

*Menu ideas: Good for cookouts, picnics, potlucks
and fish- or chicken-based entrées.*

SEASIDE SALAD

Budget
Friendly

Recipe

Great as the main course for lunch!

1 large head Iceberg lettuce - shredded (or 1 (1-pound) package prepared lettuce)
1 (8-ounce) package imitation crab meat pieces (I use Louis Kemp Crab Delights)

2 large tomatoes - sliced
1 large cucumber - cut into ¼-inch chunks
¼ cup Marzettis' fat-free slaw dressing

♥ Just before servings, gently toss all ingredients together. Serve immediately. (Putting dressing on too soon will cause lettuce to become soggy.)

Yield: 2 large salad servings

Calories: 251   Total Fat: 2.8 grams (10% fat)
Cholesterol: 38 mg   Sodium: 1387 mg

6 side salad servings

Calories: 84   Total Fat: 0.9 grams (10% fat)
Cholesterol: 13 mg   Sodium: 462 mg

Preparation time: 10 minutes or less.

*Menu ideas: As a main entrée serve with fat-free crackers.
As a side salad it goes great with fish-based entrées or soups.*

103

SEAFOOD SALAD

Budget Friendly

Recipe

This is an extra special recipe for those extra special occasions such as showers and luncheons.

1 (8-ounce) package imitation lobster meat (I use Louis Kemp Lobster Delights)

1 (8-ounce) package imitation scallop meat (I use Louis Kemp Scallop Delights)

1 (8-ounce) package imitation king crab meat (I use Louis Kemp Crab Delights)

1 pound cooked shrimp - peeled, deveined and tails removed

2 cups cucumbers - chopped with skin on and seeds removed (about 1 medium cucumber)

1 (8-ounce) bottle Kraft Thousand Island fat-free salad dressing (about 1 cup)

♥ Mix all ingredients. Keep chilled until ready to serve.

♥ *To remove seeds, cut cucumber in half lengthwise. With a spoon, scrape down the center to remove seeds.

Yield: 7 (1-cup) servings

Calories: 209   Total Fat: 2.0 grams (9% fat)
Cholesterol: 146 mg   Sodium: 1241 mg

Total preparation time: 8 minutes or less.

Menu ideas: Stuff into a pita half or put a half-cup on top of a bed of fresh green assorted lettuce for individual salads.

Cut a honeydew melon in half. Clean and put seafood salad in center, or cut off top of a fresh tomato. Take seeds out of center of tomato and stuff with seafood salad.

Serve on toasted fat-free or regular white bread with lettuce . . . or roll in a soft flour tortilla or serve a dab on crackers.

Seafood Pasta Salad: Make exactly as directed above and toss with 1 pound tricolor bow tie pasta that has been cooked in boiling water for 11 minutes, rinsed with cold water and drained. Add another 8-ounce bottle Kraft Thousand Island fat-free salad dressing.

(Seafood Salad continued)

Yield: 15 (1-cup) servings

Calories: 229   Total Fat: 1.4 grams (6% fat)
Cholesterol: 68 mg   Sodium: 711 mg

 Preparation time: 8 minutes or less.

Cooking time: Bow tie Pasta - cook 11 minutes.

Total time: 20 minutes or less.

*Menu ideas: Serve with fresh cut tomatoes, or cucumber salad.
Add Perfect Pineapple Cookies (page 237) or sherbet for dessert.*

BROCCOLI AND HAM SALAD

Budget
Friendly

Recipe

*This is delicious as an entrée by itself or
as a side salad for a cookout.*

½ cup Marzettis' fat-free cole
   slaw dressing
½ cup Hellmans low-fat
   mayonnaise
1 cup shredded fat-free mild
   cheddar cheese

½ pound lean pre-cooked ham -
   chopped
2 pounds frozen broccoli cuts -
   thawed
¼ cup chopped raisins
½ cup chopped red onions

♥ Mix dressing, mayonnaise and cheese together. Let sit for a couple of
minutes. Stir in remaining ingredients.

Yield: 5 (1-cup) entrée servings

Calories: 249   Total Fat: 4.4 grams (15% fat)
Cholesterol: 36 mg   Sodium: 1424 mg

10 (½-cup) side dish servings

Calories: 124   Total Fat: 2.2 grams (15% fat)
Cholesterol: 18 mg   Sodium: 712 mg

Preparation time: 15 minutes or less.

*Menu ideas: As an entrée, serve with
fresh melon and tomato slices on the side.*

ZESTY SUMMER COTTAGE SALAD

Budget Friendly

Recipe

There's nothing to whipping up this dish in a hurry!
It's easy to prepare, versatile and tasty!

1 (24-ounce) container low-fat cottage cheese (I use Flavorite brand -1 gram fat per ½ cup)
⅓ cup chopped fresh chives or green onion tops

½ cup fat-free sour cream
1 packet dry Butter Buds (or 1 tablespoon Butter Buds Sprinkles)
⅛ teaspoon ground pepper

♥ Mix all ingredients together. Serve chilled.

Yield: 8 (½-cup) servings

Calories: 80   Total Fat: 0.9 grams (10% fat)
Cholesterol: 4 mg   Sodium: 364 mg

Preparation time: 5 minutes or less.

Menu ideas: This creamy salad is delicious served with barbecue entrées. Also good as a dip on Baked Tostitos, or spread on a toasted bagel and top with a slice of tomato for an open-faced sandwich.

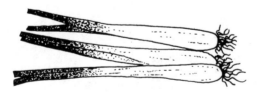

TROPICAL PASSION FRUIT SALAD

This light and creamy fruit salad is a hit with everyone!
I like to eat it as a complete lunch in itself.

³/₄ cup fat-free sour cream
1 tablespoon Equal Spoonful
(or 1 tablespoon sugar)
1 teaspoon coconut extract
(imitation coconut extract is
fine)

1 (15¹/₄-ounce) can Dole tropical
fruit in light syrup and passion
fruit juice - drained
1 (8-ounce) container fat-free
cottage cheese
1 small banana - cut into ¹/₄-inch
slices

♥ Mix sour cream, Equal (or sugar) and coconut extract together in
serving bowl with spoon. Once well mixed, add drained fruit, cottage
cheese and banana slices. Gently stir until well mixed.

♥ Serve chilled.

Yield: 6 servings

With Equal:
Calories: 104   Total Fat: 0 grams (0% fat)
Cholesterol: 3 mg   Sodium: 157 mg

With sugar:
Calories: 111   Total Fat: 0 grams (0% fat)
Cholesterol: 3 mg   Sodium: 157 mg

Preparation time: 6 minutes or less.

*Menu ideas: Picnics, potlucks, or with
fish, chicken or ham entrées.*

*Hint: Keep canned fruit refrigerated before
using so it's already chilled when you're ready to eat.*

CUCUMBER DILL SALAD

*This crispy, crunchy dish is great to nibble
on as a snack or as a side salad.*

3 large cucumbers
¼ cup shredded carrot - optional
(about ½ medium carrot)

1 (12-ounce) bottle fat-free
creamy dill dressing (I use
Medford Farms Brand)

♥ Peel cucumbers and cut into ¼-inch slices to equal 6 cups.

♥ Toss cucumber, carrot and dressing.

Yield: 12 (½-cup) servings

Calories: 57   Total Fat: 0 grams (0% fat)
Cholesterol: 0 mg   Sodium: 311 mg

Preparation time: 7 minutes or less. (Most time is derived from cutting cucumbers and shredding carrots.)

*Menu ideas: Just right for heavier main courses,
cookouts, picnics, potlucks and showers.*

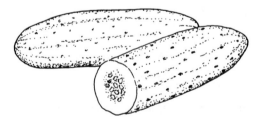

 *Isn't it funny that life seems to fly by quickly - yet some days are so long
they seem to last forever?*

SASSY SLAW

*My secret ingredients turn regular cole slaw into an
extra special salad which always gets rave reviews!*

1 (16-ounce) package ready -to-use classic cole slaw (I use Dole - found in the produce section near cut-up lettuce) (or 4½ cups shredded fresh green cabbage and ½ cup shredded carrots)

1 (20-ounce) can crushed pineapple in pineapple juice - 1 cup pineapple juice drained and discarded
¾ cup Marzettis' fat-free slaw dressing
½ teaspoon ground cinnamon

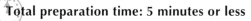

♥ Combine all ingredients in a medium bowl until well mixed.

♥ Keep chilled until ready to use.

Yield: 10 (½-cup) servings

Calories: 58   Total Fat: 0 grams (0% fat)
Cholesterol: 9 mg   Sodium: 242 mg

Total preparation time: 5 minutes or less

*Menu ideas: A delicious side vegetable for any cookout
or barbecue. Great with chicken, pork, fish or beef entrées.*

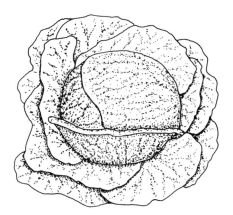

CRANBERRY APPLE SALAD

Budget
Friendly

Recipe

*Tasty on its own or as a topping for
angel food cake or frozen yogurt.*

1 (21-ounce) can apple pie filling   1 teaspoon cinnamon
1 (16-ounce) can whole berry
   Cranberry Sauce (I use Ocean
   Spray)

♥ Insert a sharp knife into opened can of pie filling and cut apples into
   small pieces while still in the can.
♥ Mix pie filling, cranberry sauce and cinnamon together.
♥ *Refrigerate for at least 20 minutes before serving.
♥ Serve chilled.

Yield: 8 (½-cup) servings

Calories: 162   Total Fat: 0 grams (0% fat)
Cholesterol: 0 mg   Sodium: 49 mg

Total preparation time: 5 minutes.

Menu ideas: Good with any holiday dinner.

*Cranberry Apple Pancakes: Make pancakes as directed on box.
Heat Cranberry Apple Salad in microwave until warm.
Spoon warmed Cranberry Apple Salad over pancakes.
Top with Cool Whip Free.*

**To eliminate this step, store cans of apple pie filling and cranberry
sauce in refrigerator before preparing recipe.*

Money can buy a piece of land, but no amount of money in the world can
buy "peace of mind".

Ham & Cheese Potato Salad

Budget Friendly

Recipe

*This hearty, meat and potatoes dish
is the answer to a hungry man's hot summer day!*

2 teaspoons mustard
1 (9-ounce) jar Kraft fat-free tartar sauce
2 teaspoons dried parsley
2 pounds extra lean pre-cooked ham - cut into ¼-inch chunks

1 (8-ounce) package fat-free Healthy Choice shredded cheddar cheese
2 pounds cooked, cooled and cubed potatoes (about 6 medium potatoes)
¾ cup chopped red onion

♥ In a large, bowl mix mustard, tartar sauce and parsley together until well mixed.

♥ Add remaining ingredients. Gently stir until all ingredients are well coated with dressing.

♥ Serve immediately or cover and keep chilled until ready to serve.

Yield: 10 (1-cup) entrée servings

Calories: 254   Total Fat: 4.6 grams (17% fat)
Cholesterol: 45 mg   Sodium: 1662 mg

20 (½-cup) side dish servings

Calories: 127   Total Fat: 2.3 grams 17% fat)
Cholesterol: 22 mg   Sodium: 831 mg

Total time: 20 minutes or less.

Menu ideas: As an entrée serve with a fresh vegetable tray with fat-free salad dressing as a dip and Blueberry Fluff Cups (page 225).

More important than being a great athlete is being a great sport!

WARM CRANAPPLE SALAD

Budget Friendly

Recipe

*This warm cranberry salad is a unique and tasty change
to an old favorite. I like serving this side salad
with pork, ham, chicken or turkey entrées.*

1 (16-ounce) can Whole Berry
Cranberry Sauce (Ocean Spray)
1 large apple (about 1 cup peeled
and chopped into ¼-inch
pieces - I use a Granny Smith
Apple)

1 teaspoon cinnamon
1 cup miniature marshmallows
1 tablespoon finely chopped
walnuts

♥ Preheat oven to 400 degrees.

♥ Spray a 1-quart casserole dish with non-fat cooking spray.

♥ Mix cranberry sauce, chopped apple and cinnamon together. Pour
into prepared casserole dish. Arrange marshmallows evenly on top.

♥ Bake at 400 degrees for 7 to 10 minutes or until tops of marshmallows
are toasty golden brown.

♥ Sprinkle chopped walnuts on top. Serve warm.

Yield: 6 servings

Calories: 168   Total Fat: 1.0 grams (5% fat)
Cholesterol: 0 mg   Sodium: 26 mg

Preparation time: 10 minutes or less.

Baking time: 7 - 10 minutes.

Total time: 20 minutes or less.

*Menu ideas: Perfect side dish with pork, ham,
chicken or turkey. Great for the holidays instead of the
traditional Cranberry Salad or Jellied Cranberries.*

TANGY TOSSED SALAD

Terrific as a meal for lunch or a side salad.

2 cups chopped turkey ham
  (about ½ pound)
1 (12-ounce) bottle of fat-free
  cole slaw dressing (I use
  T. Marzettis')
1 cup fat-free fancy shredded
  cheddar cheese (I use Healthy
  Choice)

¼ cup chopped red onion (about
  ¼ medium-size red onion)
2 heads leafy lettuce
  (or 2 (1-pound) packages
  prepared lettuce)

♥ Mix turkey ham, dressing, cheese, and onion together until well coated with dressing. Stir in lettuce just before serving.

♥ Serve chilled. I like the tangy zest of this salad. The dressing definitely adds zip to a normally boring salad.

Yield: 4 main meal entrée servings

Calories: 252   Total Fat: 2.8 grams (10% fat)
Cholesterol: 81 mg   Sodium: 1819 mg

8 side dish servings

Calories: 126   Total Fat: 1.4 grams (10% fat)
Cholesterol: 40 mg   Sodium: 909 mg

 Preparation time: 20 minutes or less.

*Menu ideas: As an entrée serve with fat-free crackers
and Peppermint Chocolate Cheesecake (page 250) for dessert.*

 You know you are "too busy" when you can't enjoy what you're doing.

MOTHER-DAUGHTER SALAD

*I like to serve this salad on a fresh romaine or leafy
lettuce leaf to accent the pretty colors of the burgundy
colored cranberries and green chives. This unique and creative
blend of flavors is a raving hit every time.*

4 cups cooked pasta shells - small size (2 cups dry)

¾ pound boneless, skinless chicken breast

½ cup dried peaches or dried apricots - cut into tiny pieces - (Sunsweet)

⅓ cup dried, sweetened cranberries - chopped (Ocean Spray)

1 (3-ounce) can real bacon bits (Oscar Mayer)

1⅓ cup light apricot syrup (Knott's Berry Farm)

2 tablespoons chopped fresh chives - optional

♥ Cook pasta as directed on box. Rinse with cold water after pasta is cooked. Set aside.

♥ Bake, microwave, or grill chicken until thoroughly cooked. Cut into tiny pieces, smaller than bite-size.

♥ Mix all ingredients except pasta together When well blended, add pasta gently and toss. Make sure all ingredients are coated well with apricot syrup, which acts as the dressing in this recipe.

♥ Serve chilled.

Yield: 6 (1-cup) entrée servings

Calories: 393   Total Fat: 5.4 grams (12% fat)
Cholesterol: 58 mg   Sodium: 515 mg

13 (½-cup) servings

Calories: 181   Total Fat: 2.5 grams (12% fat)
Cholesterol: 27 mg   Sodium: 238 mg

Preparation time: 14 minutes or less.

Cooking time: (for pasta shells and chicken) 11 minutes.

Total time: 25 minutes or less.

*Menu ideas: Great to serve at showers or potlucks.
As the main dish (entrée) a Fruity Frothy (page 61)
compliments this meal nicely.*

(Mother-Daughter Salad continued)

My 7 year old daughter was bored one day. Knowing I needed to take a pasta salad the next day for a salad bar at a special shower, I wanted to be confident that mine wouldn't be a double of someone else's. I invited my "I'm bored" daughter to help. Together we put our creative minds together and came up with this completely unique, delicious and visually beautiful salad.

BACON-LETTUCE AND TOMATO SALAD

Budget Friendly

Recipe

If you like B.L.T. sandwiches you'll love this salad!

3/4 cup fat-free sour cream
(I used Land-O-Lakes)
3/4 cup fat-free mayonnaise
(I used Kraft)
1/3 cup Equal Spoonful
(or 1/3 cup sugar)
1 teaspoon liquid smoke (found in barbecue sauce section of grocery store)

1 (3.25-ounce) container of Bac-O's bacon flavor chips
1 quart cherry tomatoes - halved
2 medium heads Romaine lettuce
- cut into bite-size pieces
(or 2 (1-pound) packages prepared lettuce)

♥ To make dressing, mix first 5 ingredients together until well blended. Keep chilled until ready to serve.

♥ When ready to serve, gently toss dressing, tomatoes and lettuce together. Serve immediately.

♥ Note: If you want a thinner dressing, add 1/4 cup skim milk.

Yield: 10 side dish servings

Calories: 111   Total Fat: 2.5 grams (20% fat)
Cholesterol: 0 mg   Sodium: 312 mg

Total preparation time: 15 minutes or less.

Menu ideas: Good as a side salad with fish, chicken, beef or pork.

MOTHER'S DAY SALAD

Budget Friendly

Recipe

This salad was named by a class I taught to mothers with their daughters.

1 (11-ounce) can mandarin oranges in light syrup, juice reserved

½ cup fat-free raspberry salad dressing (or more to taste if desired)

1 large head fresh romaine lettuce (cut or torn into bite-size pieces)

½ (3-ounce) can real bacon bits

½ ounce feta cheese - crumbled into very tiny pieces

♥ Drain the juice from the mandarin oranges into a large bowl. Add salad dressing to the juice and stir until well blended. Toss oranges, lettuce, bacon bits and dressing mixture until lettuce is well coated.

♥ Sprinkle with very tiny pieces of crumbled Feta cheese before serving.

♥ Serve chilled.

♥ I acquired the idea for this salad from an exquisite, beautiful restaurant in Michigan named The Hathaway House. I enjoyed the flavor combination so much that I was determined to create my own version at a fraction of the fats and calories of their salad. I am thrilled at my results! Knowing my version is not fattening makes mine taste even better!

♥ Thank you Hathaway House for this wonderful salad idea! It is one of my all-time favorites!

Yield: 4 servings

Calories: 157   Total Fat: 3.0 grams (17% fat)
Cholesterol: 11 mg   Sodium: 613 mg

Preparation time: 5 minutes or less.

Menu ideas: Nice served for a special Mother's Day luncheon or served as a side salad with a main entrée.

APPLE COTTAGE SALAD

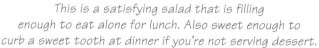
Budget
Friendly

Recipe

*This is a satisfying salad that is filling
enough to eat alone for lunch. Also sweet enough to
curb a sweet tooth at dinner if you're not serving dessert.*

1 large red Delicious apple,
   peeled and finely chopped
½ teaspoon lite salt
1 teaspoon ground cinnamon
1 tablespoon sugar (or 1
   tablespoon Equal Spoonful)

½ (24-ounce) carton fat-free
   cottage cheese
¾ cup of your favorite apple
   butter
2 tablespoons finely chopped
   walnuts or pecans - optional

♥ Sprinkle chopped apple with salt, cinnamon and sugar. Toss until well
   coated. Stir in cottage cheese and apple butter.

♥ Sprinkle chopped nuts on top.

♥ Keep refrigerated until ready to serve.

Yield: 6 servings

With sugar:
Calories: 133   Total Fat: 0.2 grams (2% fat)
Cholesterol: 5 mg   Sodium: 293 mg

With Equal:
Calories: 125   Total Fat: 0.2 grams (2% fat)
Cholesterol: 5 mg   Sodium: 293 mg

Preparation time: 10 minutes or less.

*Menu ideas: Serve this on a bed of crisp lettuce
along with a glass of Spiced Tea (page 63).*

POPEYE'S FAVORITE SALAD

Budget
Friendly

Recipe

Even Olive Oyl couldn't create a more
delicious spinach salad than this one! The
grilled onions on this salad are what make it so special!

1 large sweet white onion cut
into ½-inch slices

1 pound lean eye of round steaks,
fat trimmed away

1 (10-ounce) bag fresh, washed
and ready to eat baby spinach

6 hard boiled egg whites -
chopped

Your favorite fat-free salad dressing.
(I like to use T. Marzettis' fat-free
raspberry dressing on this salad or
fat-free Western)

♥ Spray onion slices on both sides with non-fat cooking spray. If desired,
lightly sprinkle one side of each onion slice with salt.

♥ Over medium heat, grill steaks and onion slices on an outdoor grill.
Cook to desired doneness.

♥ Cut cooked steaks into long thin strips. If desired sprinkle lightly with
garlic salt.

♥ Cut grilled onion slices into quarters.

♥ Place spinach in a large, pretty salad bowl. Top with chopped egg
whites, grilled onions and steak strips.

♥ Serve immediately with salad dressing on the side, or keep chilled for
later use. Good with the meat and onions either hot off the grill or chilled.

Yield: 4 entrée servings

Calories: 198   Total Fat: 4.3 grams (20% fat)
Cholesterol: 59 mg   Sodium: 192 mg

8 side dish servings

Calories: 99   Total Fat: 2.2 grams (20% fat)
Cholesterol: 29 mg   Sodium: 96 mg

Preparation time: 5 minutes or less.

Grilling time: 10 minutes or less.

Boiling time: 10 or less (boil eggs while steak is cooking).

Total time: 15 minutes or less.

Menu ideas: Meal in itself, served with rolls or garlic bread.

BROCCOLI & CAULIFLOWER SALAD

Budget
Friendly

Recipe

Great for picnics and potlucks!
The sweet banana peppers give this extra zing!

½ (3-ounce) container real bacon
  pieces (Oscar Mayer)
1 (16-ounce) package frozen
  broccoli and cauliflower - thawed
½ cup fat-free slaw dressing
  (T. Marzettis')

¼ cup chopped sweet banana
  pepper rings (I used Aunt
  Jane's) - drained
¼ cup chopped red onion
1 large fresh carrot - chopped

♥ Microwave bacon pieces for 10 seconds in a medium serving bowl to soften.

♥ Stir everything else in with bacon bits until well mixed.

♥ Keep chilled until ready to eat.

Yield: 6 (⅔-cup) servings

Calories: 82   Total Fat: 1.6 grams (16% fat)
Cholesterol: 15 mg   Sodium: 590 mg

Preparation time: 10 minutes.

Menu ideas: Great as a side dish with
lean ham, chicken or lean pork on the grill.
Baked potatoes, cake or pudding-type dessert.

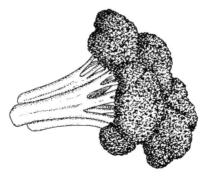

119

SPRING SALAD

*Don't let this title fool you! This salad is delicious in
all seasons . . . Spring, Summer, Fall or Winter.*

1 (8-ounce) bottle T. Marzettis' fat-free Cole Slaw Dressing
1 (8-ounce) container fat-free sour cream
1 cup chopped red onion (any sweet onion will do)
6 boiled egg whites - chopped (discard the yolks of the boiled eggs)
1 cup shredded fat-free mozzarella cheese - (Kroger brand is good)
2 large heads fresh romaine lettuce - about 10 cups chopped (for a faster salad you can buy the pre-packaged cut-up lettuce in the produce section)

♥ Mix together the cole slaw dressing and fat-free sour cream until well blended. Continue stirring and add the onion, egg whites and cheese until well coated with dressing.

♥ Gently toss the lettuce with the dressing. Serve immediately.

Yield: 8 servings

Calories: 131   Total Fat: 0 grams (0% fat)
Cholesterol: 16 mg   Sodium: 592 mg

Preparation time: 10 minutes or less.

Cooking time: 10 minutes or less (derived from boiling eggs).

Total time: 20 minutes.

*Menu ideas: This salad is excellent with
anything your heart desires.*

*Please note: Do not put the dressing on the salad until
ready to serve. It is okay to prepare the dressing with the cheese,
egg, and onions ahead of time, however keep it separate from the
lettuce until ready to serve. If lettuce is stirred with dressing
too far in advance, the salad will become soggy.*

(Spring Salad continued)

SPRING SALAD WITH CHICKEN:
Simply add 1 (10-ounce) can Premium Chunk White Chicken in water. Drain water from chicken before stirring into dressing.

Yield: 4 large entrée servings

Calories: 303   Total Fat: 1.3 grams (4% fat)
Cholesterol: 51 mg   Sodium: 1256 mg

8 side dish servings

Calories: 151   Total Fat: 0.7 grams (4% fat)
Cholesterol: 25 mg   Sodium: 628 mg

Preparation time: 10 minutes or less.

Cooking time: 10 minutes or less.

Total time: 20 minutes or less.

Menu ideas: This salad is excellent as an entrée served with reduced fat Ritz crackers for lunch!

Don't be so busy that you can't take time to dream dreams, and think thoughts.

ZESTY POTATO SALAD

No boring potato salad here folks!
This side salad adds zest to any blah meal.

*1 (9-ounce) jar Kraft Free Tartar Sauce
3/4 cup finely chopped red onion (or for faster preparation use 3/4 cup frozen onion. However, I prefer the pretty look of red onion in this salad.)
1 teaspoon sugar (or 1 teaspoon Equal Spoonful)

1 cup celery - chopped (or 1/2 teaspoon celery salt)
2 teaspoons mustard
1 teaspoon dried parsley - optional
2 pounds potatoes - cooked, cooled and cubed with skins on (About 6 medium potatoes. Leftover baked or microwaved potatoes are good.)

♥ Mix together all ingredients except potatoes until dressing is well blended.

♥ Add potatoes to dressing and gently stir until potatoes are coated with dressing.

♥ Cover and keep chilled until ready to serve.

♥ *Using prepared tartar sauce saves me time in measuring numerous ingredients such as mayonnaise, salad dressing, sweet pickle relish and vinegar.

Yield: 10 (1/2-cup) servings

With sugar:
Calories: 109   Total Fat: 0.2 grams (1% fat)
Cholesterol: 0 mg   Sodium: 197 mg

With Equal Spoonful:
Calories: 107   Total Fat: 0.2 grams (1% fat)
Cholesterol: 0 mg   Sodium: 197 mg

Preparation time: Hopefully, you have some leftover cooked potatoes in the refrigerator, because the cooking and cooling time of the potatoes are what requires the most amount of time. The quickest way to cook potatoes is in the microwave, about 3 1/2 minutes per potato. To cool quickly, place hot potatoes in sink of ice water. Total cooking and cooling time combined; about 23 minutes.

(Zesty Potato Salad continued)

Otherwise, this potato salad can be assembled in 15 minutes or less. (including cubing the potatoes.)

Menu ideas: Great for picnics and cookouts. Adds zest to any grilled or baked plain meat entrée meal. Also great with sandwiches or barbecued foods.

ZESTY EGG SALAD SANDWICHES

Budget Friendly

Recipe

This brings boring egg salad to life!

1 whole hard boiled egg, yolk separated after cooking
1 teaspoon water
¼ cup Kraft fat-free tartar sauce

4 hard boiled egg whites (discard yolks)
6 slices fat-free bread - toasted

♥ With a fork, mix egg yolk, water and tartar sauce together until smooth and creamy.

♥ Chop egg whites into tiny pieces.

♥ Stir egg whites into creamy mixture.

♥ Keep chilled until ready to serve.

♥ Spread on toasted bread. Top with fresh crisp lettuce.

Yield: 3 sandwiches

Calories: 204   Total Fat: 1.7 grams (8% fat)
Cholesterol: 71 mg   Sodium: 548 mg

Preparation time: 5 minutes or less.

Cooking time: 10 minutes.

Total time: 15 minutes or less.

Menu ideas: For a unique twist, serve open-faced egg salad sandwiches on toasted rye or pumpernickel. Top with thin slices of cucumber or tomato.

123

PEPPERED POTATO SALAD

Budget Friendly Recipe

This hearty dish is the answer to all of those who don't like sweet tasting potato salad! Don't let the pepper in the recipe title scare you, there's only enough to give the salad flavor.

6 cups cubed potatoes - with skin on
1 (8-ounce) carton fat-free sour cream (I use Land-O-Lakes)
3 tablespoons Miracle Whip Light

⅛ teaspoon ground pepper
½ cup chopped onion
¼ cup imitation Bacon Bits
1 teaspoon dried parsley flakes - optional - divided

♥ In a large Dutch oven, cook cubed potatoes in boiling salt water for 5 to 10 minutes or until tender. Drain well. Rinse with cold water until potatoes are cool. Set aside.

♥ In a medium serving bowl, stir together sour cream, Miracle Whip, pepper, onion, bacon bits and ½ teaspoon dried parsley until well mixed.

♥ Add cooked, cubed potatoes to cream mixture.

♥ Stir together until well mixed. Sprinkle top with remaining ½ teaspoon dried parsley.

♥ Keep chilled until ready to eat.

Yield: 12 (½-cup) servings

Calories: 101   Total Fat: 1.2 grams (10% fat)
Cholesterol: 0 mg   Sodium: 84 mg

Total Preparation time - including cooking of potatoes, 35 minutes or less. (Most of the time derives from cubing and cooking the potatoes.)

Menu ideas: Great for any cookout or picnic. Serve instead of a baked potato with beef, pork, fish or chicken.

Simply Delicious Side Dishes

ZESTY CORN

Budget Friendly
Recipe

*This dish will put a smile on your face
and have your family asking for seconds.*

1 (16-ounce) can cream style
  yellow corn

1 (16-ounce) can white or yellow
  corn - drained
1 cup your favorite chunky salsa

♥ Over medium heat, stir all ingredients together until well mixed.

♥ Bring to a boil. (Or cook in microwave 3 to 4 minutes until hot.)

♥ Serve hot.

Yield: 8 servings

Calories: 82   Total fat: 0.6 grams (6% fat)
Cholesterol: 0 mg   Sodium: 428 mg

Preparation time: 3 minutes or less.

Cooking time: 5 minutes or less.

Total time: 8 minutes or less.

*Menu ideas: Great with meat entrées, such as
chicken, turkey, fish, lean beef or pork tenderloin.*

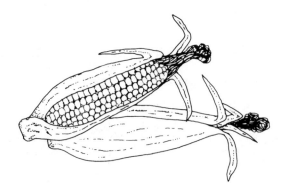

CREAMED GREEN BEANS WITH HAM

Budget Friendly Recipe

This delightful dish is fit for a king as a side dish or entrée.

4 (15-ounce) cans green beans - drained
¹/₂ pound extra lean ham - chopped
1 (8-ounce) can of mushroom stems and pieces - drained - optional

1 (12-ounce) can fat-free evaporated skim milk (I use Carnation)
1 tablespoon dry Butter Buds Sprinkles
2 tablespoons cornstarch
¹/₂ teaspoon liquid smoke

♥ Warm green beans, ham and mushrooms over medium heat in a large (12-inch or larger) non-stick skillet for 3 minutes.

♥ In a medium bowl, mix milk, Butter Buds, cornstarch and liquid smoke together with a whisk until dissolved.

♥ Stir milk mixture into skillet with cooked green beans, ham and mushrooms. Continue stirring over heat about 5 to 7 minutes or until thick.

♥ Serve hot.

Yield: 12 side dish servings

Calories: 77   Total fat: 1.3 grams (15% fat)
Cholesterol: 10 mg   Sodium: 657 mg

4 entrée servings

Calories: 230   Total fat: 3.8 grams (15% fat)
Cholesterol: 30 mg   Sodium: 1971 mg

Preparation time: 7 minutes or less.

Cooking time: 10 minutes or less.

Total time: 17 minutes or less.

Menu idea: As a side dish with any meat, fish or poultry. As an entrée, good with French bread or rolls, sliced tomatoes, and Peaches & Cream Trifle (page 262).

CALICO CORN

Budget Friendly Recipe

This slightly sweet and definitely unique vegetable dish received it's name because of its beautiful color combination.

2 (15¼-ounce) cans whole kernel corn - drained
1 tablespoon sugar

¼ cup Western fat-free salad dressing
1 cup your favorite chunky salsa

♥ In a 2-quart microwavable bowl, mix together all ingredients until well blended.

♥ Heat in microwave on full power for 3 minutes or until completely warmed.

Yield: 7 (½-cup) servings

Calories: 102   Total fat: 0.9 grams (7% fat)
Cholesterol: 0 mg   Sodium: 436 mg

Preparation time: 3 minutes or less.

Cooking time: 3 minutes.

Total time: 6 minutes or less

Menu ideas: Compliments any lean meat cooked on the grill, baked or broiled. Salad topper idea: Sprinkle chilled on top of and toss with a fresh, crisp, green lettuce salad instead of the traditional fresh tomatoes or vegetables. Serve salad dressing of your choice on the side.

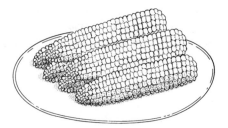

CORN CASSEROLE (BAKED)

Budget Friendly

Recipe

I got this idea from a dear friend, Kathy Beerbower.
Hers is absolutely delicious but is loaded with too much
fat and calories. This is just as delicious - and a lot less fattening.

1 (15¼-ounce) can whole kernel corn - undrained

1 (16-ounce) can cream style corn

1 (8½-ounce) box Jiffy corn muffin mix - dry

½ cup fat-free Ultra Promise - softened

1 cup fat-free sour cream (Land-O-Lakes)

♥ Preheat oven to 350 degrees.

♥ Spray a 9x13-inch pan with non-fat cooking spray.

♥ Mix all ingredients together and spread into prepared pan.

♥ Bake at 350 degrees for 35 to 40 minutes or until top is golden brown. Serve warm.

Yield: 15 servings

Calories: 132   Total fat: 2.2 grams (15% fat)
Cholesterol: 0 mg   Sodium: 378 mg

Preparation time: 5 minutes or less.

Cooking time: 40 minutes or less.

Total time: 45 minutes or less.

Menu ideas: Good with fish, chicken, turkey,
omelets, quiches or brunches.

When it comes to talking about the future . . . never say never, because
you never know.

CREAMED SPINACH

Budget
Friendly

Recipe

*Popeye would have gone nuts over this
smooth, creamy spinach.*

2 tablespoons cornstarch
1 tablespoon sugar
1 envelope Butter Buds
  (or 1 tablespoon dry Butter
  Buds Sprinkles)
1 (5-ounce) can evaporated skim
  milk

2 (10-ounce) packages frozen
  chopped spinach (once thawed,
  with hands squeeze all excess
  water from spinach)
1/3 cup fat-free Kraft Parmesan
  cheese

♥ Before even turning the stove on, in a large (12-inch) non-stick skillet
  dissolve cornstarch, sugar and Butter Buds in milk.

♥ Turn on stove to medium heat. Add spinach.

♥ Stirring constantly, bring to a boil.

♥ Sprinkle with fat-free Parmesan cheese.

♥ Reduce heat to low. Cover. Let simmer for 10 minutes.

Yield: 7 servings

Calories: 67   Total fat: 0.3 grams (4% fat)
Cholesterol: 5 mg   Sodium: 129 mg

Preparation time: 5 minutes or less.

Cooking time: 15 minutes or less.

Total time: 20 minutes or less.

*Menu ideas: Any Italian food or main meat entrées such as
chicken, turkey, fish, pork tenderloin or lean beef.*

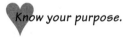

Know your purpose.

130

MUSHROOM, ONION & BACON GREEN BEAN CASSEROLE

Budget Friendly

Recipe

Don't mistake this for the classic Durkee Onion Green Bean Casserole. Although this is equally delicious. This has it's own distinguished and delicious flavor with a fraction of the fats and calories!

4 (15-ounce) cans French style green beans - drained

2 (4-ounce) cans mushroom stems and pieces

1 (1.5-ounce) envelope dry onion soup mix

1 (16-ounce) container fat-free sour cream

1 teaspoon liquid smoke (found in the Barbecue sauce aisle)

1 (3-ounce) jar bacon-pieces (I used Hormel) - divided

♥ With your hands, squeeze as much liquid from the green beans as possible.

♥ Spray a 2-quart microwaveable bowl or casserole dish with non-fat cooking spray. Stir all ingredients together except use only ½ of the jar of bacon pieces. Keep stirring until well combined.

♥ Microwave on high for 2 to 2½ minutes. Stir. Turn bowl a ½ turn. Microwave again for 2 to 2½ minutes or until completely heated. Stir again. (If you have a carousel microwave cook for 4 to 5 minutes, stirring halfway through.)

♥ Sprinkle remaining bacon bits on top of casserole.

♥ Serve hot.

Yield: 14 (½-cup) servings

Calories: 87   Total fat: 1.8 grams (19% fat)
Cholesterol: 5 mg   Sodium: 839 mg

Preparation time: 5 minutes or less.

Cooking time: 5 minutes or less.

Total time: 10 minutes or less.

Menu ideas: Good with main meat dish entrées, such as pork tenderloin, beef tenderloin, chicken, fish or turkey.

GREEN BEANS ITALIANO'

Budget
Friendly

Recipe

*I got this idea from Kenny Roger's restaurant. I'm not
sure what he has in his, but this is a pretty close match
and just as good. And I can almost bet that mine are a lot less
fattening. These beans are popular primarily with adults.*

1-1½ cups thinly sliced onion
   (2 medium onions)
¾ cup fat-free Italian salad
   dressing (I use Wish Bone)

1 (14½-ounce) can diced
   tomatoes - drained (I use Hunts)
2 (16-ounce) bags frozen green
   beans
½ tablespoon lite salt - optional

♥ In a large non-stick skillet (about 12-inch) sauté onions in salad
dressing over medium heat about 2 to 3 minutes or until tender. Add
drained diced tomatoes and green beans. Increase heat to medium-
high. Stir until well coated. Salt if desired. Cover. Cook for 5 to 7
minutes or until beans are tender.

♥ Serve hot.

Yield: 12 (²⁄₃-cup) servings

Calories: 39   Total fat: 0.2 grams (4% fat)
Cholesterol: 0 mg   Sodium: 186 mg

Preparation time: 5 minutes or less.

Cooking time: 10 minutes or less.

Total time: 15 minutes or less.

*Menu ideas: They go great with entrées that have a
marinara sauce (red sauce) like lasagna or spaghetti.*

*Don't "if only" or "what if" your life away. Do the best you can with the
cards you are dealt.*

GARLIC RED SKINS

Budget Friendly

Recipe

2 pounds red skin potatoes - washed
2 tablespoons chopped garlic (to save time purchase pre-chopped garlic in a jar from the produce section)

1 teaspoon lite salt
½ cup Fleischmann's Fat-Free Buttery Spread
1 teaspoon dried parsley

♥ Cut unpeeled red skins into 1-inch cubes.

♥ Put cubed potatoes into boiling water. Turn heat off. Let set for 15 to 20 minutes or until potatoes are tender when poked with a fork.

♥ In a large 12-inch non-stick skillet, cook garlic over medium heat with salt and butter spread for just a few minutes to heat (and make the home smell yummy!).

♥ Drain water from red skins.

♥ Stir red skins into garlic butter until well coated.

♥ Pour into serving dish. Sprinkle with dried parsley.

♥ Serve immediately.

Yield: 8 servings

Calories: 108   Total fat: 0 grams (0% fat)
Cholesterol: 0 mg   Sodium: 220 mg

Preparation time: 8 minutes or less.

Cooking time: 15-20 minutes.

Total time: 28 minutes or less.

Menu ideas: Good with meat entrées such as beef tenderloin, chicken, fish or turkey.

Thankfulness is an attitude we choose to have!

Spring Asparagus

What a wonderful way to eat fresh asparagus!

1 tablespoon mustard
⅓ cup fat-free sour cream
⅛ teaspoon dried dill weed

2 pounds fresh asparagus - steamed

♥ Mix mustard, sour cream and dill together until well blended. Toss gently with freshly steamed asparagus. Serve immediately. (If needed, this dish can be microwaved for a few minutes to re-warm.)

Yield: 6 servings

Calories: 51   Total fat: 0.4 grams (6% fat)
Cholesterol: 0 mg   Sodium: 46 mg

Preparation time: 5 minutes or less.

Cooking time: 5 to 7 minutes.

Total time: 12 minutes or less.

Menu ideas: Compliments pork, beef or chicken entrées.

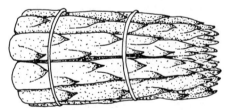

134

MASHED POTATOES DELUXE

Budget Friendly

Recipe

The perfect quickie substitute for those of you
who like the traditional, high fat "twice baked potatoes".

2 pounds red skin potatoes
1 (8-ounce) fat-free cream cheese
½ cup Fleischmann's Fat-Free
   Buttery Spread

1¼ cup - 1½ cups skim milk
3 teaspoons garlic salt - optional

♥ Wash unpeeled potatoes and pierced with a fork. Microwave whole potatoes in a *carousel microwave for 12 minutes or until fully cooked.

♥ Using a fork and sharp knife, cut cooked potatoes into cubes, leaving skins on.

♥ Put all ingredients into a medium mixing bowl. With a mixer, beat on medium speed for about two minutes or until desired creamy consistency.

♥ Microwave entire bowl of Mashed Potatoes Deluxe in the microwave an additional 1 to 2 minutes to reheat before serving.

♥ Serve additional Fleischmann's fat-free Buttery Spread on the side if desired.

Yield: 8 servings

Calories: 149   Total fat: 0 grams (0% fat)
Cholesterol: 1 mg   Sodium: 124 mg

Preparation time: Less than 20 minutes including cooking time.

Menu ideas: Good with a pork roast, beef tenderloin
or chicken, with a nice salad on the side.

*If you do not have a carousel microwave, turn potatoes
a quarter turn every 3 minutes.

CALIFORNIA GARLIC BLEND

Budget
Friendly

Recipe

Every bit as good as any fine restaurant.

1 (1 pound) bag frozen California blend vegetables (broccoli, cauliflower and carrots)

1 teaspoon crushed garlic (I buy the already crushed garlic in a jar usually found in the produce section)

½-1 teaspoon lite salt - optional

¼ cup Fleischmann's Fat-Free Buttery Spread

♥ Mix all ingredients together in a microwavable serving bowl. Cover. Place in center of a *carousel microwave. Cook on high for 4½ minutes.

♥ Stir well. Serve immediately.

Yield: 5 servings

Calories: 38   Total fat: 0.2 grams (5% fat)
Cholesterol: 0 mg   Sodium: 87 mg

Preparation time: 3 minutes or less.

Cooking time: 4½ minutes.

Total time: 7½ minutes or less.

Menu ideas: Good on top of a baked potato or with a main entrée for lunch or dinner.

*If you do not have a carousel microwave, turn the dish a half turn after 2 minutes.

If you want to be blessed then be a blessing to others.

136

CARROTS WITH A LIGHT
BUTTERY CARAMEL GLAZE

Budget
Friendly

Recipe

This slightly sweet glaze gives nature a helping hand, which entices children of all ages to eat more vegetables!

1 pound mini carrots (peeled - found in produce section)

2 tablespoons Fleischmann's Fat-Free Buttery Spread (found in butter and margarine section of grocery store)

½ teaspoon lite salt - optional

2 tablespoons Smuckers fat-free caramel topping (found in ice cream section of grocery store)

♥ Place carrots in a medium (2-quart) saucepan. Put just enough water in pan to cover carrots. Bring to a boil. Turn off heat and cover. Let sit for 10 to 13 minutes or until carrots are tender when pierced with a fork.

♥ Meantime while carrots are cooking, in a small bowl stir together butter, salt and caramel sauce until well blended.

♥ When cooked, drain carrots and mix with caramel glaze.

♥ Serve hot.

Yield: 5 servings

Calories: 71   Total fat: 0.2 grams (2% fat)
Cholesterol: 0 mg   Sodium: 84 mg

Preparation time: 3 minutes.

Cooking time: 10-13 minutes.

Total time: 16 minutes or less.

Menu ideas: Serve with Ham Kebabs (page 172)
or Manhandler Meatloaf (page 192).

SAVORY SAUSAGE & GREEN BEAN CASSEROLE

Budget
Friendly

Recipe

*The distinctive, savory flavor of
sausage pleasingly compliments these beans!*

3 (15-ounce) cans French style green beans - drained
1 (10¾-ounce) can reduced-fat Campbell's cream of mushroom soup
½ cup chopped onion (I use the frozen pre-cut onions)
½ teaspoon garlic salt - optional
1 (4-ounce) can sliced mushrooms - drained
1 (6.4-ounce) Healthy Choice low-fat breakfast sausage - cut into tiny pieces (found in frozen foods section)

♥ Mix all ingredients together, until well coated. Cook in a *carousel microwave on high for 4 to 5 minutes or until completely heated. Serve immediately.

Yield: 12 side dish servings

Calories: 50   Total fat: 1.3 grams (22% fat)
Cholesterol: 6 mg   Sodium: 576 mg

4 entrée servings

Calories: 151   Total fat: 3.8 grams (22% fat)
Cholesterol: 17 mg   Sodium: 1727 mg

Preparation time: 10 minutes or less.

Cooking time: 5 minutes or less.

Total time: 15 minutes or less.

Menu ideas: As a side dish: Good with any main meat entrée such as chicken, turkey, fish, pork tenderloin or beef tenderloin. Also good with Italian food, such as lasagna or spaghetti.

As a main entrée: Baked potato, (for faster preparation cook potatoes in microwave) and Punchbowl Cake (page 218).

*If you do not have a carousel microwave, turn a half turn after 2 minutes.

Sensational
Sweet Potato Casserole

Budget
Friendly

Recipe

Definitely a unique and flavorful twist to an old holiday favorite!

1 (24-ounce) can of sweet
potatoes with syrup
1 (20-ounce) can apple cranberry
homestyle pie filling (I used
Thank You)

Cinnamon - optional

♥ Drain syrup from sweet potatoes into a measuring cup.

♥ Put the sweet potatoes in a medium bowl. With hands or a potato masher, break sweet potatoes into little pieces.

♥ Pour ½ of the drained syrup into the sweet potatoes. Discard remaining syrup.

♥ With a hand held mixer on low speed, mix juices with sweet potatoes until well mashed. Potatoes will be lumpy and not a very thick consistency.

♥ With a spoon, stir apple cranberry pie filling into sweet potatoes.

♥ Microwave on high for 2 to 3 minutes. Stir, turn bowl a ½ turn. Microwave for 2 to 3 minutes more, or until completely heated.

♥ Sprinkle with cinnamon. Serve hot.

Yield: 10 (½-cup) servings

Calories: 111   Total fat: 0 grams (0% fat)
Cholesterol: 0 mg   Sodium: 58 mg

Preparation time: 5 minutes or less.

Cooking time: 6 minutes or less.

Total time: 11 minutes or less.

Menu ideas: Great as a side dish for your festive holiday dinner.

139

SOUR CREAM PASTA SALAD

Great as a side dish or add meat for a terrific entrée.

Budget Friendly
Recipe

1 (16-ounce) carton fat-free sour cream

¾ cup light Miracle Whip

2-3 teaspoons Durkee Salad Seasoning (found in spice section)

1 pound box ziti style pasta - cooked as directed on box (Bowtie pasta or elbow macaroni is fine also)

1 pound Healthy Choice fat-free shredded cheddar cheese

1 cup finely chopped red sweet pepper (1 medium)

1 cup chopped celery (about 3 stalks)

2 tablespoons chopped chives - optional

♥ In a large bowl mix together sour cream, Miracle Whip and Durkee Salad Seasoning until well blended. Stir in remaining ingredients until well coated with dressing. Serve chilled.

Yield: 12 (1-cup) entrée servings

Calories: 280   Total fat: 3.3 grams (11% fat)
Cholesterol: 7 mg   Sodium: 484 mg

24 (½-cup) side dish servings

Calories: 140   Total fat: 1.6 grams (11% fat)
Cholesterol: 4 mg   Sodium: 242 mg

Preparation and cooking time: 23 minutes or less (derived from cooking pasta and chopping vegetables.)

Menu ideas: Cookouts, Barbecues, luncheons, buffet and potlucks.

SOUR CREAM TUNA PASTA SALAD:
Drain water from 3 (6-ounce) cans of tuna and toss into pasta salad.

Yield: 12 (1-cup) entrée servings

Calories: 328   Total fat: 3.6 grams (10% fat)
Cholesterol: 19 mg   Sodium: 624 mg

24 (½-cup) side dish servings

Calories: 164   Total fat: 1.8 grams (10% fat)
Cholesterol: 10 mg   Sodium: 312 mg

(Sour Cream Pasta Salad continued)

SOUR CREAM CHICKEN PASTA SALAD:
Add 2 cups cooked, chopped chicken breast.

Yield: 12 (1-cup) entrée servings

Calories: 321   Total fat: 4.4 grams (13% fat)
Cholesterol: 27 mg   Sodium: 502 mg

24 (½-cup) side dish servings

Calories: 160   Total fat: 2.2 grams (13% fat)
Cholesterol: 13 mg   Sodium: 251 mg

SOUR CREAM TURKEY PASTA SALAD:
Add 2 cups cooked and chopped turkey breast.

Yield: 12 (1-cup) entrée servings

Calories: 313   Total fat: 3.6 grams (11% fat)
Cholesterol: 27 mg   Sodium: 497 mg

24 (½-cup) side dish servings

Calories: 157   Total fat: 1.8 grams(11% fat)
Cholesterol: 14 mg   Sodium: 249 mg

SOUR CREAM SAUSAGE PASTA SALAD:
Add on (14- to 16-ounce) package fat-free smoked sausage (Butter Ball and Healthy Choice brands are good.) Cut into tiny pieces.

Yield: 12 (1-cup) entrée servings

Calories: 315   Total fat: 3.3 grams (10% fat)
Cholesterol: 21 mg   Sodium: 872 mg

24 (½-cup) side dish servings

Calories: 157   Total fat: 1.6 grams (10% fat)
Cholesterol: 11 mg   Sodium: 436 mg

I'd rather be an optimist and be wrong, than be a pessimist and be right.

BROCCOLI PARMESAN

Budget
Friendly

Recipe

*Perfect for when you need a
great tasting vegetable dish - fast!*

¼ cup Fleischmann's fat-free
   Buttery Spread (found in dairy
   section)
½ teaspoon garlic salt - optional

1 (16-ounce) bag frozen broccoli
   cuts
¼ cup shredded Parmesan cheese
   (not grated - found in cheese
   section)

♥ Stir butter spread, garlic salt and broccoli in a microwavable bowl.
   Cover.

♥ Cook on high for 4 minutes. Stir. Cook for 4 more minutes on high.

♥ Sprinkle with Parmesan Cheese. Let sit for 2 minutes. Serve hot.

Yield: 5 servings

Calories: 52   Total fat: 1.4 grams (22% fat)
Cholesterol: 3 mg   Sodium: 150 mg

Preparation time: 2 minutes or less.

Cooking time: 10 minutes or less.

Total time: 12 minutes or less.

*Menu ideas: Great with any meat main entrée meal such as pork
   tenderloin, lean beef, chicken, fish, turkey or Italian entrées.*

*You know you're getting old when you have to carry your vision, hearing
and chewing aids with you. (Glasses, hearing aid and false teeth.)*

- Ron Webb

MUSHROOM-ASPARAGUS CASSEROLE

This definitely reminds me of old time country cookin'!

3 (4-ounce) cans mushroom stems and pieces - drained

5 (14½-ounce) cans asparagus - drained

1 (12-ounce) jar Heinz HomeStyle gravy - Blue Ribbon Country Flavor

¼ cup Kraft fat-free grated topping (made with Parmesan cheese and other wholesome ingredients)

¼ cup shredded fat-free mozzarella cheese (I use Healthy Choice)

♥ Spray a 2-quart casserole dish with non-fat cooking spray.

♥ Mix first four ingredients together in a casserole dish. Cover and cook in a microwave for 2 minutes. Stir. Cook another 2 minutes.

♥ Sprinkle top lightly with mozzarella cheese. Cover. Let sit a couple of minutes before serving.

♥ The heat and moisture from the gravy and vegetables will soften the mozzarella cheese.

♥ Serve hot.

Yield: 18 (½-cup) servings

Calories: 35   Total fat: 1.0 gram (21% fat)
Cholesterol: 1 mg   Sodium: 435 mg

Preparation time: 6 minutes or less.

Cooking time: 4 minutes.

Total time: 10 minutes or less.

Menu ideas: Great served as a side dish with any main meat entrée and garlic bread. Large enough to serve for big gatherings such as potlucks and family get-togethers.

143

ORIENTAL VEGETABLES

Budget Friendly

Recipe

Super as a side dish or add pork for a scrumptious entrée

1 teaspoon garlic salt	1 (12-ounce) jar Heinz
2 pounds frozen oriental	HomeStyle Bistro au jus gravy
vegetables	1 tablespoon Equal Spoonful
	2 tablespoons soy sauce

♥ In a large Dutch oven (big saucepan) dissolve garlic salt in 1½ inches of water. Put oriental vegetables in garlic salt water. (The oriental vegetables will not be covered with water!) Bring water to a full boil. Turn off heat. Cover. Let sit for 10 to 12 minutes or until fully steamed to desired tenderness.

♥ Stir gravy, Equal and soy sauce together in a serving bowl. No need to heat. The heat from the cooked vegetables will heat the sauce.

♥ Drain vegetables and stir into with sauce. Serve hot.

Yield: 8 servings

Calories: 55   Total fat: 0.6 grams (9% fat)
Cholesterol: 0 mg   Sodium: 986 mg

Preparation time: 7 minutes or less.

Cooking time: 10 - 12 minutes.

Total time: 19 minutes or less.

Menu ideas: This vegetable dish is a perfect accompaniment with the Caribbean Rice (page 206).

When it comes to life if you think, "you've seen it all" then I encourage you to open your eyes. There's always more to see!

TWICE BAKED POTATOES

Budget Friendly

Recipe

This is also from Paula Kamler from Joplin, Missouri.

♥ Bake 1 large potato. If desired you can cook it in a microwave for about 3 to 4 minutes. Make sure you poke it with a fork a few times so it won't explode when cooking.

♥ Open and scoop out contents.

To contents add:

1 slice fat-free cheese	½ teaspoon dry buttermilk Ranch
2 tablespoons fat-free sour cream	dressing mix
1 tablespoon dry Butter Buds	1 tablespoon bacon bits

♥ Mix together and put back into skin. Microwave about 20 seconds and sprinkle with another tablespoon bacon bits.

Yield: 1 serving

Calories: 321   Total fat: 2.8 grams (8% fat)
Cholesterol: 10 mg   Sodium: 910 mg

Preparation time: 4 minutes or less.

Cooking time: 3-4 minutes.

Total time: 8 minutes or less.

Menu ideas: Good for lunch with a salad.
Also good with any main meat entrée such as lean sirloin steak,
lean pork tenderloin or chicken breast. Serve with a salad or cup of
broth-based vegetable soup for a well rounded meal.

Budget
Friendly

Recipe

SPICED APPLES

An all American heartland favorite!

4 Jonathan apples - unpeeled and sliced into 1/8-inch slices
2 tablespoons dry Butter Buds Sprinkles

1 teaspoon ground cinnamon
1/4 cup dark brown sugar

♥ Toss all ingredients together until well mixed.

♥ Put in a microwavable 1-quart casserole dish. Cover with wax paper. Cook on high in carousel microwave for 4 minutes.

Yield: 4 servings

Calories: 144   Total fat: 0.5 grams (3% fat)
Cholesterol: 0 mg   Sodium: 36 mg

Preparation time: 5 minutes or less.

Cooking time: 4 minutes.

Total time: 9 minutes or less.

Menu idea: Delicious as a side dish, served over frozen fat-free vanilla ice cream or topped with a dab of Cool Whip Free.

MASHED POTATOES AND CARROTS

Budget
Friendly

Recipe

A tasty, good and old-fashioned comfort food.

*5 medium cooked potatoes - peeled

1 (14.5-ounce) can of sliced carrots - drained

⅓ cup Fleischmann's fat-free Buttery Spread

⅓ cup fat-free chicken broth (I use Swanson)

½ teaspoon celery salt

♥ *To easily cook potatoes, either cook whole in a microwave (poke with fork before cooking) on high until tender or cook whole in ½ cup water in a crockpot on low all day. (Up to 9 hours.) To easily peel potatoes, simply put hot, cooked potato under cold running water and peel the skin off with your fingers.

♥ In a medium mixing bowl break up potatoes.

♥ Add remaining ingredients to potatoes.

♥ With a mixer on low, beat for 3 to 4 minutes or until creamy smooth. If needed, add more chicken broth. (Note: There may be some lumps.) Reheat in microwave for 3 to 4 minutes or until hot.

Yield: 7 servings

Calories: 118   Total fat: 0 grams (0% fat)
Cholesterol: 0 mg   Sodium: 305 mg

Preparation time: 5 minutes or less.

Cooking time: Varies, depending on cooking method.

*Menu ideas: This side dish tastes great with
any main entrée . . . such as chicken, ham, steak, etc.*

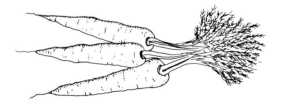

HOMESTYLE GREEN BEANS AND POTATOES

Budget Friendly

Recipe

This simple side dish is a delicious way to get two for one.
(Two vegetables in one dish.)

2 (15-ounce) can green beans - drained
3 leftover cooked red skin potatoes - unpeeled and cut into ½-inch cubes
2 tablespoons Fleischmann's fat-free Buttery Spread

2 tablespoons Bac-O's (the off brand of imitation Bac-O's or Bacon Bits is fine)
⅛ teaspoon garlic salt - optional
Dash of pepper - optional (a dash is 3 or 4 pepper shakes)

♥ Mix all ingredients in a medium microwavable bowl until well mixed. Cover. (If you do not have a lid for your bowl, wax paper or paper towels are okay to use.)

♥ Cook on high in a carousel microwave for 3 to 4 minutes.

Yield: 6 servings

Calories: 70   Total fat: 0.5 grams (6% fat)
Cholesterol: 0 mg   Sodium: 323 mg

Preparation time: 5 minutes or less.

Cooking time: 4 minutes or less.

Total time: 9 minutes or less.

Menu ideas: This side dish tastes excellent with any
meat based entrée . . . chicken, steak, ham, etc.

On The Go Entrées

Crockpot Cooking

Multiple Cooking Methods

Regular Cooking

Ten Minutes or Less

Fifteen Minutes or Less

Twenty Minutes or Less

Thirty Minutes or Less

SPICY, THICK VEGETARIAN CHILI

Budget Friendly

Recipe

This thick, hearty, stick to your bones (but not your thighs!) chili is power packed with protein and fiber.

2 (15-ounce) cans Mexican style hot chili beans

1 (16-ounce) can vegetarian refried beans (I use Old El Paso)

1 (15-ounce) can black beans (I use Progresso ready to serve)

2 cups chunky salsa (I use Chi-Chi's)

1 (6-ounce) can tomato paste

♥ Stir all ingredients together in a 3-quart or larger saucepan over a medium heat until thoroughly heated and well mixed. Presto! You're done! Now enjoy!

Yield: 9 (1-cup) servings

Calories: 176 Total fat: 1.6 grams (8% fat)
Cholesterol: 0 mg Sodium: 1034 mg

Total preparation and cooking time: 5 minutes or less.

Menu ideas: Southwestern Corn Muffins (page 80).

Additional ideas: - optional

- for spicier chili add Tabasco sauce.

- for an eye appealing garnish, sprinkle bowl of chili with Healthy Choice fancy shredded cheddar cheese.

- for a chili not as thick, add water or tomato juice - 1 cup at a time until desired consistency is reached.

"The problem with a lot of guys is they want to marry the "Barbie" doll and she's already been taken by Ken."

- Lisa Eisel

HARVEST HAM STEAKS

Budget Friendly

Recipe

*A lip smackin' and toe tappin' creative way
to use apple butter in a tasty entrée!*

♥ For each 4 ounces extra lean ham steak: spread 1 teaspoon of your favorite apple butter on top of ham steak while cooking it over medium heat on a grill (or skillet) that has been sprayed with non-fat cooking spray.

♥ After turning ham steak over, spread a second teaspoon of apple butter on top.

♥ Once bottom of ham steak is cooked, turn steak over a second time. Cook only for a couple of minutes - just enough to caramelize the apple butter.

♥ Serve right away. Left over steaks taste great as cold ham sandwiches!

♥ Note: If you don't have a terrific apple butter recipe, the one I have published in my "Down Home Cookin' Without the Down Home Fat" cookbook is fabulous!!!

Yield: 1 (4-ounce) steak

Calories: 171   Total fat: 5.7 grams (30% fat)
Cholesterol: 53 mg   Sodium: 621 mg

Cooking time: 10 minutes or less.

*Menu ideas: Homestyle Green Beans & Potatoes (page 148),
Sassy Slaw (page 109), fat-free bread with apple butter, and
Peaches & Cream Trifle (page 262) for dessert.*

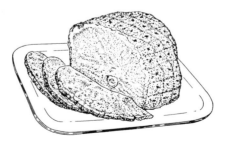

151

CREAMED PEPPERY CHICKEN

Budget Friendly

Recipe

This peppery chicken is as delicious as it is easy to make.

4 boneless, skinless chicken breasts (about 1 pound) - all visible fat removed (frozen pieces are fine. However, allow a few more minutes cooking time)

Pepper (up to 1 teaspoon)
1 (8-ounce) container fat-free sour cream (I used Land-O-Lakes)

♥ Sprinkle chicken breasts generously with pepper. (Amount of pepper used depends on your preference).

♥ In a large 12-inch non-stick skillet that has been sprayed with non-fat cooking spray, cook chicken breast covered, over medium heat for 4 to 5 minutes. Turn pieces over. Reduce heat to low.

♥ Put sour cream on top of chicken and in middle of pan. Cover and continue cooking for 4 to 5 minutes or until completely cooked and chicken is white all through. The sour cream will absorb the pepper flavor.

Yield: 4 servings

Calories: 187   Total fat: 1.4 grams (7% fat)
Cholesterol: 66 mg   Sodium: 118 mg

Total preparation and cooking time: 10 minutes or less.

Menu idea: This is excellent served on a toasted bun as a sandwich, or over pasta or rice. Or serve alone as an entrée. The sour cream will be like a thick sauce.

As an entrée serve with your choice of one from the following: Cooked rice, cooked pasta, Mashed Potatoes Deluxe (page 135), Sensational Sweet Potato Casserole (page 139) or Garlic Red Skins (page 133) along with Spring Asparagus (page 134) or Mushroom-Asparagus Casserole (page 143).

CINNAMON KISSED CHICKEN

Budget Friendly

Recipe

This lightly sweetened chicken has a touch of orange and cinnamon flavor.

½ teaspoon ground cinnamon
1 tablespoon dark brown sugar
*1 teaspoon fresh orange peel slivers

½ cup Kraft Free Red Wine Vinegar fat-free salad dressing
1 pound boneless, skinless chicken breast - cut into ½x4-inch long strips

♥ *To get orange peel slivers, simply grate the peel of an orange with a vegetable peeler or paring knife. Use just the "orange" - not the white meaty part of the skin.

♥ In a large non-stick skillet, mix cinnamon, brown sugar, orange peel slivers and salad dressing together.

♥ Add chicken pieces. Cook over medium heat for 3 to 4 minutes. Turn chicken pieces over and cook an additional 2 to 3 minutes.

♥ Chicken will be white and not translucent when fully cooked.

♥ Serve warm.

Yield: 4 servings

Calories: 154   Total fat: 1.4 grams (9% fat)
Cholesterol: 66 mg   Sodium: 475 mg

Preparation time: 5 minutes.

Total time: 15 minutes or less.

Menu ideas: Eat "as is" or if desired pour remaining sauce over cooked rice or baked sweet potatoes. Also serve with: Polynesian Fruit Salad (page 97) or sliced melon.

Life is like a "Teeter-Totter" . . . it has its highs and its lows. Through it all, it is important for us to stay focused on being balanced.

HONEY MUSTARD CHICKEN

Budget
Friendly

Recipe

So simple yet so scrumptious!

8 (4-ounce) boneless, skinless chicken breasts

2 cups fat-free honey Dijon salad dressing

♥ Marinate chicken in salad dressing overnight or up to 2 days.

♥ Cook chicken in a non-stick skillet or on a grill for 4 to 5 minutes over medium heat. Turn. Continue cooking until chicken is white in center.

♥ In order to use the dressing (you used as a marinate) as a dipping sauce you must bring it to a boil. Boil for 1 minute. Turn off heat. Let cool.

♥ Serve on the side to dip chicken pieces in.

Yield: 8 servings

Calories: 225   Total fat: 1.4 grams (6% fat)
Cholesterol: 66 mg   Sodium: 734 mg

Total preparation and cooking time: 10 minutes or less.

*Menu ideas: Tangy Tossed Salad (page 113)
and Corn Casserole (page 129).*

People don't care how much you know -- until they know how much you care.

- Solid Rock Ministries

154

SPANISH TOMATOES AND BEEF

Budget Friendly Recipe

It doesn't get any easier than this folks. This complete one skillet meal taste good accompanied with corn bread.

*1 (16-ounce) package vegetarian ground meatless (I use MorningStar Farms found in the frozen section, next to ground turkey, at Meijers)
1 (11-ounce) can white shoepeg corn (I use Green Giant)

4 cups water
1 (18-ounce) can tomato paste
1 (16-ounce) jar your favorite chunky salsa (remember the spicier the salsa the spicier this recipe will be)
1½ cups Minute brand white rice

♥ Put all ingredients into a large non-stick Dutch oven. Cook over medium heat, stirring constantly, until well mixed.

♥ Bring to a boil. Cover. Turn off heat and let simmer for a couple of minutes.

♥ Presto!! You're done.

♥ If desired, sprinkle with Healthy Choice fat-free fancy shredded cheddar cheese.

Yield: 4 servings

Calories: 508   Total fat: 0.5 grams (1% fat)
Cholesterol: 0 mg   Sodium: 1758 mg

Total preparation and cooking time: 10 minutes or less.

Menu ideas: Tossed salad, corn bread or steamed broccoli.

*If desired, substitute 1 pound cooked ground skinless turkey breast.

It's no wonder the "dog" is man's best friend" . . . Who else can you feed only dog food and water to and still have them as a "best friend"?

SPICY RICEY VEGETARIAN DINNER

You won't miss the meat in this hearty meal!

Budget
Friendly

Recipe

3 cups fat-free chicken broth
1½ cups chunky salsa
1 (15-ounce) can Healthy Valley three bean chili

¼ cup fat-free Italian salad dressing
3 cups instant rice (I used Minute Rice-instant rice)

♥ Bring all ingredients except rice to a boil. Reduce heat.

♥ Add rice. Let sit for 5 minutes.

♥ Serve hot.

Yield: 4 entrée size servings

Calories: 411   Total fat: 0 grams (0% fat)
Cholesterol: 0 mg   Sodium: 1074 mg

Total preparation and cooking time: 10 minutes or less.

Menu ideas: Eat as is or wrap in warm, soft flour tortillas.
Serve with fresh tossed salad.

ZESTY SAUSAGE SANDWICHES

Budget Friendly

Recipe

These zesty sandwiches are full of flavor.
They are perfect for anyone who would like to add a
little spice and zip to an old favorite!!

1 (14-ounce) package Butterball fat-free smoked sausage

8 tablespoons honey Dijon barbecue sauce (I use Staff)

8 tablespoons Healthy Choice fat-free mozzarella cheese

8 fat-free hot dog buns (I used Aunt Millie's)

♥ Cut each sausage in half (you should have a total of four sausages).

♥ Cut each sausage lengthwise in half (there should now be a total of eight halves).

♥ Cover and microwave all sausages together in carousel microwave on high for 3 minutes or until completely heated.

♥ Meantime while sausages are cooking spread 1 tablespoon of honey Dijon barbecue sauce on the insides of each bun.

♥ Sprinkle 1 tablespoon of mozzarella cheese on each sandwich over the barbecue sauce.

♥ Remove the warmed sausages from the microwave and place one sausage in each bun with the barbecue sauce and cheese.

♥ Return to microwave and re-heat for about 1 minute or until cheese is melted. (The moisture from the barbecue sauce and the juices from the sausage will prevent the cheese from being rubbery.)

Yield: 8 servings

Calories: 183   Total fat: 0 grams (0% fat)

Cholesterol: 22 mg   Sodium: 1027 mg

Preparation time: 5 minutes or less.

Cooking time: 4 minutes.

Total time for all sandwiches: 10 minutes or less.

Menu ideas:
For cold weather months-Tomato Soup & Angel Fluff (page 248).
For warm weather - Zesty Summer Cottage Salad (page 106),
Cucumber Dill Salad (page 108), and
Orange Fluff on top of sugar free orange Jell-O (page 252).

MEXICAN PASTA

*I hit gold when I created this! Delicious hot as a
main entrée or chilled as a pasta salad.*

Budget
Friendly

Recipe

2 cups hot water
1 (16-ounce) jar of your favorite
  thick and chunky salsa
2 beef bouillon cubes
1 (8-ounce) box elbow macaroni
  (2 cups)

1 (8-ounce) can whole kernel
  corn - do not drain
1 (8-ounce) can kidney beans -
  do not drain

♥ In a large 12-inch non-stick skillet over high heat bring water, salsa
  and beef bouillon to a boil.

♥ Stir in macaroni. Reduce heat to low.

♥ Cover. Let simmer for 10 minutes.

♥ Turn off heat. Stir in corn and kidney beans. Cover. Let sit, covered
  with heat off, for two minutes longer.

Yield: 6 (1-cup) entrée servings

Calories: 214   Total fat: 1.0 gram (5% fat)
Cholesterol: 0 mg   Sodium: 765 mg

12 (½-cup) side dish servings

Calories: 107   Total fat: 0.5 grams (5% fat)
Cholesterol: 0 mg   Sodium: 383 mg

Total time: 13-15 minutes.

*Menu ideas: As a hot entrée with a tossed salad,
pita bread and Jell-O or fruit salad. Also terrific to take to
potlucks or chilled as a pasta salad.*

♥ *Appreciation without expression of it is like having a gift you decide not
to give to a person. They know nothing of it, it does nothing for them.*

MEXICALI CHICKEN

Budget Friendly Recipe

I converted this high fat recipe sent in by
Grace Du Prey of California into a low-fat favorite (made quickly).

1 pound boneless, skinless chicken breast - all visible fat removed	1 (3-ounce) Healthy Choice fat-free cream cheese
1 (15-ounce) can Healthy Choice beef chili	1/4 cup mild thick n' chunky salsa
	1 cup fat-free Healthy Choice fancy shredded cheddar cheese
	Cooked hot rice

♥ In a 12-inch non-stick skillet, cook chicken over medium high heat for 3 to 4 minutes. Turn chicken over, cook an additional 3 to 4 minutes or until fully cooked.

♥ Remove chicken. Cut chicken into 1/4-inch strips, cut strips into 1/2-inch lengths. Return chicken to skillet. Add chili, cream cheese and salsa over medium-low heat. Stir constantly, until cream cheese is completely dissolved.

♥ Sprinkle with cheddar cheese. Cover. Cook on medium-low for 2 to 3 minutes. Serve over cooked rice.

Yield: 6 servings

Calories: 176   Total fat: 1.3 grams (7% fat)
Cholesterol: 50 mg   Sodium: 432 mg

Total preparation and cooking time: 15 minutes or less.

Menu ideas: Serve over cooked rice.
Also great with Mexican Chicken Salad (page 99).

Mexicali Chicken Burritos: Divide mixture among 8 fat-free warmed flour tortillas. Roll into burritos and serve with taco sauce on the side.

Yield: 8 burritos

Calories: 329   Total fat: 1.0 gram (3% fat)
Cholesterol: 37 mg   Sodium: 934 mg

ORANGE ROUGHY

This fish dish was submitted by Mable Jackson (one of my assistants).

1 pound orange roughy fillets
1 medium onion - cut into thin
  strips

1 teaspoon lemon pepper
  seasoning
1 tablespoon dry Butter Buds
¼ cup plain bread crumbs

♥ Spray a skillet with non-fat cooking spray and place orange roughy fillets into skillet over medium heat. Place onion on top of fish in skillet.

♥ Sprinkle lemon pepper seasoning and Butter Buds evenly on top of fish.

♥ Cook for 7 minutes. Turn over and cook for an additional 3 to 5 minutes. During the last 3 to 4 minutes of cooking time, sprinkle with bread crumbs.

♥ Fish will be cooked when completely white throughout and when it flakes when cut with fork.

Yield: 3 servings

Calories: 161   Total fat: 1.6 grams (9% fat)
Cholesterol: 30 mg   Sodium: 348 mg

Preparation time: 10-15 minutes, depending on thickness of fish.

*Menu ideas: Delicious served with Garlic Red Skins (page 133),
Spring Asparagus (page 134) or
Tropical Passion Fruit Salad (page 107).*

Wisdom is knowing when <u>not</u> to say what's on your mind.

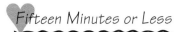

CHICKEN FETTUCCINE

Budget Friendly

Recipe

Now this is some good eatin'!

1 (12-ounce) box fettuccine florentine noodles - found in pasta section
1½ pounds boneless, skinless chicken breast - cut into bite-size pieces

1 (26½-ounce) jar Hunts Original spaghetti sauce with mushrooms
Kraft fat-free grated topping (made with Parmesan cheese) - optional

♥ Cook pasta as directed on box.

♥ Over medium heat cook chicken pieces in a non-stick 12-inch skillet until all pieces are fully cooked. (Chicken will be completely white when fully cooked.)

♥ Add spaghetti sauce. Heat for about 4 to 5 minutes or until completely heated.

♥ Serve over hot, drained pasta. If desired sprinkle with Kraft Free non-fat grated topping.

♥ This dish is delicious reheated in the microwave. Simply stir sauce in with pasta and freeze or refrigerate until ready to use.

Yield: 8 (1-cup) servings

Calories: 289   Total fat: 2.1 grams (7% fat)
Cholesterol: 49 mg   Sodium: 518 mg

Total preparation and cooking time: 15 minutes or less.

Menu idea: Tossed salad, Green Beans Italiano (page 132), or Garlic Toast (page 79).

PASTA WITH CREAMY CLAM SAUCE

Budget Friendly

Recipe

*This warm, satisfying and delicious dish is perfect
for making you feel all snugly and cozy on a chilly day!*

1 (14½-ounce) can fat-free, reduced-sodium chicken broth (I used Swanson)

2 (2.8-ounce) packages Campbell's baked ramen chicken noodle soup 98% fat-free - do not make as directed on package

1 (6.5-ounce) can minced clams - do not drain

2 teaspoons minced garlic (I buy mine in a jar already minced from the produce section)

2 tablespoons Ultra Fat-Free Promise

¼ cup cornstarch

½ cup skim milk

♥ In a large saucepan bring chicken broth to a boil. (It'll take about 3 minutes on high heat to bring broth to a boil.)

♥ Break Ramen Noodles into small pieces and drop into boiling chicken broth. Add clams, garlic and Ultra Promise. Simmer 3 minutes; stirring occasionally.

♥ In the meantime while noodles are cooking . . . in a small bowl dissolve cornstarch in milk by briskly stirring with a fork. Once noodles are done cooking, reduce heat to low. Add seasoning packets from noodles and stir milk/cornstarch mixture into broth and noodles. Keep stirring about 2 to 3 minutes or until thick and creamy.

Yield: 4 (1-cup) servings

Calories: 244   Total fat: 1.5 grams (6% fat)
Cholesterol: 17 mg   Sodium: 1232 mg

Preparation time: 5 minutes or less

Cooking time: 9 minutes or less

Total time: 15 minutes or less

*Menu ideas: Steamed asparagus, crackers or
French bread and slices of fresh melon.*

COWBOY GRUB (CASSEROLE)

Budget Friendly Recipe

For the meat and potato lover and those who love barbecue!
For added extra fun, serve on pie pans instead of plates.

1 pound lean eye of round beef (roast or steaks) - cut into ¼- to ⅓-inch chunks (or pork tenderloin)

1 pound quick cooking shredded hash browns (I use Mr. Deli's)

½ cup chopped onion (or frozen chopped onion for easier use)

½ cup your favorite barbecue sauce (I used Kraft's Thick and Spicy Brown Sugar sauce)

♥ Spray a 12-inch non-stick skillet with non-fat cooking spray.

♥ Turn heat on medium-high. Place meat on bottom of pan. Cover. Cook for 3 to 4 minutes or until brown on bottom. Turn meat over. Top with shredded hash browns and onions. Cover. Cook 3 to 4 minutes or until meat is no longer pink.

♥ Stir entire dish. Cover and cook an additional 3 to 4 minutes, stirring occasionally.

♥ Turn heat down to low. Add barbecue sauce. Gently stir until well mixed. Serve immediately.

Yield: 4 servings

With beef:
Calories: 265   Total fat: 5.3 grams (18% fat)
Cholesterol: 59 mg   Sodium: 333 mg

With pork:
Calories: 264   Total fat: 5.4 grams (19% fat)
Cholesterol: 67 mg   Sodium: 328 mg

Preparation time: 3 minutes (derived from cutting meat into chunks).

Cooking Time: 12 minutes or less.

Total Time: 15 minutes or less.

Menu ideas: Serve with Garlic Toast (page 79) and tossed salad along with Crunchy Cucumbers with Cream (page 101).

MEXICAN GOULASH

Budget Friendly

Recipe

This vegetarian dish is high in protein and flavor!

1 (15-ounce) can Hormel 97% fat-free chili (made with turkey)
1 (16-ounce) can fat-free refried beans
1 (12-ounce) can whole kernel corn - drained

1½ cups your favorite salsa
1 cup fat-free Healthy Choice fancy shredded cheddar cheese - optional
5 (10-inch) fat-free flour tortillas

♥ Mix all ingredients except tortillas together until well blended.

♥ Spray a 2½-quart round microwavable casserole dish (with lid) with non-fat cooking spray.

♥ Lay 1 tortilla flat on the bottom of casserole dish.

♥ Top with one-fifth of Mexican mixture.

♥ Continue layering tortillas and Mexican mixture until all ingredients are used.

♥ Cover. Microwave on high in a carousel microwave for 10 minutes. Let sit, covered an additional 5 minutes before serving. (If you don't have a carousel microwave rotate dish a quarter turn every 2½ minutes to evenly cook).

♥ Using a sharp knife (a steak knife works well) cut through all layers, making a checker board design on top. Each cut will be about 1 inch apart. (The cut-up tortillas will taste a lot like pasta when recipe is finished.)

♥ With a large spoon, stir entire dish to mix cut-up tortilla pieces. Serve in soup bowls.

♥ Sprinkle lightly with additional fat-free cheddar cheese if desired.

Yield: 8 servings

Calories: 260   Total fat: 1.4 grams (5% fat)
Cholesterol: 7 mg   Sodium: 1135 mg

Preparation time: 5 minutes or less.

Cooking time: 10 minutes.

Total time: 15 minutes or less.

Menu ideas: Mexican Chicken Salad (page 99) and cornbread.

CHICKEN ASPARAGUS CASSEROLE

Budget
Friendly

Recipe

*A delicious, one skillet casserole that is complete
enough to eat as an entire meal by itself.*

1 pound boneless, skinless
chicken breast - all visible fat
removed
1 (14½-ounce) can fat-free
chicken broth (I used Swanson)
¼ cup hot water
½ teaspoon dried thyme

2 cups instant rice
1 (14.5-ounce) can asparagus -
drained (or French style green
beans)
1 (10¾-ounce) can Campbell's
Healthy Request cream of
chicken soup

♥ In a 12-inch non-stick skillet, cook chicken breast in chicken broth
and water over medium-high heat for 3 minutes, covered. Turn
chicken over, cover, and cook an additional 3 minutes.

♥ Remove chicken breast and cut into ¼-inch thick strips. Return to
broth.

♥ Reduce heat to very low. Stir in thyme and rice making sure it is
covered with broth.

♥ Gently stir in drained asparagus and cream of chicken soup, stirring
until well mixed. Do not cover. Continue cooking on low for 3 more
minutes to thicken sauce.

♥ Turn off heat and let cool a couple of minutes before serving.

Yield: 4 entrée servings

Calories: 370   Total fat: 4.5 grams (11% fat)
Cholesterol: 75 mg   Sodium: 1123 mg

Total preparation and cooking time: 15 minutes or less.

*Menu ideas: A complete meal in itself,
however if desired, serve with a dinner roll and
either fruit cocktail or frozen yogurt with sliced fruit.*

Budget
Friendly

Recipe

PIZZA BURRITOS

I hit a home run when I created these!
All my fans (family) cheer for more.

1 (16-ounce) can fat-free refried beans
2 (14-ounce) jars of Ragu Pizza Quick Sauce (chunky tomato flavor)

1 (8-ounce) package of fat-free mozzarella cheese (I used Healthy Indulgence)
20 (10-inch) fat-free tortillas

- ♥ In a medium bowl, combine refried beans, Ragu Pizza Sauce and fat-free cheese. Stir until well mixed.
- ♥ To soften, put the stack of tortilla shells in the carousel microwave on high for 1 minute.
- ♥ Take one flour tortilla, put 2 heaping tablespoons of the above mixture, into the center. Roll up the tortilla and place in the carousel microwave for 10 seconds.
- ♥ If desired, you can make numerous pizza burritos and multiply the number of burritos you have by 10 seconds each to figure out cooking time.

Yield: 20 servings

Calories: 252   Total fat: 0 grams (0% fat)
Cholesterol: 1 mg   Sodium: 817 mg

Preparation time including cooking: 10-12 minutes

Menu ideas: This goes good with salsa and fat-free tortilla chips, tossed salad and frozen yogurt topped with fruit.

Aren't you glad for times when you think you have made a mistake and you end up __not__ making the mistake afterall?

STEAK & POTATOES STIR-FRY

This hearty stick to your ribs (but not your arteries)
dish will satisfy any meat and potatoes lover!

1 pound beef tenderloin fully cooked and cut into tiny pieces

1 pound frozen homestyle, diced, quick cooking potatoes (look under ingredients to be sure potatoes are pre-cooked)

1 (15.2-ounce) can whole kernel corn - drained

1 teaspoon garlic salt

½ teaspoon pepper - optional

¼ cup chopped chives

3 tablespoons Ultra Fat-Free Promise

♥ If your beef is not cooked, this is a good time to start cooking beef in a separate skillet or on a grill.

♥ Spray a large non-stick skillet (about 12-inch) with non-fat cooking spray.

♥ Cook potatoes on medium-high heat for about 5 to 6 minutes without allowing them to brown. Turn potatoes over and continue cooking until golden brown.

♥ Add cooked beef, corn, garlic salt, pepper, chives and Ultra Promise. Continue cooking for about 3 to 4 minutes or until fully heated.

Yield: 5 servings

Calories: 322   Total fat: 9.8 grams (27% fat)
Cholesterol: 76 mg   Sodium: 618 mg

Total preparation time: less than 15 minutes.

Menu ideas: You may want to serve ketchup or steak sauce on the side. Whole wheat toast is a good accompaniment. Add a green vegetable as a side dish and you have a complete meal.

It's wonderful when your best friend, your lover and your children's father are all the same person - your husband.

SWEET & SASSY ENTRÉE
(FAST AND EASY)

Budget
Friendly

Recipe

If you like sweet and sour dishes you'll like this one!
Sometimes sweet and sour sauces can be sickening sweet and thick, but
this one is perfect! The sauce combined with the pasta and vegetables is a
unique twist my family really likes! (This would be good with shrimp also,
or eliminate the chicken for an excellent vegetarian entrée.)

½ cup fat-free raspberry salad
  dressing (I use T. Marzettis')
1 teaspoon onion salt
½ cup chicken broth (I make my
  own with one bouillon cube
  dissolved in 1 cup water. Use
  only ½ cup of prepared broth.)

4 honey mustard flavored
  boneless, skinless chicken
  breasts - cut into bite-size
  pieces (I use Tyson)
8 cups your favorite frozen
  vegetable and pasta
  combination. (I use Flav-R-Pac
  brand - asparagus and linguine
  stir fry with vegetable blend)

♥ In a large non-stick skillet combine salad dressing, onion salt and chicken broth together over medium heat until salad dressing is dissolved. Increase heat to medium-high. Add chicken and vegetable combination. Cook for 7 to 9 minutes, stirring occasionally.

Yield: 4 (2½-cup) servings

Calories: 376 Total fat: 12.1 grams (28% fat)
Cholesterol: 47 mg Sodium: 2032 mg

Total preparation and cooking time: 15 minutes or less.

Menu ideas: Add garlic toast and you have a complete meal.

God never stops speaking to us, however sometimes we stop listening.

168

Southwestern Fiesta

Budget
Friendly

Recipe

Eat as a main dish or as a dip.
An excellent source of protein!

1 pound ground skinless turkey
breast
1 (1¼-ounce) package taco
seasoning mix
2 cups salsa

4 cups tomato sauce (or tomato
juice)
1 (15-ounce) can black beans -
drained
2 cups instant rice

♥ Spray a non-stick large soup pan or Dutch oven with non-fat cooking
spray. Add turkey and taco seasoning mix and cook over medium heat
until fully cooked.

♥ Add salsa, tomato sauce and black beans. Bring to a boil. Add instant
rice, making sure rice is covered by liquid. Turn off heat.

♥ Stir. Cover. Let sit for 5 minutes.

Yield: 8 (1¼-cup) entrée servings

Calories: 249   Total fat: 1.0 gram (4% fat)
Cholesterol: 39 mg   Sodium: 1575 mg

26 (about ⅓-cup) dip servings

Calories: 77   Total fat: 0.3 grams (4% fat)
Cholesterol: 12 mg   Sodium: 485 mg

Total preparation and cooking time: 15 minutes or less.

Menu ideas: As a dip: Serve with Baked Tostitos tortilla chips and
fat-free sour cream. Some people like to sprinkle fat-free fancy
shredded cheddar cheese (Healthy Choice) on top.

As a entrée: Serve as is or wrapped in a warm,
soft flour tortilla. Add a fresh green salad.

If I know I'm causing God sadness then I know I've got to change.

DILLED PORK STEAKS

A creative way to quickly prepare a special and mouth-watering meal.

1 cup dill pickle juice   dried dill - optional
2 pounds pork tenderloin - all
   visible fat removed and cut into
   8 (4-ounce) steaks

♥ Marinate overnight in dill pickle juice.

♥ Remove meat from dill juice used to marinate. Discard dill juice.

♥ Cook on a grill or in a non-stick skillet for 4 to 5 minutes. Turn over and continue cooking until center is no longer pink.

♥ Sprinkle with dried dill before serving if desired.

Yield: 8 steaks

Calories: 140   Total fat: 4.1 grams (28% fat)
Cholesterol: 67 mg   Sodium: 110 mg

Preparation time: 5 minutes.

Cooking time: 10 minutes or less.

Total time: 15 minutes or less.

Menu ideas: Sassy Slaw (page 109),
Corn Casserole (page 129),
Sensational Sweet Potato Casserole (page 139) or
Spring Asparagus (page 134).

DILLED CHICKEN STEAKS:
Substitute 2 pounds boneless, skinless chicken breast or turkey breast.

Yield: 8 servings

With chicken:
Calories: 125   Total fat: 1.4 grams (11% fat)
Cholesterol: 66 mg   Sodium: 136 mg

With turkey:
Calories: 125   Total fat: 1.1 grams (8% fat)
Cholesterol: 77 mg   Sodium: 112 mg

Note: Sodium content of above recipes is an estimate.

MEXICAN STYLE SPAGHETTI

Budget
Friendly

Recipe

Sauce is boss in this creative combination.
It's definitely a unique zesty twist to an old-time favorite.

1 (16-ounce) package dry thin
  spaghetti
1 (16-ounce) jar your favorite
  thick and chunky salsa
  (I used Pace mild flavor)

2 (26-ounce) jars extra chunky
  garlic and onions pasta sauce
  (I used Healthy Choice)
1 cup Healthy Choice fat-free
  shredded cheddar cheese
1 cup Healthy Choice fat-free
  shredded mozzarella cheese

♥ Cook spaghetti as directed on package. Drain.

♥ While spaghetti is boiling; heat salsa and pasta sauce together in large
  saucepan over medium heat until it comes to a low boil. Reduce heat
  to a simmer.

♥ Pour sauce over drained spaghetti. Sprinkle with both cheeses.

♥ Serve immediately.

Yield: 8 servings

Calories: 338   Total fat: 0.9 grams (3% fat)
Cholesterol: 3 mg   Sodium: 1105 mg

Total preparation and cooking time: 13 minutes or less.

Menu ideas: Garlic Toast (page 79), and Tossed Salad.

*The key is do NOT overcook the sauce. All you
need to do is heat the sauce.*

If you overcook it the chunks will disappear.

Children need discipline so they can have self-discipline.

171

HAM KEBABS

Great outdoor grill entrée!

Budget
Friendly

Recipe

1 (18-ounce) bottle honey Dijon barbecue sauce (I used Staff K.C. Style)

2 pounds extra lean ham - cut into 1½-inch chunks

8 kebab sticks

♥ Arrange ham chunks on kebabs. Brush with barbecue sauce.

♥ Cook over medium heat on a grill for 2 to 3 minutes. Turn. Continue cooking 2 to 3 minutes or until fully heated.

Yield: 8 kebabs (4 ounces meat each)

Calories: 245   Total fat: 5.6 grams (21% fat)
Cholesterol: 53 mg   Sodium: 2239 mg

Preparation time: 10 minutes.

Cooking time: 5 minutes.

Total preparation time: 15 minutes or less.

Optional: Add fresh 1½-inch cubes of fresh pineapple or onion chunks in-between meat chunks.

Menu ideas: Sassy Slaw (page 109), Apple Cottage Salad (page 117), or Zesty Potato Salad (page 122).

BEEF STROGANOFF

Budget
Friendly

Recipe

If they only knew it could be this easy years ago!
Only one pan to clean-up!

1 pound eye of round beef - cut
into ½-inch chunks
2 medium onions (as a time
saver, use 1 pound of frozen
chopped onions)
1 (4-ounce) can mushroom stems
and pieces - do not drain

2 teaspoons minced garlic
(I use the kind in a jar - already
prepared)
3 cups beef broth (or 3 beef
bouillon cubes dissolved in
3 cups water)
4 cups medium egg noodles
(I use Light and Fluffy)
1 cup fat-free sour cream

♥ Spray a large kettle or soup pot with non-fat cooking spray. Over
medium heat cook beef, onions, mushrooms and garlic together. Stir
occasionally.

♥ Once meat is fully cooked, add beef broth, egg noodles and sour
cream. Turn heat to high.

♥ Once boiling, turn heat down to low. (Do not cover.) Cook on low for
5 to 7 minutes until pasta is desired doneness. Stir occasionally.

♥ Remove from heat. Let sit 4 to 5 minutes before serving. (Broth will
thicken as it sits.) If desired sprinkle lightly with salt and pepper.

Yield: 7 (1-cup) servings

Calories: 218   Total fat: 3.3 grams (14% fat)
Cholesterol: 54 mg   Sodium: 491 mg

Preparation time: 5 minutes (mostly derived from cutting meat).

Cooking time: 15 minutes or less.

Total time: 20 minutes or less.

Menu ideas: Steamed broccoli, fat-free sourdough bread
or rolls, Spiced Apples (page 146).

CHICKEN STROGANOFF:
Substitute 1 pound boneless, skinless chicken breast cut into ½-inch
chunks instead of beef. Use chicken broth instead of beef broth.
Follow directions exactly.

Presto Ham Casserole

*Easy is the name of this game and it'll
score high points from your fans for being tasty!*

Budget
Friendly

Recipe

1 (7.25-ounce) box macaroni and cheese (the off brands are fine) - do not make as directed on box

1 cup hot water

1 (15-ounce) can Healthy Choice cream of mushroom soup

1 pound extra lean ham - cut into ⅓-inch chunks

1 (15-ounce) can sweet peas - drained

♥ Spray a 2-quart covered microwavable casserole dish with non-fat cooking spray.

♥ In prepared casserole dish, mix powdered cheese packet (from macaroni and cheese box) with hot water and soup until cheese is completely dissolved.

♥ Stir in chopped ham and the macaroni until well mixed.

♥ Cover. Cook in a *carousel microwave on high for 7 minutes. (Very carefully remove lid, so you do not get a steam burn!)

♥ Stir. Cover and continue cooking in *carousel microwave for an additional 6 minutes.

♥ Stir in drained peas. Cover and let sit 2 to 3 minutes before serving. (If making ahead of time, freeze or refrigerate until needed. Microwave until warm.)

Yield: 5 servings

Calories: 342   Total fat: 6.5 grams (17% fat)
Cholesterol: 49 mg   Sodium: 1936 mg

Preparation time: 5 minutes or less.

Cooking time: 13 minutes.

Total time: 18 minutes or less.

Menu ideas: Tossed salad and Jell-O with fruit.

**If you do not have a carousel microwave,
turn the dish a quarter turn every 2 minutes.*

174

PRESTO SAUSAGE CASSEROLE

Budget Friendly Recipe

*It's hard to believe a casserole so good
can be made so quickly.*

1 (7.25-ounce) box macaroni and cheese (the off brands are fine) - do not make as directed on box
1 cup hot water
1 (15-ounce) can Healthy Choice Cream of Mushroom Soup

1 pound fat-free Butterball smoked sausage (or 1 pound fat-free Healthy Choice kielbasa) - cut into bite-size pieces
1 (15-ounce) can green beans - drained

♥ Spray a 2-quart covered microwavable casserole dish with non-fat cooking spray.

♥ In prepared casserole dish, mix powdered cheese packet (from macaroni and cheese box) with hot water and soup until cheese is completely dissolved.

♥ Stir in chopped sausage and macaroni until well mixed.

♥ Cover. Cook in a *carousel microwave on high for 7 minutes. (Very carefully remove lid, so you do not get a steam burn!)

♥ Stir. Cover and continue cooking in *carousel microwave for an additional 6 minutes.

♥ Stir in drained beans. Cover and let sit 2 to 3 minutes before serving. (If making ahead of time, freeze or refrigerate until needed. Microwave until warm.)

Yield: 5 servings

Calories: 286   Total fat: 1.9 grams (6% fat)
Cholesterol: 45 mg   Sodium: 1702 mg

Preparation time: 5 minutes or less.

Cooking time: 13 minutes.

Total time: 18 minutes or less.

*Menu ideas: Mother's Day Salad (page 116)
and Very Berry Fruit Salad (page 98).*

**If you do not have a carousel microwave,
turn the dish a quarter turn every 2 minutes.*

175

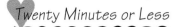
PRESTO POULTRY CASSEROLE

Budget
Friendly

Recipe

A great way to use leftover holiday turkey.

1 (7.25-ounce) box macaroni and cheese (the off brands are fine) - do not make as directed on box
1 cup hot water
1 (15-ounce) can Healthy Choice cream of mushroom soup

1 pound leftover cooked chicken (or turkey breast) - cut into bite-size pieces
1 (15-ounce) can asparagus - drained

♥ Spray a 2-quart covered microwavable casserole dish with non-fat cooking spray.

♥ In prepared casserole dish mix powdered cheese packet (from macaroni and cheese box) with hot water and soup until cheese is completely dissolved.

♥ Stir in chopped chicken (or turkey) and macaroni until well mixed.

♥ Cover. Cook in a *carousel microwave on high for 7 minutes. (Very carefully remove lid, so you do not get a steam burn!)

♥ Stir. Cover and continue cooking in *carousel microwave for an additional 6 minutes.

♥ Stir in drained asparagus. Cover and let sit 2-3 minutes before serving. (If making ahead of time, freeze or refrigerate until needed. Microwave until warm.)

Yield: 5 servings

Calories: 349   Total fat: 6.3 grams (17% fat)
Cholesterol: 83 mg   Sodium: 731 mg

Preparation time: 5 minutes or less.

Cooking time: 13 minutes.

Total time: 18 minutes or less.

Menu ideas: Warm Cranapple Salad (page 112) and Cucumber Dill Salad (page 108).

**If you do not have a carousel microwave,
turn the dish a quarter turn every 2 minutes.*

176

MEXICAN CASSEROLE

*This no bake, no boil casserole is the
answer to satisfying hungry tummies - quickly!*

Budget
Friendly

Recipe

1 (1¼-ounce) packet taco
  seasoning mix
2 cups hot water
1 (7.25-ounce) box macaroni and
  cheese (do not make as
  directed on box.)
1 cup salsa

1 (15-ounce) can whole kernel
  corn - drained
1 pound vegetarian ground
  meatless (or cooked ground
  skinless turkey breast)
¾ cup fat-free sour cream

♥ In a 2-quart microwavable covered casserole dish, mix all ingredients except sour cream, until well mixed and dry cheese mixture (from macaroni and cheese) is dissolved.

♥ Cover. Cook for 8 minutes on high in carousel microwave.

♥ Carefully remove lid (so you don't get burned from the steam.) Mix well.

♥ Cover. Continue cooking on high in carousel microwave for an additional 6 minutes.

♥ Stir in sour cream. Cover. Let sit 2-3 minutes before serving.

Yield: 6 servings

Calories: 359   Total fat: 1.7 grams (4% fat)
Cholesterol: 5 mg   Sodium: 1654 mg

Preparation time: 5 minutes or less.

Cooking time: 13 minutes plus 2 minutes sitting time.

Total time: 20 minutes or less.

*Menu ideas: Taco salad, sliced cucumbers
and sliced cantaloupe or melon.*

SHRIMP RICE CASSEROLE

This delectable dish is good to the last bite!

8 cups water
4 cups long grain rice
8 beef bouillon cubes
2 pounds frozen, fully cooked
and ready to eat (60-80 count)
shrimp - frozen

1 (3-ounce) jar bacon pieces
(I use Oscar Mayer - real bacon
pieces)
1 (12-ounce) bottle Kikkoman
Teriyaki Baste and Glaze Sauce

♥ In a large Dutch oven (big saucepan) bring water, rice, bouillon cubes, shrimp, and bacon pieces to a full boil.

♥ Turn heat to low. Cover.

♥ Simmer 14 minutes or until all water is absorbed.

♥ Stir in Teriyaki Baste and Glaze Sauce.

♥ Serve hot. (This can be frozen and reheated in a microwave).

Yield: 18 (1-cup) servings

Calories: 252   Total fat: 1.8 grams (6% fat)
Cholesterol: 102 mg   Sodium: 1190 mg

Total preparation and cooking time: 20 minutes or less.

*Menu ideas: Sassy Slaw (page 109), and
Broccoli Parmesan (page 142).*

APRICOT CHICKEN AND RICE

Budget
Friendly

Recipe

Rice-A-Roni never tasted so good!

1 (6.8-ounce) package Beef Rice-A-Roni - prepared as directed on box substituting Ultra Fat-Free Promise for margarine

4 medium onions - cut into quarters (separate the layers of onions in each quarter)

1½ pounds boneless, skinless chicken breast

½ cup Knott's Berry Farm Light Apricot Fruit Syrup (found in maple syrup section)

1 teaspoon garlic salt

♥ Prepare Rice-A-Roni, stir in onions and cook as directed on box (substituting fat-free Ultra Promise for margarine).

♥ Meantime, arrange chicken breast in a 12-inch non-stick skillet. Pour apricot syrup over chicken and sprinkle with garlic salt. Cover. Cook on medium heat for 7 minutes.

♥ Turn chicken pieces over. Cover. Cook until chicken is completely white. (About 5 to 10 minutes, depending on thickness.) Remove chicken. Pour sauce from chicken into cooked Rice-A-Roni, stir until well mixed.

♥ Serve chicken over rice.

Yield: 4 servings

Calories: 465   Total fat: 3.5 grams (7% fat)
Cholesterol: 100 mg   Sodium: 1514 mg

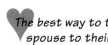**Total preparation and cooking time: 20 minutes or less.**

*Menu ideas: Crunchy Cucumbers with Cream (page 101)
and Steamed Broccoli.*

The best way to teach your children to be a good spouse is to be a good spouse to their parent from the day your child is born.

ZESTY SAUSAGE SKILLET DINNER

Budget
Friendly

Recipe

The one dish skillet dinner that'll add zip to your day!

1 (14-ounce) package fat-free smoked sausage - quartered and cut into bite-size pieces (I used Butterball)

1 (20-ounce) package seasoned diced potato home fries - thawed (found in frozen foods section - I used Bob Evans)

½ cup plus 1 tablespoon your favorite honey Dijon barbecue sauce (I used Staff)

♥ Spray a 12-inch non-stick skillet with non-fat cooking spray.

♥ Put all ingredients into skillet and cook over medium heat, stirring until all ingredients are well coated with barbecue sauce.

♥ Cover. Reduce heat to medium-low. Cook without stirring for 10 minutes.

♥ With a pancake turner, turn mixture over. Bottom will be caramelized and brown.

♥ Cover. Cook an additional 5 minutes or until bottom is caramelized.

Yield: 4 large entrée servings

Calories: 359   Total fat: 5.8 grams (15% fat)
Cholesterol: 51 mg   Sodium: 1607 mg

Preparation time: 5 minutes (most of the time is derived from cutting meat).

Cooking time: 15 minutes.

Total time: 20 minutes or less.

Menu ideas: Tossed salad, green beans and sugar-free Jell-O for dessert.

BEEF AND BROCCOLI SKILLET CASSEROLE

Budget Friendly

Recipe

Just what busy people need . . . a great tasting one dish dinner made quickly and easily with very little clean up! A unique blend between sweet and sour, and stir fry . . . without all the yucky fat!

*1 pound beef eye of round (steak or roast) - all visible fat removed - cut into ½-inch chunks

1 (1-pound) bag frozen broccoli florets - cut into 1-inch chunks

3 cups hot water

1 (1-ounce) envelope dry onion soup mix (there are 2 envelopes per box)

3 cups instant rice

¾ cup Western fat-free salad dressing

♥ In a 12-inch non-stick skillet, cook beef on high for 3 to 4 minutes or until bottom is cooked. Turn over.

♥ Pour broccoli, water and dry onion soup mix over beef. Stir until soup mix is dissolved. Cover. Cook on high for 6 minutes.

♥ Add rice. Stir until rice is covered with liquid. Turn off heat. Cover. Let sit 5 minutes.

♥ Stir in Western dressing. Serve immediately. Serve with lite soy sauce on the side if desired.

♥ *Note: Pork tenderloin can be substituted instead of eye of round beef if desired. It tastes equally as good.

Yield: 6 (1-cup) servings

With beef:
Calories: 341   Total fat: 3.1 grams (8% fat)
Cholesterol: 39 mg   Sodium: 785 mg

With pork:
Calories: 340   Total fat: 3.2 grams (8% fat)
Cholesterol: 45 mg   Sodium: 782 mg

Preparation time: 3 minutes (derived from cutting beef into chunks).

Cooking time: 15 minutes or less.

Total time: 18 minutes or less.

Menu ideas: Any green vegetable. Fortune cookie for dessert.

MEXICAN PORK TENDERLOIN WITH RICE

*Substitute chicken, turkey or beef tenderloin for
pork for additional meal ideas.*

4 (4-ounce) pork tenderloin steaks - all visible fat removed (4 steaks total)

1 (16-ounce) jar your favorite chunky salsa

1 (8-ounce) can red kidney beans - do not drain

1 (8-ounce) can whole kernel corn - do not drain

½ cup instant enriched long grain rice

(only add the last 2 ingredients if you like spicy, hot mexican food)

1 (4-ounce) can mild green chili peppers chopped - optional

2-3 dashes of Tobasco Sauce - optional

- ♥ Cook pork steaks with salsa in a 12-inch non-stick skillet that has been sprayed with non-fat cooking spray over medium heat for 5 to 7 minutes.

- ♥ Turn steaks over. Cook 5 to 7 minutes or until no longer pink in center. Remove meat from skillet and set aside.

- ♥ Add remaining ingredients to skillet. Stir until well mixed. Bring to a boil.

- ♥ Put cooked meat on top of rice.

- ♥ Remove from heat. Cover and let sit 5 minutes.

- ♥ Serve with taco sauce on the side if desired.

- ♥ This can also be made days ahead of time, refrigerated and reheated in the microwave. Or freeze and reheat.

Yield: 4 (4-ounce) pork tenderloin steaks

Calories: 149   Total fat: 4.1 grams (27% fat)
Cholesterol: 67 mg   Sodium: 180 mg

4 (1-cup) mexican rice servings

Calories: 155   Total fat: 0.5 grams (3% fat)
Cholesterol: 0 mg   Sodium: 712 mg

Total preparation and cooking time: 20 minutes

Menu ideas: This is a complete entrée in itself. If desired serve with a fresh green salad or green beans. Corn bread or soft tortillas and any dessert would go great with this.

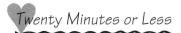

HEARTY BARBECUE SKILLET DINNER

Budget Friendly

Recipe

This is a meat and potatoes lover's meal!

2 pounds red skin potatoes	¹/₂ cup packed dark brown sugar
2 medium onions - chopped	1 (14-ounce) package Healthy
1 beef bouillon cube dissolved in	Choice low-fat smoked sausage
1 cup water	- chopped into bite-size pieces
1 (15-ounce) can tomato sauce	

♥ Poke potatoes with a fork numerous times, then microwave on high until cooked. (They will be soft to the touch when fully cooked.)

♥ In the meantime, cook onion, beef bouillon with water, tomato sauce, brown sugar and sausage over medium heat in a large non-stick skillet (12-inch or larger). Stir occasionally.

♥ Cut cooked red skins into bite-size pieces. Stir into pan with other ingredients, covering all ingredients with sauce.

♥ Recipe is completely cooked when onions are tender and everything is fully heated.

♥ *This meal can be made days in advance and easily re-heated.

Yield: 6 servings

Calories: 303   Total fat: 2.0 grams (6% fat)
Cholesterol: 24 mg   Sodium: 1140 mg

Total preparation and cooking time: 20 minutes or less.

Menu ideas: Cucumber Dill Salad (page 108),
sliced tomatoes and applesauce.

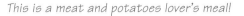*Be your child's biggest fan! Support what interest they're involved in (sports, music, etc.) even if you aren't enthusiastic about that interest.*

AuGratin Casserole Dinner

Budget
Friendly

Recipe

*If you like cheesie broccoli, au gratin potatoes
and ham you'll like this one dish entrée!*

1 (5.5-ounce) box au gratin
   potatoes - dry
1 (12-ounce) can fat-free
   evaporated skim milk
1½ cups hot water

12 ounces extra lean ham
   (or turkey ham) - cut into bite-
   size pieces
1 (16-ounce) bag frozen broccoli
   pieces

♥ In a 2-quart microwavable casserole dish, mix dry au gratin potatoes
(potatoes and seasoning cheese packet) with evaporated skim milk
and water until powdered cheese is completely dissolved.

♥ Stir in ham pieces.

♥ Cover with wax paper. Cook in carousel microwave on high for
5 minutes.

♥ Stir in broccoli pieces. Cover. Continue cooking in carousel microwave on high for an additional 15 minutes, stirring occasionally.

♥ Remove wax paper. Let sit 3 to 5 minutes before serving.

Yield: 4 servings

Calories: 338   Total fat: 6.2 grams (15% fat)
Cholesterol: 44 mg   Sodium: 2170 mg

Preparation time: 5 minutes or less.

Cooking time: 20 minutes.

Total time: 25 minutes or less.

*Menu ideas: A complete meal in itself, however
Spiced Apples (page 146) also taste delicious with this entrée.*

CHICKEN CHEESIE PIZZA

A tasty twist to an old time favorite of traditional pizza.

1 (10-ounce) can Pillsbury prepared pizza crust dough
1 boneless, skinless chicken breast (about ½ pound)
⅛-¼ teaspoon ground pepper
¼ cup light Miracle Whip

¼ cup Kraft fat-free grated topping (made with Parmesan cheese and other ingredients)
½ cup fat-free ranch dressing
1 (8-ounce) Healthy Choice fancy shredded mozzarella cheese

♥ Preheat oven to 425 degrees.

♥ Press dough into a jelly roll pan (a cookie sheet with 1-inch sides), that has been sprayed with non-fat cooking spray.

♥ Cook chicken breast in a microwave for about 2 minutes. (Until no pink is visible). Drain juice. Cut cooked chicken breast into tiny ¼-inch pieces. Sprinkle with pepper. Set aside.

♥ Mix Miracle Whip, grated topping and ranch dressing together. Spread mixture over pizza crust.

♥ Sprinkle mozzarella cheese over mixture. Top with peppered chicken pieces.

♥ Bake at 425 degrees for 12 to 15 minutes or until crust is golden brown.

Yield: 4 entrée servings

Calories: 419   Total fat: 5.5 grams (12% fat)
Cholesterol: 46 mg   Sodium: 1378 mg

Preparation time: 10 minutes or less.

Cooking time: 15 minutes or less.

Total time: 25 minutes or less.

Menu idea: Tossed salad and Green Beans Italiano (page 132).

Note: Red or green pepper slices, added before baking, would also taste good on top of chicken.

CHICKEN OR TURKEY CASSEROLE

Budget Friendly Recipe

*I converted a high-fat, time consuming casserole
(sent in by Carolyn Green from Southern Ohio) into this
fast and easy to prepare dish that is every bit as tasty.*

1 cup dry elbow macaroni
1 (10-ounce) can premium chunk chicken in water - drained (Swanson) (or 2 cups cooked turkey breast)
1 (15-ounce) can Healthy Choice cream of mushroom soup

1 cup chicken broth (either from a can or made with bouillon)
½ cup chopped onion (or frozen chopped onion)
1 (4-ounce) can sliced mushrooms - drained

♥ Spray a 2-quart covered casserole dish with non-fat cooking spray.

♥ Combine all ingredients in prepared dish and mix well.

♥ Cook covered in a carousel microwave for 17 to 20 minutes or until pasta is tender.

♥ Let sit for 3 minutes before removing lid. Be very careful when taking off the lid, because the steam is going to be extremely hot!

Yield: 4 servings

With Chicken:
Calories: 206   Total fat: 2.0 grams (9% fat)
Cholesterol: 24 mg   Sodium: 823 mg

With Turkey:
Calories: 246   Total fat: 1.8 grams (7% fat)
Cholesterol: 60 mg   Sodium 642 mg

Preparation time: 5 minutes or less.

Cooking time: 20 minutes.

Total time: 25 minutes or less.

*Menu ideas: Green beans along with a tossed salad
and fat-free sliced bread on the side. If desired serve sugar-free
Jell-O for dessert or Brownie Cookies (page 228).*

SAUSAGE OR HAM CASSEROLE

Budget Friendly Recipe

This recipe idea derived from the Chicken (or Turkey) Casserole.
If you like that, you're sure to like this! Enjoy!

1 cup dry elbow macaroni
7 ounces fat-free Butterball smoked sausage (or extra lean ham - 2 grams of fat per 2 ounces) - chopped
1 (15-ounce) can Healthy Choice cream of mushroom soup

1 cup beef broth (either from a can or made from bouillon)
½ cup chopped onion (or frozen chopped onion)
½ cup chopped green pepper (or frozen chopped green pepper)

♥ Spray a 2-quart covered casserole dish with non-fat cooking spray.

♥ Combine all ingredients in prepared dish and mix well.

♥ Cook covered in a carousel microwave for 17 to 20 minutes or until pasta is tender.

♥ Let sit for 3 minutes before removing lid. Be very careful when taking off the lid, because the steam is going to be extremely hot!

Yield: 4 servings

With Sausage:
Calories: 197   Total fat: 0.9 grams (4% fat)
Cholesterol: 21 mg   Sodium: 992 mg

With Ham:
Calories: 211   Total fat: 3.4 grams (15% fat)
Cholesterol: 23 mg   Sodium: 1119 mg

Preparation time: 5 minutes or less.

Cooking time: 20 minutes.

Total time: 25 minutes or less.

Menu ideas: Serve with fat-free rolls, steamed broccoli
and if desired for dessert an Apple Oatmeal Cookie to curb
your sweet tooth (page 243).

8 LAYER CHILI CASSEROLE

Budget Friendly

Recipe

*If only all vegetarian dishes could be
this satisfying and hearty!*

1 medium onion - chopped
1 (16-ounce) can fat-free refried
  beans
1 (15-ounce) can Health Valley
  mild vegetarian fat-free chili
  with black beans

1 (8-ounce) bottle mild taco
  sauce
1 (11-ounce) package 10-inch
  fat-free flour tortillas
  (I used Chi-Chi's)

♥ Spray a 2½-quart, round, covered microwavable casserole dish with
  non-fat cooking spray. Set aside.

♥ In a medium bowl, microwave onions, covered, for 2 minutes.

♥ Stir in refried beans, chili and taco sauce until well blended.

♥ Tear 2 of the tortillas into small pieces. (These will be used to fill in the
  outer space between the tortilla layer and casserole dish.)

♥ Lay a tortilla flat on bottom of casserole dish. If needed use torn tortilla
  to fill in space between casserole dish and edge.

♥ Top with ¾ cup of chili mixture. Top with a tortilla.

♥ Continue layering chili mixture (¾ cup at a time) and tortillas until all
  ingredients are used.

♥ Cover and microwave on high for 10 minutes. Let sit for 5 minutes
  before serving.

♥ Cut with a sharp knife (a steak knife works well) cutting through all
  layers as you would a pie.

Yield: 8 servings

Calories: 219   Total fat: 0 grams (0% fat)
Cholesterol: 0 mg   Sodium: 852 mg

Preparation time: 10 minutes or less.

Cooking time: 10 minutes. (Plus 5 minutes sitting time)

Total time: 25 minutes or less.

Menu ideas: Tossed salad, crackers or cornbread.

"QUICKIE MEAL"

Budget Friendly

Recipe

*This meal reminds me of a hamburger helper
one dish meal, but made with rice. Great for
"on the run days" when you need a quickie meal.*

1 pound extra lean ground turkey breast (I use Turkey Store) (or vegetarian ground meatless)
3 cups beef broth
1 (14.5-ounce) can Hunt's Choice diced tomatoes with roasted garlic, onion and oregano

1 (4-ounce) can mushroom pieces and stems - do not drain
1 cup dry rice
Pepper to taste

♥ Cook turkey and a little of the broth in a 12-inch non-stick skillet over medium heat until fully cooked.

♥ Remove turkey. Add remaining broth, tomatoes and undrained mushrooms and bring to a boil. Add rice. Stir well. Reduce heat to a low boil, cover and cook 10 minutes.

♥ Crumble cooked turkey into tiny pieces. Stir into rice mixture. Cook another 5 minutes.

♥ Turn heat off. Cover. Let simmer 2 to 3 minutes. Serve hot.

♥ If desired top with ground pepper and lite soy sauce.

Yield: 5 servings

Calories: 261   Total fat: 1.2 grams (4% fat)
Cholesterol: 62 mg   Sodium: 797 mg

Total preparation and cooking time: 25 minutes or less.

Menu ideas: Oriental Vegetables (page 144), and fruit cocktail.

Let your children know no matter what you'll always love them! (You may not agree with what they do) but you still love them.

189

BREADED PORK TENDERLOINS

*Move over old fashioned fried pork tenderloin! This winner is a
frequent request that tastes every bit as delicious!*

1 pound pork tenderloin roast -
  cut crosswise into 6 pieces - all
  visible fat removed
¹/₃ cup all-purpose flour
1 teaspoon Lawry's seasoned salt

³/₄ cup Italian bread crumbs
  (I use Progresso)
2 egg whites - beaten
2 tablespoons skim milk

♥ Preheat oven 400 degrees.

♥ Spray a cookie sheet with non-fat cooking spray. Set aside.

♥ Pound pork to ¹/₄- to ¹/₈-inch thickness. Set aside.

♥ In a small bowl, stir together flour, seasoned salt and bread crumbs.

♥ In a separate small bowl, beat together egg whites and skim milk. Coat
  meat in crumb mixture.

♥ Dip the coated meat into egg mixture, then re-dip into crumb mixture.

♥ Place breaded meat on prepared cookie sheet.

♥ Spray top of meat with non-fat cooking spray.

♥ Bake at 400 degrees for 10 minutes.

♥ Turn over. Spray top of meat with non-fat cooking spray. Bake an
  additional 10 minutes. Breading will be crispy and slightly golden
  brown when done.

♥ If desired serve with Mild Mustard/Dill Dipping Sauce (page 73).

Yield: 6 servings

Calories: 181   Total fat: 3.6 grams (18% fat)
Cholesterol: 45 mg   Sodium: 499 mg

Preparation time: 10 minutes or less.

Cooking time: 20 minutes.

Total time: 30 minutes or less.

*Menu ideas: Spring Salad (page 120),
Mashed Potatoes Deluxe (page 135), and
California Garlic Blend (page 136).*

CHRISTMAS CHICKEN & RICE DINNER

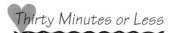

Budget Friendly Recipe

*This colorful combination of Christmas colors
(red and green) gave this flavorful entrée it's distinguished name.*

⅓ cup pineapple-orange frozen concentrate	2 tablespoons cornstarch
½ (8-ounce) tub Ultra-Promise fat-free spread	1 red pepper - cut into long ¼-inch strips
½ teaspoon garlic salt - optional	1 green pepper - cut into long ¼-inch strips
1 pound boneless, skinless chicken breast - cut into ½-inch pieces	

♥ In a 12-inch non-stick skillet, cook frozen pineapple-orange frozen concentrate, Ultra Promise, garlic salt and chicken together over medium heat until chicken is fully cooked, stir occasionally.

♥ Remove ⅓ cup of the sauce. Stir cornstarch into removed sauce until dissolved. Add back into chicken.

♥ Cook and stir well until pieces are well coated with sauce and remaining sauce thickens. Add sliced red and green peppers.

♥ Cover and continue cooking 5 minutes over medium heat. Peppers will be tender yet slightly crunchy.

♥ Serve over rice or alone.

Yield: 5 servings (not including rice)

Calories: 178   Total fat: 1.3 grams (7% fat)
Cholesterol: 53 mg   Sodium: 174 mg

Preparation time: 10 minutes (derived from cutting).

Cooking time: 15 minutes.

Total time: 25 minutes or less.

*Menu ideas: Tossed salad, wild or
white rice and steamed asparagus.*

MANHANDLER MEATLOAF

Budget Friendly

Recipe

As one little girl once said after being questioned
about the large amount she was eating, "I just can't help
myself, Aunt Dawn! It's so good, I just can't stop eating it.!"
(By the way don't tell them it's low-fat and they won't know it!)

MEATLOAF

1 (6-ounce) box pork-flavored
Stove Top stuffing
1 (8-ounce) carton egg substitute
(I use Egg Beaters)
1 cup your favorite mild thick n'
chunky salsa (I use Ortega)

½ cup honey barbecue sauce
(I use Kraft)
2 (14-ounce) packages fat-free
smoked sausage (I use Butterball)
2 pounds lean ground beef eye of
round

GLAZE

¼ cup grape jelly
½ cup honey barbecue sauce

2 tablespoons salsa

♥ Preheat oven to 350 degrees.

♥ With a blender, grind up the bread crumbs of the stuffing mix for about 20 seconds into fine bread crumbs.

♥ In a large bowl combine egg substitute, salsa, barbecue sauce, fine bread crumbs and seasoning packet from stuffing mix. Stir until well combined. Set aside.

♥ Cut sausage lengths into 1-inch pieces and grind in blender.

♥ Combine ground sausage and ground eye of round with breadcrumb mixture. (Go ahead! Roll your sleeves up and dig right in, this man handler meatloaf is easiest to combine together with your hands.)

♥ To make glaze, microwave jelly for a few seconds to help jelly dissolve. Mix together the glaze ingredients until there are no chunks of jelly remaining. Choose cooking choice below and follow directions as to when to put glaze on meatloaf.

WHAT'S SO GREAT ABOUT THIS RECIPE ARE THE MANY CHOICES IN WHICH YOU CAN COOK IT . . .

♥ **. . . in a rush?** Microwave for 12 to 13 minutes in a carousel microwave after molding half of meatloaf mixture into a ring with your hands on a microwavable plate that has been sprayed with non-fat cooking spray. Cover with wax paper before cooking. After cooking spread glaze over meat. Let stand 3 to 4 minutes before serving.

(Manhandler Meatloaf continued)

♥ **... like the traditional flavor of the baked glaze?** Bake in an 8x4x2-inch loaf pan that has been sprayed with non-fat cooking spray in the oven for 50 minutes at 350 degrees. Spread glaze over meat and continue baking for an additional 10 minutes.

♥ **... after a long days work do you want to come home to the aroma of a fully cooked entrée?** Form the meatloaf mixture into a round loaf. Cook in the crockpot on low for 8½ to 9 hours. (Line crock pot with tin foil. Spray tin foil with non-fat cooking spray before cooking for an easy clean up.) Or cook in crockpot on high for 4 hours. Put glaze on meatloaf after removing from crockpot. Let set for 3 to 4 minutes before serving.

♥ **... do you want one big mega meatloaf?** Line a roaster with tin foil. With hands, form into a large loaf. Bake covered for 1 hour, 15 minutes at 350 degrees. Top with glaze. Bake an additional 10 minutes uncovered.

♥ **Remember this recipe makes two meatloaves! Make sure you divide the meatloaf and glaze into two. If desired cook one meatloaf. Freeze second meatloaf to cook later.**

INTERESTING INSIGHTS OF THIS RECIPE . . .

♥ Using salsa saves time by eliminating cutting time of onions, green peppers, etc.

♥ Using boxed stuffing mix also saves time measuring lots of individual seasonings and spices.

♥ Less than 3 grams of fat per serving. And these are hearty servings!

Yield: 16 (4-ounce) servings (8 servings per loaf)

Calories: 214   Total fat: 2.4 grams (10% fat)
Cholesterol: 51 mg   Sodium: 1062 mg

Preparation time: 20 minutes or less.

Cooking time: Depends on method of cooking.

Menu ideas: Mushroom, Onion & Bacon Green Bean Casserole (page 131), Carrots with a Light Buttery Caramel Glaze (page 137), and Mashed Potatoes Deluxe (page 135).

HAWAIIAN STYLE BAKED BEANS

Budget
Friendly

Recipe

*A delicious twist to an old time favorite,
which is packed with protein! Great as a meal or side dish!*

2 (16-ounce) cans vegetarian baked beans (I use Bush's Best)

¼ cup chopped onion (for faster preparation use frozen chopped onions)

¼ cup Teriyaki Baste and Glaze (I use Kikkoman's) - found in barbecue section of grocery store

4 ounces extra lean cooked ham - cut into bite-size pieces (2 grams of fat per 2 ounces)

1 (8-ounce) can crushed pineapple in unsweetened pineapple juice - drained

♥ Spray container you are going to cook this recipe in with non-fat cooking spray. (For easier clean-up).

♥ Look on chart for desired cooking method and times.

♥ When cooking this dish you have 3 options:

    A. 2-quart microwavable container.

    B. Crockpot.

    C. 2-quart saucepan.

♥ Mix all ingredients in container you are going to cook it in, until well mixed.

♥ Cover and cook:

    A. in carousel microwave on high for 3 minutes or until completely heated.

    B. in crockpot on low for 4 hours.

    C. in a saucepan until sauce is boiling. Turn off heat and let simmer for 3 to 4 minutes.

Yield: 11 (½-cup) side dish servings

Calories: 112   Total fat: 0.9 grams (7% fat)
Cholesterol: 5 mg   Sodium: 622 mg

Yield: 5 (1-cup) entrée size servings

Calories: 245   Total fat: 2.0 grams (7% fat)
Cholesterol: 11 mg   Sodium: 1369 mg

(Hawaiian Style Baked Beans continued)

Preparation time: 5 minutes or less.

Cooking time varies, depending on method you used.

Menu ideas: As an entrée serve with Sassy Slaw (page 109), or celery sticks with fat-free dressing for dipping, and watermelon wedges or sliced honeydew melon or as a side dish with fat free hot dogs.

195

COWBOY CHOW

Budget Friendly Recipe

Cowboys of the olden days only wish it would have tasted this good! For fun serve in pie pans instead of plates.

1 (14-ounce) package low-fat smoked sausage - cut into bite-size pieces (I use Healthy Choice)

1 cup your favorite thick and chunky salsa

1 cup Original Western barbecue sauce (I use Bullseye)

1 (10-ounce) can whole kernel corn - drained

1 (15½-ounce) can dark red kidney beans - drained

1 (3 pound 5 ounce) can pork and beans - drain and remove all visible chunks of fat (I use Van Camp's)

½ cup chopped onion - (for faster preparation use frozen chopped onions)

♥ Spray the container you are going to cook this dish in with non-fat cooking spray. (For easier clean-up.)

♥ Mix all ingredients in prepared container until well mixed.

♥ Look on chart for desired cooking method and times.

♥ When cooking this dish you have 3 options:

    A. Stove top - use a large (Dutch oven) size pan

    B. Crockpot

    C. Microwave - Use a 3-quart microwavable container

♥ Cooking times:

    A. Stove top - Bring to a boil. Reduce heat to low. Cover and simmer for 5 minutes.

    B. Crockpot - Cover and cook on low for 3 hours. If needed it can cook up to 6 hours.

    C. Cover and place in carousel microwave. Cook on high for 5 to 6 minutes or until completely heated. If you don't have a carousel microwave, rotate dish a quarter turn every 2 minutes.

Yield: 9½ cups

9 (1 cup) entrée servings

Calories: 298   Total fat: 3.8 grams (11% fat)
Cholesterol: 27 mg   Sodium: 1743 mg

(Cowboy Chow continued)

19 (½ cup) side dish serving

Calories: 141   Total fat: 1.8 grams (11% fat)
Cholesterol: 13 mg   Sodium: 826 mg

Preparation time: 5 minutes or less.

Cooking time: Varies depending on cooking method used.

*Menu ideas: As an entrée simply serve cornbread
and sliced cucumbers on the side along with chilled lite
fruit cocktail for dessert.*

*No matter how good you are at what "you do", if "you do" with God on
your side, you'll be even better!*

"B.B.B." (Best Baked Beans)

Budget Friendly

Recipe

*My daughters loved these so much that they named
the recipe themselves! They are very filling, satisfying and
delicious! No one would ever believe they're fat-free! Eat as a meal
or side dish. A fun way to serve these when it's the
entrée is by using a pie pan as the plate.*

*1 (1-pound) package ground meatless all-vegetable burger crumbles (I use MorningStar Farms Brand found in frozen section next to ground turkey) (or 1 pound cooked ground eye of round or 1 pound cooked skinless ground turkey breast)

1 (15-ounce) can butter beans - drained

2 (16-ounce) cans fat-free vegetarian baked beans (I used Bush's Best)

¾ cup Kraft Thick n' Spicy Brown Sugar Flavored barbecue sauce

½ cup chopped onion (for faster preparation use chopped frozen onions)

♥ Spray whatever cooking container you are going to use with non-fat cooking spray. (You have 2 choices, the crockpot or a 2-quart microwavable container.)

♥ Mix all ingredients in the container you are going to cook it in, until well mixed.

♥ Cooking Method:

Carousel microwave: Cover. Cook on high for 5 minutes.
Crockpot: Cover. Cook on low for 4 hours.

♥ *Note: For those of you who don't like vegetarian meat substitute, you'll love this! In regards to the rest of the family . . . don't tell them it's not real beef and they'll never know! (Some things are better left unsaid!)

Yield: 16 (½-cup) side dish servings

With Ground Meatless:
Calories: 125   Total fat: 0.5 grams (4% fat)
Cholesterol: 0 mg   Sodium: 585 mg

With Ground Eye of Round:
Calories: 113   Total fat: 1.5 grams (12% fat)
Cholesterol: 15 mg   Sodium: 404 mg

("B.B.B." Best Baked Beans continued)

With Ground Turkey Breast:
Calories: 109   Total fat: 0.8 grams (6% fat)
Cholesterol: 19 mg   Sodium: 403 mg

Yield: 8 (1-cup) entrée size servings

With Ground Meatless:
Calories: 249   Total fat: 1.0 gram (4% fat)
Cholesterol: 0 mg   Sodium: 1169 mg

With Ground Eye of Round:
Calories: 225   Total fat: 3.0 grams (12% fat)
Cholesterol: 29 mg   Sodium: 807 mg

With Ground Turkey Breast:
Calories: 217   Total fat: 1.6 grams (6% fat)
Cholesterol: 39 mg   Sodium: 806 mg

Total preparation time: (Using Ground Meatless) 6 minutes or less.

Cooking time: 5 minutes in microwave on high or 4-5 hours on low in crockpot.

*Menu ideas: Great side dish for any cookout or potluck.
Also terrific as an entrée, serve with a salad or fresh
vegetable sticks with dip, cornbread and strawberries
over angel food cake for dessert.*

*There's nothing you can do to get a good reputation except to earn it!
And to earn it, it takes everything you have!*

- Patricia Barnes

Budget
Friendly

FARMER'S CASSEROLE

Recipe

You won't believe how flavorful and easy this casserole is!

1½ pounds extra lean ham - cut into bite-size chunks (2 grams of fat per 2 ounces)
1 (20-ounce) package seasoned diced potato home fries (I used Bob Evans, found in the frozen section.)

1 (4-ounce) can mushroom stems and pieces - drained
1 (15-ounce) can Healthy Choice cream of mushroom soup
½ cup chopped red onion (or chopped frozen regular onions)
1 (14.5-ounce) can green beans - drained

♥ Crockpot Cooking: Spray a crockpot with non-fat cooking spray. Pour all ingredients into crockpot and mix until well blended. Cover. Cook on low for 4 hours.

♥ Microwave Cooking: Spray a 2-quart microwavable casserole dish with non-fat cooking spray. Pour all ingredients into prepared casserole dish. Mix until well blended. Cover. Cook on high in carousel microwave for 7 to 8 minutes, stirring once.

Yield: 7 servings

Calories: 278   Total fat: 8.5 grams (28% fat)
Cholesterol: 50 mg   Sodium: 1727 mg

Preparation time: 8 minutes or less.

Cooking time: Crockpot: 4 hours. Microwave: 7-8 minutes.

Total time: Crockpot: 4 hours and 8 minutes. Microwave: 16 minutes or less.

Menu ideas: A complete meal in itself, or serve cooked asparagus and fat-free bread with jam on the side, along with Brownie Cookies (page 228).

SWISS STEAK AND POTATOES

Budget
Friendly

Recipe

*What a wonderful, warm and
mouth-watering meal to come home to on a cold or chilly day!*

1 (14.5-ounce) can stewed, sliced
   tomatoes - do not drain
1 (12-ounce) jar fat-free beef
   gravy
1/4 teaspoon dried thyme

1 (1-pound) bag fresh mini carrots
   (found in produce section)
2 medium onions - quartered
1 pound eye of round steaks - cut
   into 1/2-inch thicknesses
4 medium potatoes - washed

- ♥ Spray crockpot with non-fat cooking spray.
- ♥ Mix undrained tomatoes, gravy, thyme, carrots and onions together until well mixed.
- ♥ Place meat into mixture, making sure it is completely covered with sauce.
- ♥ Place potatoes on top.
- ♥ Cover. Cook on high for 4 hours or on low for 8 hours. (Completely cooked after documented time, however the meal can remain in the crockpot for up to 1 hour longer without burning.)

Yield: 4 servings

Calories: 359   Total fat: 4.6 grams (11% fat)
Cholesterol: 59 mg   Sodium: 782 mg

Preparation time: 20 minutes or less.

Cooking time: 4-8 hours (depending on your needs)

*Menu ideas: A complete meal in itself.
However you may want to round it off with
Sweet & Sour Fresh Vegetable Garden Salad (page 102),
Pinwheel Dinner Rolls (page 82) and
Punchbowl Cake (page 218) for dessert.*

SMOTHERED STEAK

Each succulent bite is as tasty as the last!

1 pound whole beef tenderloin
2 large onions - quartered and
  separated
2 large green peppers - cut into
  ³/₄-inch strips

1 (8-ounce) package fresh
  mushrooms - sliced
¼ cup dry Butter Buds
½ cup water
1 teaspoon celery salt (or garlic
  salt)

♥ Spray a crockpot with non-fat cooking spray.

♥ Place beef in crockpot and top with onions, peppers, and mushrooms. Mix Butter Buds, water and celery salt together until Butter Buds dissolve. Pour over vegetables. Gently toss vegetables to distribute seasonings.

♥ Cover. Cook on high for 4 to 5 hours or on low for 8 to 9 hours.

♥ Cut beef into 4 (4-ounce) steaks. Arrange on platter.

♥ Toss vegetables in juices. Spoon juice and vegetables over beef. Serve hot.

Preparation time: 7 minutes or less.

Cooking time: 4-5 hours on high and 8-9 hours on low.

Yield: 4 servings

Calories: 263   Total fat: 8.7 grams (29% fat)
Cholesterol: 72 mg   Sodium: 491 mg

*Menu ideas: If there is room in your crockpot,
place 12 small red skin potatoes on top. If not,
microwave potatoes or serve with Garlic Red Skins (page 133)
and Creamed Spinach (page 130).*

CALIFORNIA MEDLEY STEW

Budget Friendly

This stew is a unique twist to an old time favorite.

Recipe

4 medium unpeeled potatoes - cut in ½-inch chunks

1 medium onion - chopped in 1½- to 2-inch chunks (or 1 cup frozen chopped onion)

2 (14-ounce) packages low fat smoked sausage - cut into ½-inch chunks

2 envelopes dry Butter Buds (or 2 tablespoons Butter Buds Sprinkles)

1 (1 pound) package California blend frozen vegetables

2 (14.5-ounce) cans Swanson fat-free chicken broth

½ cup cornstarch

1 teaspoon garlic salt - optional

♥ Spray crockpot with non-fat cooking spray.

♥ Put potatoes and onions in first and top with remaining ingredients except cornstarch and garlic salt. Cover.

♥ Cook on low for 8 to 10 hours.

♥ Drain broth from crockpot. Put broth into a large 12-inch non-stick skillet over high heat. With a whisk, mix 1 cup of the broth with cornstarch and garlic salt.

♥ Once cornstarch is completely dissolved, stir into remaining broth in skillet. With whisk, keep stirring for about 4 to 5 minutes or until thick.

♥ Gently stir meat and vegetables from crockpot into thick gravy.

♥ Serve immediately.

Yield: 8 servings

Calories: 235   Total fat: 2.9 grams (11% fat)
Cholesterol: 36 mg   Sodium: 1132 mg

Preparation time: 10 minutes or less.

Cooking time: 8-10 hours.

Menu ideas: Serve with sour dough bread for a complete meal!

HERBED EYE OF ROUND WITH SEASONED POTATOES & BUTTERED MUSHROOMS

Put into a crockpot before a long day away and come home to a mouth-watering aroma that's delicious and ready to eat.

2 pounds beef eye of round - all visible fat removed
1½ teaspoons dried thyme
1½ teaspoons dried basil
1 teaspoon garlic salt

1 (1 pound) bag frozen Bob Evans Seasoned Diced Potatoes
3 tablespoons fat-free Ultra Promise - divided
6 ounces fresh mushrooms - sliced

- ♥ Spray a crockpot with non-fat cooking spray.
- ♥ Sprinkle all sides of beef with thyme, basil, and garlic salt.
- ♥ Place beef in crockpot.
- ♥ Tear 2 pieces of foil each about 18 inches long. Fold the seams together along the side.
- ♥ Spray foil with non-fat cooking spray.
- ♥ Place diced potatoes in center of foil. Spread 2 tablespoons of the Ultra Promise over frozen diced potatoes. Fold the foil (as you would a gifted package) to seal in the flavor of potatoes.
- ♥ Place potatoes on beef.
- ♥ Spray another 18-inch piece of foil with non-fat cooking spray. Stack mushrooms in foil. Dab 1 tablespoon of fat-free margarine on top of mushrooms. Sprinkle lightly with garlic salt if desired. Fold foil (as you would a gifted package) to seal in flavor.
- ♥ Place mushrooms on top of beef and potatoes.
- ♥ Cover crockpot.
- ♥ Cook on low for 8 to 10 hours. (Or cook on high for 4 to 5 hours). Serve juices in bottom of crockpot on the side.

Yield: 6 servings

5 ounces serving of beef

1 ounce serving of buttered mushrooms (to top beef)

2½ ounces serving of seasoned potatoes

(Herbed Eye of Round continued)

Calories: 312   Total fat: 8.6 grams (26% fat)
Cholesterol: 83 mg   Sodium: 456 mg

Preparation time: 10 minutes or less.

Menu ideas: Broccoli Parmesan (page 142),
Carrots with a Light Buttery Caramel Glaze (page 137)
and garlic toast.

CHICKEN AND POTATO STEW

Budget
Friendly

Recipe

One of my assistants (Robin Friend,
who loves to eat high fat) gave me this recipe.

1 pound boneless, skinless chicken breast - cut into bite-size pieces	2 (16-ounce) packages of frozen vegetables for stew - (potatoes, onions and carrots)
1 (15-ounce) can Healthy Choice cream of mushroom soup	2 tablespoons fat-free Ultra Promise

♥ Layer in crockpot in the following order: chicken, soup, frozen vegetables and Promise.

♥ Cover. Cook on low for 8 to 9 hours. Mix well before serving. If desired, add lite salt and pepper to taste.

Yield: 6 servings

Calories: 199   Total fat: 1.2 grams (6% fat)
Cholesterol: 44 mg   Sodium: 290 mg

Preparation time: 5 minutes or less.

Cooking time: 8-9 hours on low.

Total time: 9 hours or less.

Menu ideas: Serve with biscuits or
sourdough bread for a complete meal.

CARIBBEAN RICE

*Mexico inspired me to create this flavorful dish. A terrific meal to make
before leaving home for work, errands, church, etc.! How comforting it is to
come home to the flavorful aroma of a delicious meal awaiting you!*

1 (9.5-ounce) bottle Lawry's teriyaki sauce with ginger and sesame - Chicken Sauté

1 (20-ounce) can crushed pineapple in its own juice - do not drain

1 (15-ounce) can sweet peas - drained - (or 1 cup chopped green pepper)

1 pound (26-30 count) cooked, peeled and deveined frozen shrimp - frozen

3 cups beef broth (3 beef bouillon cubes dissolved in 3 cups of water)

3 cups instant rice (enriched long grain)

♥ Spray crockpot with non-fat cooking spray.

♥ Put teriyaki sauce, pineapple, peas and shrimp into crockpot. Very gently stir until well mixed.

♥ Cover. Cook on high for 3½ to 4 hours or on low for 7 to 8 hours.

♥ Ten minutes before it's time to eat, prepare rice by bringing broth to a boil in a medium saucepan.

♥ Stir in rice. Cover. Remove from heat. Let stand 5 minutes.

♥ Gently stir cooked rice into crockpot mixture.

♥ Serve immediately with lite soy sauce on the side if desired.

Yield: 8 entrée servings

Calories: 303   Total fat: 2.0 grams (6% fat)
Cholesterol: 111 mg   Sodium: 1052 mg

Preparation time: 15 minutes

Cooking time: Depends on temperature (3½-8 hours)

Meal ideas: Cooked asparagus and French bread.

BEANIE BABY STEW

*This is a breeze to put together and
a crowd pleaser every time!*

Budget
Friendly

Recipe

1 (24-ounce) jar Randall's Deluxe
Great Northern Beans
2 (10-ounce) cans Swanson white
chicken chunks in water
1 (49½-ounce) can Swanson
chicken broth - all visible fat
removed

1 (12-ounce) bag frozen chopped
onions
1 (7-ounce) can diced green
chilies (I used Ortega)
1 (1 pound) bag frozen diced
potatoes
½ cup cornstarch

♥ Put all ingredients except cornstarch into a crockpot. Cover. Cook on high for 4 hours or low for 8 to 9 hours.

♥ With a ladle or strainer, remove as much of the cooked ingredients as possible and put into a large bowl. With a potato masher, smash cooked food for about 1 minute. (This will make the broth thicker.)

♥ Combine cornstarch with ½ cup cold water. Stir briskly until cornstarch is completely dissolved.

♥ Stir dissolved cornstarch and water into broth in the crockpot. Stir until well mixed.

♥ Return smashed vegetables to crockpot.

♥ Stir. Turn crockpot to high. Cover and cook for another 20 to 30 minutes. Stew will be a thick and creamy consistency when done.

♥ If desired sprinkle each serving bowl of chowder lightly with fat-free mozzarella cheese just before eating.

Yield: 14 (1-cup) servings

Calories: 185   Total fat: 3.7 grams (18% fat)
Cholesterol: 25 mg   Sodium: 514 mg

Preparation time: 5 minutes or less.

Cooking time: Varies depending on method of cooking - high or low temperature.

Menu idea: Tossed salad or cornbread.

HAM & CABBAGE DINNER

Budget Friendly

Recipe

As a child this was one of my favorite meals!
It's great to prepare when camping . . . if you're fortunate
enough to have electricity when you camp. Some people like to put
fresh peeled carrots and chunks of onions in this dish.

2 tablespoons dry Butter Buds Sprinkles
1 (14.5 ounce) can Swanson fat-free, reduced-sodium chicken broth

1 head cabbage - cored and cut into 6 wedges
1½ pounds extra lean ham
¼ cup Fleischmann's Fat-Free Buttery Spread

♥ In a crockpot stir the Butter Buds with the chicken broth until dissolved.

♥ Put cabbage wedges in the bottom of the crockpot. (Don't worry if the broth does not cover the cabbage.)

♥ Place ham on top of cabbage.

♥ Cover. Cook on low for 8 to 10 hours or on high for 4 hours. (Don't worry about overcooking.)

♥ Cut ham into 6 slices.

♥ Stir cooked cabbage wedges in broth before removing from crock pot. With slotted spoon remove cabbage and place in a pretty serving bowl. Toss with Fleischmann's Fat-Free spread. If desired sprinkle lightly with lite salt. Serve immediately. Serve with Fleischmann's Fat-Free spread and salt and pepper on the side.

Yield: 6 servings

Calories: 207   Total fat: 6.0 grams (26% fat)
Cholesterol: 53 mg   Sodium: 1887 mg

Preparation time: 10 minutes or less.

Cooking time: Varies, depending on temperature.

Meal idea: Microwaved red skin potatoes, taste good
with sliced fat-free wheat bread. (Aunt Millie's brand is good.)
A mousse of any flavor is a rich and satisfying dessert
which is easy to prepare and compliments this meal.

LEMON PEPPER PORK TENDERLOIN WITH LEMON KISSED POTATOES

Put in right before leaving for church. There's nothing like coming home to a delicious home cooked meal that's awaiting you!

2 pounds pork tenderloin - all visible fat removed
2 medium lemons - cut into quarters and seeds discarded
1 teaspoon ground pepper
1 teaspoon garlic salt
8 medium potatoes - cut into ½-inch cubes
1 teaspoon cream of tartar
1 teaspoon dried parsley

♥ With a knife, cut pork tenderloin down the center lengthwise to divide it in half. With a knife, cut ¼-inch deep cuts all over the pork. Squeeze the lemon juice onto tenderloin. Sprinkle lightly with pepper and garlic salt. Put the meat around the sides and bottom of the crockpot.

♥ Put diced potatoes in a bowl with one cup of water and 1 teaspoon cream of tartar, let soak for 1 minute. (This will keep the potatoes from turning brown or discolored while cooking). Drain. Put potatoes on top of meat in crock pot. Sprinkle with dried parsley. Arrange what remains of lemon quarters on top.

♥ Cook on high for 2½ to 3 hours or cook on low 5 to 6 hours. Remove lemons before serving.

♥ Serve on a large serving plate. (If desired you can sprinkle potatoes lightly with salt and more dried parsley).

♥ Serve immediately.

Yield: 8 servings

Calories: 240   Total fat: 4.2 grams (16% fat)
Cholesterol: 67 mg   Sodium: 282 mg

Preparation time: 10 minutes or less.

Cooking time: Depends on temperature used.

Menu ideas: Sassy Slaw (page 109), or
Tangy Tossed Salad (page 113),
Cornbread and Cranberry Apple Salad (page 110).

209

BEEF AND POTATOES WITH MUSHROOM AND ONION GRAVY

Budget Friendly

Recipe

Beef doesn't get more tender than this!
Forget the knife-it cuts with a fork!

1 cup water
¾ cup Village Saucerie - Garden Herb Flavor (found in Shake 'n Bake asile) - divided
1 (2½ pound) eye of round roast cut into ¼- to ⅓-inch thin slices (Put in refrigerator from freezer the night before and it will be partially frozen for easier cutting in the morning. It's easier to slice when partially frozen.)

1 (12-ounce) bag frozen chopped onions
2 (7-ounce) cans mushrooms stems and pieces - do not drain
8 medium potatoes
⅓ cup cornstarch

♥ Dissolve water and ½ cup Village Saucerie in a crockpot. Place a layer of meat slices (3 or 4 slices per layer) in crockpot. Sprinkle some of remaining Village Saucerie seasoning over meat, then add a layer of onions and mushrooms. Continue layering this way until beef, Village Saucerie seasoning and vegetables are all used. Cover. Cook on low for 9 to 10 hours.

♥ Remove meat to a serving platter. Set aside 1 cup of the liquid. Put remaining juices, mushrooms and onions into a 12-inch non-stick skillet over high heat and bring to a boil. (Which will happen within a minute.) In the meantime briskly stir ⅓ cup cornstarch into the 1 cup of liquid set aside. Once dissolved, briskly whisk into boiling liquid. Constantly stir for about 1 minute or until thick. Excellent gravy for potatoes. Sprinkle with salt and pepper if desired.

♥ Cook 8 potatoes in the microwave before removing meat and making gravy. (Prick potatoes before microwaving to prevent them from exploding while cooking.)

(Beef and Potatoes continued)

Yield: 8 servings

Calories: 351   Total fat: 5.3 grams (14% fat)
Cholesterol: 74 mg   Sodium: 556 mg

Preparation time: 20 minutes or less.

Cooking time: 9-10 hours.

Menu idea: Tossed salad with sliced fresh tomatoes topped with fat-free Italian dressing and French bread.

Those who think you can buy true love are foolish . . . How much is a hug worth? How much is a kiss? Money can buy a lot of things, but not true love.

WORLD'S EASIEST LASAGNA

Budget
Friendly
Recipe

*I converted my Great Aunt Florence Craw's Easy
Oven Lasagna to this, which has got to be one of the easiest
lasagnas in the world to make! If you love lasagna, but you hate how long
it normally takes than this is the answer for you! Now you can say
good-bye to cooking the noodles first and it taste terrific!*

1 ½ (26-ounce) jars Healthy
   Choice Super Chunky
   Mushroom pasta sauce
1 pound package MorningStar
   Farms Ground Meatless (found
   in freezer section of the grocery
   store next to ground turkey or
   1 pound lean ground turkey
   breast)

1 (8-ounce) package dry lasagna
   noodles (10 strips)
1 (16-ounce) container fat-free
   cottage cheese
2 (8-ounce) packages Healthy
   Choice fat-free mozzarella
   cheese

♥ Preheat oven to 375 degrees.

♥ Line a 9x13-inch pan with foil. (For easier clean up). Spray lined pan
   with non-fat cooking spray.

♥ In a large bowl, mix together pasta sauce and ground meatless (no
   need to cook ground meatless). (Or if you prefer ground turkey:
   microwave turkey until fully cooked and add to pasta sauce). Stir until
   well mixed.

♥ Line bottom of prepared pan with one-third of pasta sauce mixture.

♥ Lay 5 strips of uncooked lasagna noodles on top of pasta sauce
   mixture.

♥ Spread one cup of cottage cheese over noodles and sprinkle two-
   thirds of the mozzarella cheese over cottage cheese.

♥ Repeat layers ending with sauce.

♥ Cover with foil and bake at 375 for 1 hour.

Yield: 12 servings

With ground meatless:
Calories: 251   Total fat: 0.3 grams (1% fat)
Cholesterol: 6 mg   Sodium: 1027 mg

212

(World's Easiest Lasagna continued)

With ground turkey breast:
Calories: 230   Total fat: 0.7 grams (3% fat)
Cholesterol: 32 mg   Sodium: 785 mg

Preparation time: 10 minutes or less.

Cooking time: 1 hour.

Total time: 70 minutes or less.

*Menu ideas: Tossed salad, Green Beans Italiano' (page 132)
and Garlic Toast (page 79).*

*Note: If desired, microwave pasta sauce remaining
in the jar and serve as a dip for garlic toast.*

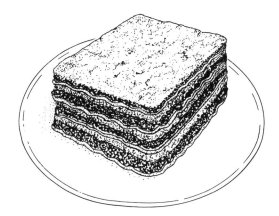

*I want to be the type of person that when people think of me it brings a
smile to their face.*

CHICKEN NUGGETS

Budget
Friendly

Recipe

*My homemade version of chicken nuggets are a lot
less fattening thank fast food restaurants and just as tasty!
A serving of these homemade babies have less fat than one
little nugget at Mickey D's! WOW!*

1 (6-ounce) box Stove Top
  Stuffing - any flavor (I used their
  cornbread flavor)

4 egg whites
1 ½ pounds boneless, skinless
  chicken breast - all fat removed

♥ Preheat oven to 425 degrees.

♥ Cover a cookie sheet with foil. Spray foil with non-fat cooking spray.
Set aside.

♥ On high speed in a blender (or food processor) grind bread crumbs
and seasoning mix from stuffing for 30 seconds. Pour into a shallow
bowl.

♥ Beat egg whites in blender (or food processor) for 15 seconds. Pour
into a separate shallow bowl.

♥ Cut chicken into nuggets. (The same size McDonalds does).

♥ With a fork, take pieces of chicken (one at a time) and dip into ground
crumbs. Dip into egg whites. Dip again into bread crumbs.

♥ Place prepared chicken nuggets onto foiled cookie sheet.

♥ Bake at 425 degrees for 15 minutes, turn nuggets over. Bake an
additional 5 minutes.

♥ Serve with mustard, barbecue sauce, sweet and sour sauce or your
favorite fat-free salad dressing for dipping.

Yield: 6 (4-ounce) servings

Calories: 247 Total fat: 2.4 grams (9% fat)
Cholesterol: 66 mg Sodium: 627 mg

Preparation time: 15 minutes or less.

Cooking time: 20 minutes.

Total time: 35 minutes or less.

*Menu ideas: Bacon-Lettuce and Tomato Salad (page 115),
Broccoli Parmesan (page 142) and lite fruit cocktail.*

Speedy Sweets

BANANA BUTTERSCOTCH DROPS

Budget
Friendly

Recipe

These sweet babies will curb any sweet tooth!
If you like banana bread and butterscotch cookies
you'll like this unique cookie combination!

3 ripe medium bananas - mashed
1 (18¼-ounce) box Betty Crocker Reduced Fat Sweet Rewards yellow cake mix - dry

2 cups old fashioned oats
1 cup butterscotch baking chips

♥ Preheat oven to 350 degrees.

♥ Spray cookie sheets with non-fat cooking spray. Line cookie sheets with foil. (For easier clean-up.)

♥ With a mixer on medium speed, mix bananas for one minute. Add cake mix and continue mixing for 1½ to 2 minutes or until all ingredients are well blended.

♥ With a wooden spoon, stir in oats and butterscotch baking chips until well blended.

♥ With a measuring teaspoon, drop rounded teaspoonfuls of cookie dough onto prepared cookie sheets.

♥ Bake at 350 degrees for 14 to 15 minutes or until bottoms are golden brown.

Yield: 6 dozen (Nutritional information per cookie)

Calories: 54   Total fat: 1.4 grams (23% fat)
Cholesterol: 0 mg   Sodium: 53 mg

Preparation time: 10 minutes or less.

Baking time: 15 minutes or less (Per 2 dozen).

Total time: 25 minutes or less for 2 dozen. Add 15 minutes baking time for each 2 dozen made.

Menu ideas: Dig right in for a holiday treat!

BUTTERFINGER TRIFLE

Budget
Friendly

Recipe

This is rich!!

4 cups skim milk - divided
2 (1-ounce) boxes instant sugar-
free vanilla pudding mix
2 (8-ounce) containers Cool Whip
Free - divided
2 (2.1-ounce) Butterfinger candy
bars - crushed - divided

1 (12-ounce) fat-free golden
dessert cake - cut into ½-inch
pieces (by Tripp Bakers - found
at Food Town, or a 12-ounce
fat-free pound cake will work)
1 (1.4-ounce) box instant sugar-
free chocolate pudding mix
1 (1.4-ounce) box instant sugar-
free butterscotch pudding mix

♥ With a whisk, beat 2 cups milk and vanilla pudding together for 1
minute. Stir in 1 container Cool Whip and 1½ crushed candy bars.
Gently stir in cake pieces. Set aside.

♥ With whisk, beat 2 cups milk and chocolate and butterscotch puddings
together for one minute. Stir in remaining container Cool Whip Free.

♥ In the bottom of a large glass bowl, spread half of the chocolate-
butterscotch pudding mixture.

♥ Top with half of the cake mixture.

♥ Smooth on remaining chocolate-butterscotch mixture.

♥ Spread remaining cake mixture on top.

♥ Sprinkle with remaining crushed candy.

♥ Keep chilled until ready to serve.

Yield: 16 servings

Calories: 186   Total fat: 1.8 grams (9% fat)
Cholesterol: 1 mg   Sodium: 427 mg

Total preparation time: 10 minutes or less.

*Menu ideas: This would be very
tasty for a gathering with family or friends.*

PUNCHBOWL CAKE

Budget
Friendly

Recipe

This recipe was given to me by Pat Paydo of Birmingham, Alabama. It is absolutely wonderful!! (Fast, easy and delicious. Also very pretty!!)

1 (13.5-ounce) angel food cake
1 (21-ounce) can strawberry or blueberry pie filling

2 medium bananas - sliced then quarter the slices
1 (8-ounce) container Cool Whip Free

♥ Cut cake into 3 layers. Tear 1 of the layers into tiny pieces. Set aside.

♥ Mix pie filling with quartered banana slices and mix with spoon until well blended. Set aside.

♥ Place a layer of angel food cake on the bottom of a punch bowl. Use torn pieces of cake to fill in any gaps.

♥ Spread ½ of the fruit mixture over cake.

♥ Place second layer of cake on top of fruit filling. Use torn pieces to fill in any gaps.

♥ Spread remaining fruit mixture on top of cake.

♥ Frost Cool Whip Free evenly on top.

Yield: 12 servings

Calories: 188   Total fat: 0.3 grams (2% fat)
Cholesterol: 0 mg   Sodium: 264 mg

Total preparation time: 5 minutes or less.

Menu ideas: Nice and tasty summer delight!

We spend too much time arguing and debating about things that really aren't important or things we can't change.

APPLE BERRY BAKE

*This is one of my most favorite creations and it is
absolutely delicious! If you like apple crisp and cranberries,
you'll like this creative combination as much as I do.
It's a guaranteed winner!*

¼ tub (2-ounce) Ultra Promise fat-free spread (2 tubs in 1-pound package)

1 (8-ounce) package apple-cinnamon crisp mix (I use Calhoun Bend Mill brand - found in baking section of grocery store)

1 (16-ounce) can whole berry cranberry sauce (I use Ocean Spray)

1 teaspoon ground cinnamon

1 large apple - peeled and chopped into ¼-inch pieces (about 1 cup) (I use Granny Smith)

♥ Preheat oven to 400 degrees.

♥ Spray a 9x9-inch cake pan (or 9-inch pie pan will work fine also) with non-fat cooking spray.

♥ With a fork, mix Ultra Promise spread and apple-cinnamon crisp mix until well mixed. Dough will be "doughy" - not crumbly. Set in freezer.

♥ Mix cranberries, cinnamon and chopped apple together until well combined. Pour this cranberry/apple mixture into prepared pan.

♥ With two forks, arrange pieces of dough on top of mixture. There may be some spots where the dough has not completely covered the cranberry/apple mixture.

♥ Bake at 400 degrees for 27 minutes or until top of dough is golden brown and fruit is bubbly hot.

♥ Let cool for 4 to 5 minutes before serving.

Yield: 9 servings

Calories: 185   Total fat: 0.8 grams (7% fat)
Cholesterol: 0 mg   Sodium: 126 mg

Preparation time: 8 minutes or less.

Baking time: 27 minutes.

Total time: 35 minutes or less.

*Menu ideas: Any chicken, turkey, ham or pork entrée.
Also it's wonderful served hot with Cool Whip Free.*

219

STRAWBERRY SQUARES

Budget Friendly

Recipe

½ cup applesauce
½ cup strawberry preserves
1 (8-ounce) carton Egg Beaters - divided
1 (18¼-ounce) Betty Crocker Reduced Fat Sweet Rewards yellow cake mix

1 (.32-ounce) box sugar free strawberry gelatin mix - dry
1 cup powdered sugar
1 (8-ounce) package fat-free cream cheese (I use Healthy Choice)

- ♥ Preheat oven to 350 degrees.
- ♥ Spray a 9x15-inch jelly roll pan with non-fat cooking spray. Set aside.
- ♥ Mix applesauce, strawberry preserves, ¼ cup Egg Beaters and cake mix together with a mixer on medium speed. Beat 2 minutes.
- ♥ Spread batter into prepared pan.
- ♥ With mixer, beat together dry gelatin, powdered sugar, cream cheese and remaining Egg Beaters on medium speed for 2 minutes. Pour over cake batter.
- ♥ Bake at 350 degrees for 22 to 25 minutes or until a knife inserted in center comes out clean.

Yield: 24 servings

Calories: 140   Total fat: 1.6 grams (10% fat)
Cholesterol: 1 mg   Sodium: 227 mg

Preparation time: 10 minutes or less.

Baking time: 25 minutes or less.

Total time: 35 minutes or less.

Menu ideas: After cooking out with friends and family, bring this taste tempting treat out.

Get in the habit of doing good habits and get in the habit of dropping bad habits.

Swiss Chocolate Almond Ice Cream Cake

Budget Friendly

Recipe

Oh man! This is too good!

2 quarts Flavorite Swiss Chocolate Almond low-fat frozen yogurt
5 fat-free chocolate brownies (I use Famous Amos brownies)

6 reduced-fat fudge sandwich cookies (I use Staff)
1 (11½-ounce) jar Smucker's fat-free hot fudge

♥ Let frozen yogurt set out to soften. (About 5 minutes).

♥ Spray a 9x13-inch pan with non-fat cooking spray.

♥ Put brownies and cookies in a food processor. Turn it on for about 30 to 40 seconds or until it is a course, crumbly consistency.

♥ With palm of hand, press brownie-cookie mixture on bottom of prepared pan.

♥ Spoon frozen yogurt over brownie-cookie crust. With a spatula, spread yogurt to look smooth.

♥ Heat hot fudge in microwave. Quickly spread hot fudge over yogurt. The hot fudge will melt the yogurt. That's okay.

♥ Freeze overnight.

♥ This can be made days in advance. Cut into squares.

Yield: 15 servings

Calories: 241   Total fat: 2.4 grams (9% fat)
Cholesterol: 5 mg   Sodium: 199 mg

Preparation time: 15-20 minutes.

Menu ideas: Great for a hot summer dessert!

BLACK FOREST TORTILLA STACK

Budget Friendly Recipe

It doesn't get any easier or any faster than this folks!

1 (1.4-ounce) box Jell-O instant sugar free chocolate pudding - dry
2 cups skim milk
7 (10-inch) fat-free flour tortillas (I use Buena Vida)

1 (21-ounce) can cherry pie filling
¼ cup Smucker's fat-free hot fudge

♥ Mix pudding and skim milk together, stirring briskly for two minutes. Set aside.

♥ Lay one tortilla on cake plate. Spread ½ cup chocolate pudding over tortilla.

♥ Lay second tortilla on top of pudding. Spread ⅓ can cherry pie filling over tortilla.

♥ Lay third tortilla on top of pie filling. Repeat layers twice. Top with remaining pudding.

♥ Microwave hot fudge for 15 seconds on high or until fully heated. Drizzle hot fudge over pudding and let drizzle over sides.

♥ Keep refrigerated until ready to serve.

Yield: 12 servings

Calories: 218   Total fat: 0 grams (0% fat)
Cholesterol: 1 mg   Sodium: 536 mg

Total preparation time: 5 minutes or less

Menu ideas: Good after any light meal, such as soups, salads or vegetable-based casseroles.

If we wait for perfect conditions to do what we want to do chances are we will never do it.

 Kids Cookin'

MINT MOUSSE

This rich thick dessert is fabulous!!!

 Budget Friendly

Recipe

½ teaspoon mint extract (found next to vanilla)

1 (12-ounce) container Cool Whip Free

1 (1-ounce) box sugar-free vanilla instant pudding - dry (I used Jell-O brand)

6 drops of green food coloring - optional

- ♥ Mix all ingredients together.
- ♥ Keep stirring for 2 minutes.
- ♥ Spoon into dessert cups. (For a fancier look, spoon into wide mouth wine glasses instead of dessert cups.)
- ♥ Ready to serve as is or refrigerate until ready to eat.
- ♥ Garnishing Ideas: Christmas - Place a small candy cane into each dessert - allowing the cane to show or crush 1 candy cane into tiny pieces and sprinkle on top.
- ♥ St. Patrick's Day - Set a spearmint candy leaf on top of each dessert.

Yield: 5 servings (without garnish)

Calories: 132   Total fat: 0 grams (0% fat)
Cholesterol: 0 mg   Sodium: 272 mg

Total preparation time: 5 minutes or less.

Menu ideas: Christmas or St. Patrick's Day celebration meals. Any fancy meal.

PUMPKIN FLUFF (PUMPKIN FLUFF PIE)

This creamy, fluffy dessert is a "just right"
substitution after a heavy meal.

1½ cups canned pumpkin
1 teaspoon cinnamon
½ cup Equal Spoonful
1 tablespoon lite maple syrup

1 (12-ounce) container Cool
  Whip Free
1 (1.5-ounce) box sugar-free
  vanilla pudding - dry

♥ Mix pumpkin, cinnamon, Equal Spoonful and maple syrup together until well blended. Set aside.

♥ In a different bowl, mix Cool Whip and pudding together until well blended.

♥ Combine the pumpkin mixture with the pudding mixture. Stir until well mixed.

♥ Sprinkle top lightly with extra cinnamon if desired.

♥ Keep refrigerated until ready to eat. Serve chilled.

Yield: 8 servings

Calories: 112   Total fat: 0 grams (0% fat)
Cholesterol: 0 mg   Sodium: 251 mg

For Pumpkin Fluff Pie: Use a prepared graham cracker reduced-fat pie crust. (I use Keebler). Simply prepare pumpkin fluff as directed and put into pie crust. Sprinkle top with cinnamon if desired.

Yield: 8 servings

Calories: 213   Total fat: 3.0 grams (14% fat)
Cholesterol: 0 mg   Sodium: 348 mg

Preparation time: 10 minutes or less.

Menu ideas: Perfect dessert for
Thanksgiving or Christmas dinner.

BLUEBERRY FLUFF CUPS

Budget Friendly Recipe

Fun, fast and fabulous for the Fourth of July!

1½ cups Cool Whip Free
3 tablespoons Smuckers's Simply Fruit blueberry spreadable fruit (jam)

4 (1-ounce) Dolly Madison Bakery short cakes
1 cup fresh blueberries (sprinkled lightly with Equal to sweeten if needed)

♥ Mix Cool Whip Free and blueberry jam together until well blended. Divide mixture evenly among short cakes. If desired, put a dab of Cool Whip Free on top.

♥ Top with blueberries. Cover and keep chilled until ready to eat.

♥ For a prettier, more elegant presentation put each dessert onto its own pretty little plate before serving.

Yield: 4 servings

Calories: 185   Total fat: 2.2 grams (12% fat)
Cholesterol: 15 mg   Sodium: 141 mg

Total preparation time: 5 minutes or less.

Menu ideas: Great for Patriotic holidays - Memorial Day, Labor Day, Fourth of July, etc. For a colorful patriotic celebration dessert, substitute strawberry jam for the blueberry. Top with fresh sliced strawberries. Double recipe, making red and blue colored dessert cups. Make a pattern of red and blue dessert cups. Top with a dab of Cool Whip Free on each dessert for red, white and blue!

APRICOT CAKE

Budget Friendly Recipe

Always an appreciated afternoon delight.

1 (17-ounce) can apricot halves in heavy syrup
1 (18¼-ounce) Betty Crocker Reduced Fat Sweet Rewards yellow cake mix-dry
1 cup apricot preserves, divided
1 (1-ounce) box sugar free instant vanilla pudding and pie filling-dry
1 (12-ounce) container Cool Whip Free

♥ Preheat oven to 350 degrees.

♥ Spray a 9x13-inch pan with non-fat cooking spray. Set aside.

♥ In a blender, purée apricots with the heavy syrup until smooth and thick.

♥ In a medium bowl using a mixer, combine dry cake mix and puréed apricots on medium speed for two minutes.

♥ Spread the cake batter into prepared pan. Bake at 350 degrees for 33 to 35 minutes, or until cake is golden brown and edges move away from sides of pan.

♥ Let the cake cool for about 10 minutes. Spread ⅓ cup apricot preserves over the cake.

♥ To make frosting, in a medium bowl using a mixer, stir together remaining two-thirds cup apricot preserves with the dry pudding mix and Cool Whip Free. Mix on low for about 1 minute or until well mixed.

♥ This cake is delicious served warm from the oven with a dab of this frosting or let the cake cool completely and frost the entire cake with the above frosting.

♥ Refrigerate leftover cake.

Yield: 15 servings

Calories: 262   Total fat: 2.6 grams (9% fat)
Cholesterol: 0 mg   Sodium: 347 mg

Preparation time: 8 minutes or less.

Baking time: 33-35 minutes.

Total time: 53 minutes or less.

Menu ideas: Delicious after any type of luncheon or dinner party.

226

FROZEN CHEESECAKE DESSERT

If you like cheesecake flavored ice cream you're gonna love this! This recipe was originally sent in from Tami Heiss of Toledo, Ohio. Her version using a low-fat pie crust was a lot higher in fat. I think you'll love it!

³/₄ cup graham cracker crumbs (for easier use buy the prepared crumbs)

1 (12-ounce) container Cool Whip Free

2 (8-ounce) packages fat-free cream cheese

¹/₃ cup sugar (or ¹/₃ cup Equal Spoonful)

1 (21-ounce) can cherry pie filling (or blueberry)

♥ Spray a 9x13-inch pan with non-fat cooking spray.
♥ Sprinkle graham cracker crumbs in bottom of pan. Set aside.
♥ In a large bowl with a mixer, combine Cool Whip Free, cream cheese and sugar (or Equal Spoonful) on medium speed for 2 minutes.
♥ Spread into prepared pan.
♥ Top with pie filling. Freeze for 2 hours to set.
♥ Let sit 10 minutes before cutting.

Yield: 15 servings

Calories: 154   Total fat: 0.7 grams (4% fat)
Cholesterol: 2 mg   Sodium: 199 mg

Preparation time: 10-12 minutes.

Menu ideas: Great on a hot summer day!

You are never too old to dream.

BROWNIE COOKIES

Budget Friendly

Recipe

This scrumptious cookie is very versatile.
Seven different cookies can be derived from the base,
and they're all terrific!

¼ cup brown sugar
3 tablespoons applesauce
1 egg white

2 tablespoons flour
1 (10.25-ounce) Gold Medal
　Smart Size brownie mix - dry

♥ Preheat oven to 350 degrees.

♥ Line 2 cookie sheets with foil, spray with non-fat cooking spray. Set aside.

♥ Mix together brown sugar, applesauce and egg white until well blended. Stir in flour and brownie mix until well mixed.

♥ Drop by rounded teaspoonfuls onto prepared cookie sheets. With a damp fork press cookies down into 1½-inch diameter circles.

♥ Bake at 350 degrees for 10 minutes.

Yield: 2 dozen (Nutritional information per cookie)

Calories: 66　Total fat: 1.6 grams (21% fat)
Cholesterol: 4 mg　Sodium: 39 mg

Preparation time: 5 minutes or less.

Baking time: 10 minutes

Total time: 15 minutes or less

Menu ideas: Perfect for those school lunches
or an after-school snack.

The following are cookie recipes using the
"Brownie Cookies" recipe as the base.

DOUBLE CHOCOLATE BROWNIE COOKIES:
Follow recipe exactly and place 3 Hershey's reduced-fat baking chips on top of each cookie before baking.

Yield: 2 dozen (Nutritional information per cookie)

Calories: 76　Total fat: 1.9 grams (22% fat)
Cholesterol: 4 mg　Sodium: 39 mg

228

(Brownie Cookies continued)

MINT BROWNIE COOKIES:
Follow recipe exactly except add 3 drops mint extract to base before mixing.

Yield: 2 dozen (Nutritional information per cookie)

Calories: 66   Total fat: 1.6 grams (21% fat)
Cholesterol: 4 mg   Sodium: 39 mg

DOUBLE CHOCOLATE MINT BROWNIE COOKIES:
Follow recipe exactly except add 3 drops mint extract before mixing.
Place 3 mint flavored baking chips, on top of each cookie before baking.

Yield: 2 dozen (Nutritional information per cookie)

Calories: 82   Total fat: 2.6 grams (28% fat)
Cholesterol: 4 mg   Sodium: 39 mg

BROWNIE SANDWICH COOKIES:
Once cookies are done baking and are cool, spread 2 teaspoons marshmallow creme on bottom of cookie. Place second cookie on top of marshmallow creme and press together.

Yield: 12 cookies (Nutritional information per cookie)

Calories: 170   Total fat: 3.2 grams (16% fat)
Cholesterol: 8 mg   Sodium: 84 mg

MINT BROWNIE SANDWICH COOKIES:
Follow recipe exactly except add 3 drops mint extract before mixing. Once cookies are done baking and are cool, spread 2 teaspoons marshmallow creme on bottom cookie. Place second cookie on top of marshmallow creme and press together.

Yield: 12 cookies (Nutritional information per cookie)

Calories: 170   Total fat: 3.2 grams (16% fat)
Cholesterol: 8 mg   Sodium: 84 mg

BROWNIE NUT COOKIES:
Follow recipe exactly. Just before baking, lightly sprinkle finely chopped walnuts or pecans over cookies and press in. (No more than ¼ cup for entire recipe.)

Yields: 2 dozen (Nutritional information per cookie)

Calories: 74   Total fat: 2.4 grams (28% fat)
Cholesterol: 4 mg   Sodium: 39 mg

SAND, ROCKS AND CANDY (DESSERT)

Budget Friendly Recipe

For fun, decorate this by placing a child's small plastic sand bucket with the little sand shovel next to the bucket on top and into the dessert! Great for beach side picnics and cookouts!

2 (2-ounce) Chick-O-Stick candy bars
2 (1.7-ounce) boxes sugar-free butterscotch pudding mix - dry - (I use Royal)

4 cups skim milk
1½ cups graham cracker crumbs (for faster preparation I used Sunshine brand already crushed)

♥ Keep wrappers on and crush candy bars by hitting with a rolling pin. Set aside.

♥ Briskly stir together pudding and skim milk for 2 minutes. Stir one crushed candy bar into pudding.

♥ Sprinkle half of the graham cracker crumbs on bottom of a 9x 13-inch pan.

♥ Spread pudding over graham crackers crumbs.

♥ Sprinkle remaining graham cracker crumbs over pudding.

♥ Sprinkle second crushed Chick-O-Stick over crumbs.

♥ Serve immediately or cover and keep chilled until ready to serve.

Yield: 12 servings

Calories: 160   Total fat: 2.6 grams (15% fat)
Cholesterol: 2 mg   Sodium: 484 mg

Total preparation time: 6 minutes or less.

Menu ideas: Great for beach side picnics or cookouts.

Why can't we stop complaining and instead be thankful for what we have?

FRENCH PEPPERMINT CRÈME PUDDING CAKE DESSERT

Budget Friendly

Recipe

This cool, creamy dessert cake satisfies even the most discriminating taste.

3 peppermint candy canes - finely crushed in the blender - divided
1½ cups skim milk
1 (3.4-ounce) box of French vanilla instant pudding - dry

1 (12-ounce) container Cool Whip Free
1 (10.5-ounce) angel food cake

♥ Mix 2 crushed candy canes, milk and pudding together in bowl for about 2 minutes by hand with a whisk. Add Cool Whip Free and keep stirring until well blended, smooth and creamy. Set aside.

♥ Cut angel food cake into 4 thin layers. Line bottom of 9x13-inch pan with angel food cake pieces. You will need to tear some of the pieces of cake so that you can line the entire bottom of the pan with cake pieces.

♥ Frost with crème mixture.

♥ Sprinkle remaining crushed candy cane on top. Eat as is or keep chilled until ready to eat.

Yield: 12 servings

Calories: 180   Total fat: 0.3 grams (2% fat)
Cholesterol: 1 mg   Sodium: 350 mg

Preparation time: 5-10 minutes.

Menu ideas: Serve as a delightful holiday dessert.

Most limitations are self-imposed when it comes to obtaining your hopes and dreams. (God can do far greater things through you than you ever thought of or imagined.)

BOSTON CREAM CAKE

Budget
Friendly
Recipe

I got this idea from our local bakery.
Of course their version was at least 3 times more fattening.
Mine is every bit as tasty as their's - if not more!
This recipe makes 2 (8-inch) round cakes.

CAKE
6 egg whites
½ cup applesauce

1 (18.25-ounce) box Betty
Crocker Reduced Fat Sweet
Rewards yellow cake mix - dry

FILLING
1 (1-ounce) box sugar free-fat-free
instant vanilla pudding - dry
(I use Jell-O)

1½ cups skim milk

GLAZE
⅔ cup fat-free hot fudge - divided
(I use Smucker's)

♥ Preheat oven to 350 degrees.

♥ Spray 4 (8-inch) round pans with non-fat cooking spray. Set aside.

♥ With a mixer, beat egg whites for 30 seconds. Add applesauce and beat 10 seconds. Gradually add cake mix. (Do not pour in all at once.) Once entire cake mix is added, beat on high speed for 2 minutes.

♥ Divide and spread batter evenly among prepared pans.

♥ Bake at 350 degrees for 15 minutes or until a knife inserted in center comes out clean.

♥ Cool in pans for 10 minutes. Remove from pans and cool completely. (They will cool more quickly on cooling racks.)

♥ While cakes are baking and cooling, prepare filling. Clean and use same bowl cake batter was made in and the same mixer beaters.

♥ With mixer on lowest speed, mix dry pudding and milk together for 2 minutes. Refrigerate until cakes are completely cooled.

♥ To assemble cakes, put one cake layer on a cake plate (or large dinner plate). Spread half of the cream mixture on cake. Put second cake layer on top of creamed mixture. Spread ⅓ cup hot fudge topping on top of cake. Repeat for second cake.

♥ Keep refrigerated until ready to serve.

(Boston Cream Cake continued)

Yield: 2 (8-inch) round cakes with 8 servings per cake, 16 servings total

Calories: 196   Total fat: 2.5 grams (11% fat)
Cholesterol: 0 mg   Sodium: 371 mg

Preparation time: 12 minutes.

Baking time 15 minutes (plus 20 minutes cooling time).

Total time: 47 minutes or less.

Menu ideas: Good dessert cake after a light dinner such as fish, chicken, soups and vegetable entrées.

The person who succeeds is the person who perseveres and keeps on trying.

233

SPICE COOKIES

Budget Friendly Recipe

Not only does this very versatile cookie satisfy your sweet tooth, but when they're baking, the fragrant aroma of potpourri fills your home with a warm and cozy feeling.

2 cups whole wheat flour
1 cup sugar
1 teaspoon baking soda
4 egg whites

½ cup applesauce
½ teaspoon ground cloves
1 teaspoon ground cinnamon

♥ Preheat oven to 350 degrees.

♥ Line cookie sheets with foil. Spray foil with non-fat cooking spray. Set aside.

♥ In a large mixing bowl, mix all ingredients together with a spatula until well mixed.

♥ Drop cookie dough by rounded teaspoonfuls onto prepared cookie sheets.

♥ Bake at 350 degrees for 6 to 7 minutes or until bottoms are lightly browned.

Yield: 6 dozen (Nutritional information per cookie)

Calories: 24   Total fat: 0.1 grams (2% fat)
Cholesterol: 0 mg   Sodium: 21 mg

Preparation time: 10 minutes or less.

Baking time: 6-7 minutes (for 2 cookie sheets of 1 dozen each).

Total time: 17 minutes or less (for 2 dozen) add an additional 7 minutes for each 2 dozen.

Menu ideas: Great to eat in the fall and during the holidays.

Variations using the "Spice Cookies" recipe above as the base. Bake as directed in Spice Cookie Recipe.

CHOCOLATE CHIP SPICE COOKIES:
Press 3 chocolate chips on top of each cookie before baking.

Yield: 6 dozen (Nutritional information per cookie)

Calories: 39   Total fat: 1.0 gram (22% fat)
Cholesterol: 0 mg   Sodium: 21 mg

(Spice Cookies continued)

CINNAMON IMPERIAL COOKIES:
Press 4 cinnamon red hot candies on top of each cookie before baking.

Yield: 6 dozen (Nutritional information per cookie)

Calories: 31   Total fat: 0.1 grams (2% fat)
Cholesterol: 0 mg   Sodium: 21 mg

ICED SPICE COOKIES:
Microwave ¼ cup Betty Crocker low-fat vanilla frosting. Lightly drizzle frosting over cooled cookies.

Yield: 6 dozen (Nutritional information per cookie)

Calories: 30   Total fat: 0.2 grams (6% fat)
Cholesterol: 0 mg   Sodium:24 mg

APPLE SPICE COOKIES:
Leaving skins on, cut 2 apples into ¼-inch pieces. Stir apple pieces into prepared dough. The best choices of apples to use are Rome Beauty (also known as Red Rome), Golden Delicious, Granny Smith, Jonathan and Macintosh apples. Note: Red Delicious are not good to bake with.

Yield: 6 dozen (Nutritional information per cookie)

Calories: 26   Total fat: 0.1 grams (3% fat)
Cholesterol: 0 mg   Sodium: 21 mg

APPLE-WALNUT COOKIES:
Leaving skins on, cut 2 apples into ¼-inch pieces. Stir apple pieces into prepared dough. (See apple spice cookies for selection of best apple choices to use.) Not using more than ¡/¤ cup finely chopped walnuts for the entire recipe, sprinkle walnuts on top of cookies before baking.

Yield: 6 dozen (Nutritional information per cookie)

Calories: 31   Total fat: 0.6 grams (16% fat)
Cholesterol: 0 mg   Sodium: 21 mg

(Spice Cookies continued on next page)

(Spice Cookies continued)

ICED APPLE-WALNUT COOKIES:
Follow Apple Walnut Cookies recipe exactly. Microwave ¼ cup Betty Crocker low-fat vanilla frosting. Lightly drizzle frosting over cooled cookies.

Yield: 6 dozen (Nutritional information per cookie)

Calories: 38   Total fat: 0.7 grams (17% fat)
Cholesterol: 0 mg   Sodium: 24 mg

RAISIN SPICE COOKIES:
Stir ¾ cup raisins into prepared dough. After baking, sift or sprinkle cooled cookies lightly with ¼ cup powdered sugar.

Yield: 6 dozen (Nutritional information per cookie)

Calories: 31   Total fat: 0.1 grams (2% fat)
Cholesterol: 0 mg   Sodium: 21 mg

CRANBERRY COOKIES:
Stir ¾ cup chopped, dried cranberries into prepared dough.

Yield: 6 dozen (Nutritional information per cookie)

Calories: 28   Total fat: 0.1 grams (3% fat)
Cholesterol: 0 mg   Sodium: 21 mg

CRANBERRY WALNUT COOKIES:
Stir ¾ cup chopped, dried cranberries into prepared dough. Not using more than ½ cup of finely chopped walnuts for the entire recipe, sprinkle walnuts on top of cookies before baking.

Yield: 6 dozen (Nutritional information per cookie)

Calories: 33   Total fat: 0.6 grams (15% fat)
Cholesterol: 0 mg   Sodium: 21 mg

CARROT COOKIES:
Stir 1½ cups finely grated carrot into prepared cookie dough. After baking, sift or sprinkle cooled cookies lightly with ¼ cup powdered sugar.

Yield: 6 dozen (Nutritional information per cookie)

Calories: 26   Total fat: 0.1 grams (2% fat)
Cholesterol: 0 mg   Sodium: 22 mg

PERFECT PINEAPPLE COOKIES

Budget Friendly

Recipe

*It's hard to eat just one! If you like
pineapple upside down cake you'll love these!*

¼ cup dark brown sugar
1 (20-ounce) can crushed
  pineapple in its natural juices -
  with one cup juice drained and
  discarded
3 egg whites

1 (18.25-ounce) box Betty
  Crocker Reduced-Fat Sweet
  Rewards yellow cake mix - dry
½ cup graham crackers crumbs
  (I use Sunshine)

♥ Preheat oven to 350 degrees.

♥ Line cookie sheets with foil and spray with non-fat cooking spray. Set aside.

♥ With a spatula or spoon, mix together dark brown sugar, drained pineapple, and egg whites until well mixed and sugar is dissolved.

♥ Add cake mix and graham cracker crumbs. Continue stirring until well mixed.

♥ Drop by teaspoonfuls onto prepared cookie sheets. Dip fingers in water and press top of cookie down to 1½-inch diameter circles.

♥ Bake at 350 degrees for 11 to 12 minutes, or until bottoms are golden brown.

Yield: 7 dozen cookies (Nutritional information per cookie)

Calories: 33   Total fat: 0.5 grams (14% fat)
Cholesterol: 0 mg   Sodium: 50 mg

Preparation time: 5 minutes or less.

Baking time: 11-12 minutes per 2 dozen cookies.

Total time: 17 minutes or less for first 2 dozen. Add an additional 12 minutes baking time for each 2 dozen cookies.

*Menu idea: 3 of these make a great snack -
under 100 calories and only 1½ grams of fat.
Or serve after a meal to curb your sweet tooth.*

237

DOUBLE CHOCOLATE
OATMEAL COOKIES

Budget
Friendly

Recipe

For the chocolate lover!

4 egg whites
³/₄ cup applesauce
¹/₂ cup dark brown sugar
1¹/₂ cups quick cooking oats

1 (18.25-ounce) box Betty Crocker
Reduced Fat Sweet Rewards
devil's food cake mix - dry
1 cup semi-sweet chocolate chips

♥ Preheat oven to 350 degrees.

♥ Line cookie sheets with foil. Spray foil with non-fat cooking spray. Set
aside.

♥ In a large bowl, mix egg whites, applesauce and brown sugar with
spatula until well mixed.

♥ Stir in oats and dry cake mix. Continue stirring until well mixed.

♥ Stir in chocolate chips until well mixed and chips are evenly distrib-
uted throughout dough.

♥ Drop cookie dough onto prepared cookie sheets by rounded teaspoonfuls.

♥ Dip a fork into water and press dough down to about 1¹/₂-inch
diameter circles.

♥ Bake at 350 degrees for 12 to 13 minutes.

Yield: 5 dozen (Nutritional information per cookie)

Calories: 64   Total fat: 1.7 grams (23% fat)
Cholesterol: 0 mg   Sodium: 68 mg

Preparation time: 5 minutes or less

**Baking time: 12-13 minutes -(2 cookie sheets with 1 dozen cookies
per sheet.)**

**Total time: 17-18 minutes for 2 dozen cookies plus an additional
12-13 minutes for each additional 2 dozen baked.**

*Menu ideas: Great to pack for lunches or an after-school snack
when you've got a sweet tooth and fruit just isn't enough to curb
it. Also good after dinner to curb your sweet tooth.*

(Double Chocolate Oatmeal Cookies continued)

The following are cookie recipes using the "Double Chocolate Oatmeal Cookie" recipe as the base.

DOUBLE CHOCOLATE CRÈME FILLED SANDWICH COOKIES:
Follow recipe exactly. After cookies have cooled, place 2 teaspoons marshmallow creme on bottom of one cookie and place a second cookie on top. Press gently together.

Yield: 2½ dozen (Nutritional information per cookie)

Calories: 167   Total fat: 3.4 grams (18% fat)
Cholesterol: 0 mg   Sodium: 142 mg

CHOCOLATE PECAN COOKIES:
(An adult favorite!) Follow recipe exactly, but before baking, sprinkle lightly with chopped pecans. (Use no more than ½ cup pecans for entire recipe.)

Dip fork into water and press dough down to about 1½-inch diameter circles.

Bake at 350 degrees for 12 to 13 minutes.

Yield: 5 dozen (Nutritional information per cookie)

Calories: 70   Total fat: 2.4 grams (29% fat)
Cholesterol: 0 mg   Sodium: 68 mg

CHOCOLATE PECAN CREAM FILLED SANDWICH COOKIES:
Follow recipe exactly, but before baking, sprinkle lightly with chopped pecans. (Use no more than ½ cup pecans for entire recipe.)

Dip fork into water and press dough down to about 1½-inch diameter circles.

Bake at 350 degrees for 12 to 13 minutes.

After cookies have cooled, place 2 teaspoons marshmallow cream on bottom of one cookie and place a second cookie on top. Press gently together.

Yield: 2½ dozen (Nutritional information per cookie)

Calories: 180   Total fat: 4.8 grams (23% fat)
Cholesterol: 0 mg   Sodium: 142 mg

HOT FUDGE CAKE

Budget Friendly Recipe

*This mouth-watering, delicious dessert
is just what the tummy ordered!*

1 (18.25-ounce) Betty Crocker Reduced-Fat Sweet Rewards devil's food cake mix - dry
1⅓ cups water
3 tablespoons applesauce
6 egg whites

1 (half-gallon) container fat-free frozen vanilla yogurt - slightly thawed
1 (11½-ounce) Smucker's fat-free hot fudge
1 (8-ounce) container Cool Whip Free

♥ Preheat oven to 350 degrees.

♥ Spray two 9x13-inch pans with non-fat cooking spray. Set aside.

♥ With a mixer, beat cake mix, water, applesauce and egg whites on low speed for 30 seconds. Beat on medium speed 2 minutes longer.

♥ Divide the batter into prepared pans. Bake at 350 degrees for 15 minutes. Let cakes cool for 10 minutes.

♥ Spread frozen yogurt evenly over one of the cakes.

♥ Place second cake on top of frozen yogurt. At this point you can serve cake or freeze entire cake to eat later. (Cover with plastic wrap or foil before freezing.)

♥ To serve cut into 16 pieces. Place each individual piece on a serving plate.

♥ Microwave hot fudge in jar for 30 to 45 seconds. Stir. Drizzle 1 tablespoon hot fudge on each serving.

♥ Top with a dab of Cool Whip Free. (Top with maraschino cherry if desired.) Serve immediately.

Yield: 16 servings

Calories: 321   Total fat: 2.8 grams (8% fat)
Cholesterol: 2 mg   Sodium: 398 mg

Preparation time: 5 minutes.

Baking time: 15 minutes.

Total time: 30 minutes including cooling time.

*Menu ideas: Great served after a light
main entrée such as a boiled dinner.*

CHOCOLATE CHEESE SQUARES

Budget Friendly Recipe

Fast and easy to prepare. Needs time to bake and cool.

1 (17.5-ounce) Double Chocolate Chunk Cookie mix by Gold Medal - dry - divided
9 egg whites - divided
½ cup sugar

2 (8-ounce) fat-free cream cheese - softened (I use Kraft Philadelphia Free)
¼ cup chocolate-flavored powdered sugar (I use domino 10-X Confectioners sugar)

- ♥ Preheat oven to 300 degrees.
- ♥ Set aside 1 cup of dry cookie mix. In a large bowl, mix remaining cookie mix with 3 egg whites.
- ♥ Spray a 9x13-inch jelly roll pan (a cookie sheet with a 1-inch edge) with non-fat cooking spray.
- ♥ With a spatula, spread mixture evenly over bottom of pan. (This layer will be thin.)
- ♥ Beat together sugar, softened cream cheese, 6 egg whites and reserved cookie mix. Beat on medium speed for 1½ minutes (or until well blended). Pour over batter in prepared pan.
- ♥ Bake at 300 degrees for 40 minutes or until center is firm.
- ♥ Let cool 10 minutes. Cut into 24 (2½-inch) squares.
- ♥ Sift powdered sugar over squares. If desired you can arrange squares on serving plate. (They will chill faster if removed from baking pan and separated. Do not stack!) Cover with foil. Refrigerate at least 30 minutes to chill before serving. Keep refrigerated. Best served chilled.

Yield: 24 servings

Calories: 147   Total fat: 5.0 grams (30% fat)
Cholesterol: 1 mg   Sodium: 172 mg

Preparation time: 10 minutes or less.

Baking time: 40 minutes.

Total time: 50 minutes or less.

Menu ideas: Goes great with any entrée.

PUMPKIN APPLE BAKE

Budget Friendly Recipe

*This dessert is wonderful served warm with a dab of
Cool Whip Free, or serve chilled! Although I use no eggs,
it reminds me a lot of a thick pumpkin custard (with apples in it.)
Definitely a unique replacement during the holidays for pumpkin pie.*

1½ cups fat-free pancake mix
  (I use Krusteaz fat-free buttermilk
  pancake mix) - divided
1 (14-ounce) can fat-free
  sweetened condensed milk -
  divided

1 (29-ounce) can pumpkin
1 (21-ounce) can apple pie filling
1 tablespoon pumpkin pie spice
1 cup dark brown sugar

♥ Preheat oven to 350 degrees.

♥ Spray a 9x13-inch pan with non-fat cooking spray. Set aside.

♥ In a microwavable small bowl, mix ½ cup pancake mix and ⅓ cup sweetened condensed milk until well mixed. Set aside.

♥ Mix all remaining ingredients together. Spread mixture into prepared pan. Microwave dough mixture (previously set aside) for a few seconds, until bubbly. Drizzle bubbly, hot dough mixture over pumpkin mixture.

♥ Bake at 350 degrees for 50 minutes. Top will be toasty brown in color when done.

♥ Let sit 5 minutes before cutting. Refrigerate unused portions.

Yield: 15 servings

Calories: 228   Total fat: 0 grams (0% fat)
Cholesterol: 1 mg Sodium: 141 mg

If desired try adding ½ cup of raisins also.

Preparation time: 5 minutes.

Baking time: 50 minutes.

Total time: 55 minutes.

Menu ideas: This would be great served with a holiday dinner.

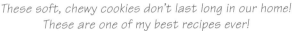

Apple Oatmeal Cookies

Budget
Friendly

Recipe

These soft, chewy cookies don't last long in our home!
These are one of my best recipes ever!

³/₄ cup applesauce
¹/₂ cup dark brown sugar
1¹/₂ cups quick cooking oats
1 (18.25-ounce) box Betty
  Crocker Reduced-Fat Sweet
  Rewards yellow cake mix - dry

1¹/₂ teaspoons cinnamon
¹/₂ cup raisins
1 cup peeled and finely chopped
  apple (Johnathan or MacIntosh)

♥ Preheat oven to 350 degrees.

♥ Line cookie sheets with foil. Spray foil with non-fat cooking spray. Set aside.

♥ In a large bowl, mix applesauce and brown sugar until well mixed.

♥ Stir in remaining ingredients. Continue stirring until well mixed and dough is smooth.

♥ Drop cookie dough onto prepared cookie sheets by rounded teaspoonfuls. Dip a fork into water and press dough down to about 1¹/₂-inch diameter circles.

♥ Bake at 350 degrees for 10 to 12 minutes or until lightly golden on bottom. (I bake mine for 10 minutes).

Yield: 6 dozen (Nutritional information per cookie)

Calories: 46   Total fat: 0.7 grams (13% fat)
Cholesterol: 0 mg   Sodium: 52 mg

Preparation time: 10 minutes.

Baking time: 10-12 minutes (2 cookie sheets with 1 dozen cookies per sheet).

Total time: 22 minutes for 2 dozen cookies plus an additional 12 minutes for each 2 dozen baked.

Menu ideas: Two cookies make a great snack at only about 90 calories and less than 1¹/₂ grams of fat. One or two are also great for curbing a sweet tooth after a big meal.

VERY BERRY CHEESECAKE TRIFLE

Budget Friendly Recipe

This beautiful trifle is super rich. (A little bit goes a long way!)
It always gets of wonderful comments such as,
"Ooh! Aah! How pretty!", when I serve it.

2 (8-ounce) packages fat-free cream cheese - softened
¾ cup powdered sugar
1 teaspoon imitation Vanilla, Butter and Nut flavor extract (this is the name of one extract, not 3 different extracts. If you don't have it, you can substitute 1 teaspoon almond extract instead)

1 (8-ounce) container Cool Whip Free
1 (10.5-ounce) angel food cake - torn into bite-size pieces
1 (21-ounce) can strawberry pie filling (I use Thank You)
1 (21-ounce) can blueberry pie filling

♥ In a large bowl with mixer on low, beat softened cream cheese, powdered sugar and extract for 2 minutes until well blended. Add Cool Whip Free and continue mixing for another minute. (Or until well blended.) Clean off beaters of mixer.

♥ With a spatula, stir in cake pieces. Set aside.

♥ Using a large, pretty, glass bowl spread strawberry pie filling evenly over the bottom of the bowl.

♥ Spread cream cheese/cake mixture evenly over strawberry pie filling. (This is the middle layer of the trifle.)

♥ Spread blueberry pie filling evenly over cream cheese/cake mixture.

♥ Ready to serve as is, or refrigerate until ready to eat.

♥ Refrigerate any unused portions.

Yield: 15 servings

Calories: 214   Total fat: 0.3 grams (1% fat)
Cholesterol: 2 mg   Sodium: 325 mg

Total preparation time: 15 minutes or less

Menu ideas: This is a very pretty dessert. Great for potlucks or when you have to serve "dessert only" with coffee .. say after playing cards or after a Bible study. Because it is a heavy dessert, I'd serve this either after a light meal (such as vegetable soup or a boiled dinner) or after a special dinner, such as when company comes, but give yourself time for conversation after dinner so you have time for your meal to digest before dessert.

244

ZUCCHINI SNACK CAKE

Budget
Friendly
Recipe

This versatile snack cake is as nutritious as it is delicious.

1 ½ teaspoons ground cinnamon
6 egg whites
1 (18.25-ounce) Betty Crocker Reduced-Fat Sweet Rewards yellow cake mix - dry

1 cup applesauce
3 cups finely shredded zucchini
½ cup raisins

♥ Preheat oven to 350 degrees.

♥ Spray 4 (8-inch) round cake pans with non-fat cooking spray.

♥ In a large bowl using a spatula, mix cinnamon, egg whites, cake mix and applesauce for about 2 minutes or until well mixed.

♥ Gently stir in shredded zucchini and raisins until well mixed.

♥ Divide batter evenly into prepared pans.

♥ Bake at 350 degrees for 20 minutes. Cool 10 minutes.

♥ Cut each cake into 6 pieces.

Yield: 24 pieces

Calories: 108   Total fat: 1.7 grams (14% fat)
Cholesterol: 0 mg   Sodium: 168 mg

Preparation time: 20 minutes or less.

Baking time: 20 minutes.

Total time: 40 minutes or less.

Menu ideas: Great for breakfast, snack cake
or after-school snack.

FOUR-LAYER ZUCCHINI CAKE:
While cakes are baking . . . with mixer on medium speed, beat together 1 (8-ounce) package cream cheese and 1 cup marshmallow creme for 1 minute or until well mixed. Once cakes are cooled, spread cream mixture evenly on top of cake layers. Stack cakes 4 layers high.

Yield: 12 servings

Calories: 312   Total fat: 3.4 grams (10% fat)
Cholesterol: 1 mg   Sodium: 438 mg

BANANA SPLIT ICE CREAM CAKE

Budget Friendly

Recipe

This is a real hit with children!

1 cup crushed pretzel sticks (about 1½ cups before crushed)

1 (½ gallon) container Kroger Deluxe Banana Split fat-free ice cream - slightly thawed

1 (8-ounce) container Cool Whip Free

¼ cup Hershey's lite chocolate syrup

♥ Spray a 9x13-inch pan with a non-fat cooking spray.

♥ Crush pretzels into tiny pieces. (To make it easier I use my food processor). Sprinkle pretzel crumbs onto bottom of pan. (There will not be enough pretzels to cover entire bottom of pan). You will see the pan in some places.

♥ Spoon ice cream on top of pretzels. Spread Cool Whip Free topping over ice cream. Drizzle chocolate syrup over whipped topping.

♥ Keep frozen until ready to serve.

♥ Cut into 15 square pieces.

Yield: 15 servings

Calories: 208   Total fat: 0.2 grams (1% fat)
Cholesterol: 5 mg   Sodium: 172 mg

Preparation time: 10 minutes or less.

Menu ideas: Perfect for a birthday party, or very refreshing on a hot summer day.

246

JAMMIN' SNACK CAKE BARS

Budget
Friendly

Recipe

Turn up the radio and "JAM" while baking these tasty treats!

5 egg whites
1 (8-ounce) package fat-free
cream cheese (Kraft
Philadelphia Free) - softened
⅓ cup powdered sugar

1 (9-ounce) box Jiffy golden
yellow cake mix
½ cup strawberry jam (or your
favorite jam)

♥ Preheat oven to 350 degrees.

♥ Spray 9x13-inch pan with non-fat cooking spray. Set aside.

♥ With a mixer, beat egg whites, softened cream cheese and powdered
sugar together for about 1 minute on medium speed.

♥ Slowly add cake mix. Beat on high for 2 minutes.

♥ Spread into prepared pan.

♥ Bake at 350 degrees for 15 minutes.

♥ While cake is still hot, spread jam on top.

Yield: 15 servings

Calories: 132   Total fat: 2.0 grams (13% fat)
Cholesterol: 2 mg   Sodium: 205 mg

 Preparation time: 10 minutes or less.

Baking time: 15 minutes.

Total time: 25 minutes or less.

Menu ideas: Good for breakfast, brunch or dessert.

Be generous and sincere with your compliments.

ANGEL FLUFF

Budget
Friendly

Recipe

This recipe is quick and easy to prepare.
Tastes best if prepared a few days ahead of time,
giving the creamy mixture time for absorption of jello flavoring.

2 (8-ounce) packages fat-free
   cream cheese (I use Kraft
   Philadelphia)
1 (16-ounce) container fat-free
   sour cream (Breakstone)
1½ cups marshmallow creme

1 tablespoon plus 1 teaspoon
   sugar-free strawberry Jell-O
1 (10-ounce) angel food cake -
   torn into bite-size pieces
1 (21-ounce) can cherry pie
   filling

♥ With a mixer, combine cream cheese, sour cream, marshmallow
  creme and dry Jell-O on high speed until well mixed.

♥ Spread half of the cream mixture on bottom of a large glass bowl.
  Arrange half the torn cake pieces on top. Smooth half of the pie filling
  over cake. Repeat layers, ending with pie filling.

♥ Chill.

Yield: 15 servings

Calories: 252   Total fat: 0.3 grams (1% fat)
Cholesterol: 2 mg   Sodium: 347 mg

 Total preparation time: 15 minutes or less.

Menu ideas: Great to take to potlucks.

 You don't need to know someone for a long time to love them.

BUTTERSCOTCH BLITZ

The bonus is - you can whip it up quickly!

Budget
Friendly

Recipe

1 cup skim milk
1 (1.7-ounce) package sugar-free instant butterscotch pudding - dry (Royal)
1 (12-ounce) container Cool Whip Free

15 whole graham crackers (there are 4 small sections per cracker)
2 tablespoons butterscotch chips - finely chopped

♥ Briskly mix milk and butterscotch pudding together for 1 minute with a spoon. Stir in Cool Whip Free.

♥ Arrange 7½ graham crackers on bottom of a 9x13-inch pan. Spread half of butterscotch mixture over crackers.

♥ Arrange second layer of 7½ graham crackers on top of butterscotch mixture. Spread remaining butterscotch mixture on second layer of graham crackers.

♥ Sprinkle chopped butterscotch chips over dessert. Keep chilled and covered until ready to eat.

♥ Eat within 2 days.

Yield: 6 servings

Calories: 300   Total fat: 4.6 grams (15% fat)
Cholesterol: 1 mg   Sodium: 599 mg

Total preparation time: 10 minutes or less.

Menu ideas: This would be a nice summer dessert.

 *It's not enough to just appreciate what others do for you. We have to express our appreciation to those we appreciate!*

249

PEPPERMINT CHOCOLATE CHEESECAKE

Budget Friendly Recipe

*This is one of my favorite creations.
At a ritzy restaurant I ate an extremely high fat version of
this creation, which got my creative wheels turning. I think you'll agree -
this dessert tastes unbelievably sinful. Thank the good Lord - its not!*

12 peppermint disk candies
(Brach's) - divided
2 (8-ounce) packages Kraft
Philadelphia fat-free cream
cheese - softened
1 cup marshmallow creme
½ cup chocolate-flavored

powdered sugar (Domino)
6 reduced-fat Oreo cookies -
divided
3 low-fat Hostess Lights
chocolate cupcakes with
creamy filling

♥ Spray a 9x9-inch pan with non-fat cooking spray. Set aside.

♥ Put peppermint disks in a blender and crush into a fine powder. Set aside 1 teaspoon of the peppermint powder for later use.

♥ With a mixer, combine remaining crushed peppermint powder, cream cheese, marshmallow creme and powdered sugar on high for one minute. Set aside.

♥ Crush Oreos into tiny pieces, setting aside a quarter of crushed Oreos for later use. Cut cupcakes into tiny pieces. Mix remaining three-fourths of crushed Oreos and all of the cupcake pieces together and press (with hands) into bottom of prepared pan.

♥ Spread cream mixture on top of crust. Mix the reserved peppermint powder and reserved crushed Oreos. Sprinkle over top of cake.

♥ Serve as is, or keep refrigerated until ready to eat.

Yield: 9 servings

Calories: 285   Total fat: 1.3 grams (4% fat)
Cholesterol: 4 mg   Sodium: 393 mg

Total preparation time: 15 minutes or less.

*Menu ideas: Good after a light meal, such as
soup, salad or one dish entrées.*

MINT MOUSSE CAKE

Budget Friendly

Recipe

An easy icebox delight. The key to this fast and easy dessert is to keep all ingredients chilled and move quickly to return back to the refrigerator once finished.

2 (8-ounce) containers Cool Whip Free (make sure they are very cold)

½ cup well-chilled Hershey's fat-free Chocolate Mint Sundae Shoppe syrup

1 (12-ounce) fat-free chocolate pound cake - chilled (I bought mine at Food Town)

8 maraschino cherries - optional

♥ Combine very cold Cool Whip Free with the well-chilled syrup in a chilled bowl. Gently stir together until well combined as a smooth creamy light mousse.

♥ Remove cake from refrigerator and cut horizontally into three slices.

♥ Lightly spread layers of the cake with mousse. Stack layers and frost top and sides of cake.

♥ YOU WILL NOT USE ALL OF THE MOUSSE!

♥ Garnish with maraschino cherries. Cover and refrigerate immediately. Keep chilled until ready to serve.

♥ When ready to serve, top each slice of cake (once on it's own plate) with a dab of remaining mint mousse.

Yield: 8 servings

Calories: 265   Total fat: 0 grams (0% fat)
Cholesterol: 0 mg   Sodium: 189 mg

Preparation time: 10 minutes or less.

Total time: 10 minutes or less.

Menu ideas: This would compliment any special entrée.

Showing and expressing appreciation is a little gift we give of ourselves, that ultimately means a lot to the receiver!

251

Kids Cookin'

ORANGE FLUFF

Budget Friendly

Recipe

Excellent by itself or as a topping on a pound cake,
angel food cake, or plain jello.

1 (8-ounce) package fat-free sour cream

1 (0.35-ounce) box sugar-free orange gelatin - dry (D-Zerta)

1 (8-ounce) container Cool Whip Free

1 (11-ounce) can mandarin orange segments in light syrup - drained

♥ Stir sour cream, jello and whipped topping together until well mixed. Gently fold in mandarin orange segments.

♥ Serve chilled.

Yield: 5 servings

Calories: 149   Total fat: 0 grams (0% fat)
Cholesterol: 0 mg   Sodium: 106 mg

Total preparation time: 5 minutes or less.

Menu ideas: Wonderful served with
Mexican Pork Tenderloin (page 182).

STRAWBERRY-BANANA CREAM DESSERT

Budget Friendly

Recipe

*This recipe is fast and easy to prepare, however it takes time to set.
I like to make this the night before. This can be made up
to 2 days in advance.*

1 (0.7-ounce) box sugar-free raspberry gelatin (D-Zerta) - divided

3 cups boiling water (It's easier if you bring water to boil in the microwave.)

1 (10-ounce) package frozen sliced strawberries in sugar - thawed

½ (13.5-ounce) angel food cake - cut into ½-inch pieces

3 medium bananas - thinly sliced

1 cup Cool Whip Free

♥ Spray a 9x13-inch pan with non-fat cooking spray.

♥ Dissolve gelatin in boiling water in a medium bowl. Set aside 1 cup of gelatin.

♥ Add thawed strawberries and cut-up angel food cake pieces to remaining 2 cups of gelatin in bowl. Stir until well mixed.

♥ Evenly spread prepared cake mixture into prepared pan. Evenly arrange banana slices on top of cake mixture. Set aside.

♥ Stir reserved 1 cup of gelatin with 1 cup of Cool Whip Free until a smooth, creamy consistency is reached.

♥ Pour evenly over sliced bananas and cake. Make sure all banana slices are covered to prevent browning.

♥ Refrigerate for at least 2 hours.

Yield: 15 servings

Calories: 87   Total fat: 0.2 grams (2% fat)
Cholesterol: 0 mg   Sodium: 131 mg

Preparation time: 20 minutes or less.

Refrigeration time: 2 hours.

*Menu ideas: Will compliment any entrée.
Also great for showers, parties and holidays.*

253

OREO MOUSSE

Budget
Friendly

Recipe

*It's hard to believe this thick, rich,
creamy mousse is almost fat-free!*

1 (1.5-ounce) sugar free chocolate
instant pudding mix - dry
1 (12-ounce) Cool Whip Free

4 reduced-fat Oreos - crushed -
divided

♥ Mix pudding and Cool Whip Free together for about 2 minutes by hand
(with spatula) until well mixed. Stir in cookie crumbs, reserving about
1 crumbled cookie to sprinkle on top. Put into individual dessert cups.
(If you don't have dessert cups, wide mouth wine glasses work great!)

♥ Serve chilled.

Yield: 6 servings

Calories: 147   Total fat: 0.7 grams (5% fat)
Cholesterol: 0 mg   Sodium: 380 mg

Preparation time: 10 minutes or less.

Total time: 10 minutes or less.

Menu ideas: Taste great after a hearty meal!

ZEBRAS

*Lions and tigers will love this mixture of brownies
and ice cream. Fast, low-fat and special.*

Budget
Friendly

Recipe

1 (10¼-ounce) package Gold
   Medal Smart Size Fudge
   Brownie mix
½ cup applesauce

1 (½-gallon) container Kemp's
   Caramel Praline Crunch fat-free
   ice cream
12 teaspoons Hershey's lite
   chocolate syrup

- ♥ Preheat oven to 350 degrees.
- ♥ Spray 12 muffin tins with non-fat cooking spray. Set aside.
- ♥ Stir brownie mix with applesauce until well blended. Divide brownie batter evenly into prepared muffin tins. Bake 17 minutes at 350 degrees.
- ♥ Once brownies are put into the oven, take ice cream out of the freezer to soften.
- ♥ Let brownies cool 4 to 5 minutes. Leave brownies in tins. Spoon ¼ cup of ice cream on top of each warm brownie. Cover with plastic wrap and freeze for 2 hours.
- ♥ Dip a sharp steak knife into hot water. Run knife along outside edge of each cup. Remove dessert.
- ♥ Drizzle each zebra lightly with 1 teaspoon Hershey's lite chocolate syrup.

Yield: 12 brownies

Calories: 319   Total fat: 3.2 grams (9% fat)
Cholesterol: 15 mg   Sodium: 184 mg

Preparation time: 5 minutes.

Baking time: 17 minutes.

Total time: 22 minutes.

*Menu ideas: Wonderful served with
Beanie Baby Stew (page 207).*

BUTTERSCOTCH FLUFF

Budget Friendly

Recipe

This smooth, silky, rich dessert
tastes totally fattening. Don't worry, it isn't!

1 (1.34-ounce) box sugar-free butterscotch pudding mix - dry

1 (12-ounce) container Cool Whip Free

♥ Mix ingredients together with a spatula for about 2 minutes or until well blended.

♥ Spoon into individual dessert cups. If you don't have dessert cups, wide mouth wine glasses work well.

♥ Serve chilled.

Yield: 6 servings

Calories: 114   Total fat: 0 grams (0% fat)
Cholesterol: 0 mg   Sodium: 293 mg

Preparation time: 5 minutes or less.

Menu ideas: A nice light dessert that would taste
great after Cowboy Chow (page 196).

BANANA CREAM CAKE

Banana cream pie lovers will love this!

Budget
Friendly

Recipe

2 egg whites
4 bananas - cut into ¼-inch slices
1 (18.25-ounce) box Betty
   Crocker Super Moist white cake
   mix with pudding - dry

1 cup skim milk
1 (1.35-ounce) box sugar-free
   instant vanilla pudding
1 (8-ounce) container Cool Whip
   Free

♥ Preheat oven to 350 degrees.

♥ Spray a 9x13-inch pan with non-fat cooking spray.

♥ Beat egg whites on medium with hand held mixer. Add three-fourths of banana slices and beat until well mixed. Add cake mix. Continue mixing for about 1 minute. Spread into prepared pan.

♥ Bake at 350 degrees for 30 minutes.

♥ In the meantime while cake is baking, make cream topping . . . with a mixer combine milk and pudding on medium speed for 2 minutes. Add Cool Whip Free and keep mixing until well blended and cream is of consistent color. Set cream aside.

♥ Let cake cool for 10 minutes.

♥ Arrange remaining banana slices on top of cake. Spread cream mixture over banana slices, covering entire cake.

♥ Serve warm or cover and refrigerate for serving later.

Yield: 15 servings

Calories: 216   Total fat: 3.5 grams (15% fat)
Cholesterol: 0 mg   Sodium: 359 mg

Preparation time: 12 minutes or less.

Baking time: 30 minutes.

Total time: 42 minutes or less.

Menu ideas: Great for a tasty summer or picnic dessert.

Caramel/Apple Dessert

Budget Friendly

Recipe

This recipe was sent to me by Lou Ann Hartman.

1 (5-ounce) bag Snackwell Caramel Nut Clusters
1 (2.1-ounce) box sugar-free instant vanilla pudding
1 cup skim milk

1 (8-ounce) container Cool Whip Free (or your favorite fat-free brand)
3 Granny Smith apples - chopped into tiny pieces

♥ Cut each piece of candy into 6 pieces.
♥ Mix pudding with milk. Add Cool Whip, chopped apples and candy pieces.
♥ Mix all together. Refrigerate.
♥ Stir before serving.

Yield: 6 servings

Calories: 238   Total fat: 2.6 grams (10% fat)
Cholesterol: 1 mg   Sodium: 538 mg

Preparation time: 10-15 minutes or less.

Menu ideas: You might like to serve this after a dinner of Sausage or Ham Casserole (page 187).

Life is funny but often we're so focused on taking it seriously that we don't see the humor in it.

PINEAPPLE SNACK CAKE

Budget Friendly

Recipe

A tasty, light, healthy snack cake.

1 (18.25-ounce) Betty Crocker Reduced Fat Sweet Rewards yellow cake mix - dry

1 (20-ounce) can crushed pineapple in its own juice - do not drain

²/₃ cup firmly packed dark brown sugar

♥ Preheat oven to 350 degrees.

♥ Spray an 11x17-inch jelly roll pan (a cookie sheet with a 1-inch rim) with non-fat cooking spray. Set aside.

♥ With a spatula, mix dry cake mix with undrained pineapple.

♥ Stir until well mixed.

♥ Spread batter thinly in prepared pan. For easier spreading you may want to spray a spatula with non-fat cooking spray before using it to spread the batter.

♥ With fingers, sprinkle dark brown sugar evenly over batter.

♥ Bake at 350 degrees for 25 minutes or until sides are golden brown.

♥ Let cool before cutting into 24 square bars. If stacking, put wax paper between layers.

Yield: 24 square bars

Calories: 124   Total fat: 1.7 grams (12% fat)
Cholesterol: 0 mg   Sodium: 155 mg

Preparation time: 10 minutes or less.

Baking time: 25 minutes.

Total time: 35 minutes or less.

Menu ideas: This is also good warm with a dab of Cool Whip Free.

PINEAPPLE FLUFF

Budget
Friendly

Recipe

Mmmmm, this is oh so-ooo good!

1 (1.7-ounce) package sugar-free
vanilla pudding - dry
1 (20-ounce) can crushed
pineapple in natural juice - do
not drain
1 (12-ounce) container Cool
Whip Free

½ cup very finely chopped celery
- (about 1 large stalk)
2 medium bananas - thinly sliced
½ (10-ounce) angel food cake -
torn into bite-size pieces

♥ Mix pudding, undrained pineapple and Cool Whip for about two
minutes or until pudding is dissolved and well mixed.

♥ Stir in celery and bananas. Stir until well coated.

♥ Stir torn angel food cake pieces into dessert. Keep stirring until well
coated.

♥ Serve chilled.

Yield: 14 (½-cup) servings

Calories: 118   Total fat: 0.2 grams (2% fat)
Cholesterol: 0 mg   Sodium: 236 mg

Preparation time: 12 minutes or less.

Menu ideas: Great with fish entrées.

♥ *Enjoy the little perks in life . . . Coffee perking, Perky People, etc.*

MARASCHINO CHOCOLATE CHERRY CREAM PIE

Budget Friendly
Recipe

This baby is rich! Watch out!

29 Nabisco reduced-fat Chocolate Nilla wafers
1 (10-ounce) jar maraschino cherries - cut in half - drained with 5 tablespoons juice reserved
1 (1.7-ounce) box sugar-free chocolate pudding - dry

1 teaspoon almond extract - divided
2 (12-ounce) containers Cool Whip Free - divided
2 tablespoons reduced-fat chocolate chips - finely chopped

- ♥ Line a 9-inch pie pan with wafers.
- ♥ Mix dry pudding, ½ teaspoon almond extract and 1 container Cool Whip Free together for about 2 minutes or until well blended.
- ♥ Set aside 9 cherry halves (to decorate top with). Stir remaining cherries into chocolate mixture. Spread in pie pan over cookies.
- ♥ Combine 5 tablespoons cherry juice, remaining container of Cool Whip Free and remaining ½ teaspoon almond extract for about 1 minute or until well mixed. Smooth over chocolate mixture in pie pan.
- ♥ Sprinkle finely chopped chocolate pieces around perimeter of pie pan.
- ♥ Decorate with reserved cherry halves.
- ♥ Cover. Keep refrigerated until ready to eat.

Yield: 8 servings

Calories: 269   Total fat: 2.1 grams (8% fat)
Cholesterol: 0 mg   Sodium: 373 mg

Total preparation time: 20 minutes or less.

Menu ideas: Serve after a light main entrée as a delightfully rich dessert. Also good when serving a dessert only.

PEACHES & CREAM TRIFLE

As beautiful as it is delectable!

Budget
Friendly

Recipe

1 (29-ounce) can sliced peaches - drained

2 tablespoons sugar (or 2 tablespoons Equal Spoonful)

1 (10-ounce) store bought angel food cake

1 (21-ounce) can peach pie filling (I used Thank You)

1 (8-ounce) container Cool Whip Free

2 tablespoons finely chopped walnuts

♥ After draining juice from peaches, while peaches are still in the can take a sharp knife and cut peaches into tiny pieces (¼- to ½-inch pieces). Stir in sugar (or Equal).

♥ Cut cake into 3 layers. Cut top layer into ½-inch pieces. Set aside.

♥ In a large glass bowl, lay bottom layer of cake on bottom of bowl. Fill in empty spots using half of the cut cake pieces.

♥ Spread half of pie filling over cake. Spread half of cut peaches over pie filling.

♥ Spread half of Cool Whip Free over peaches.

♥ Place second layer of cut cake over Cool Whip Free. Fill in empty spots using remaining cut cake pieces.

♥ Repeat layers of pie filling, peaches and Cool Whip Free.

♥ Sprinkle finely chopped walnuts on top.

♥ Serve as is or cover and keep chilled until ready to use.

Yield: 15 servings

Calories: 139   Total fat: 0.8 grams (5% fat)
Cholesterol: 0 mg   Sodium: 158 mg

Preparation time: 10 minutes or less.

Menu ideas: Taste great after those cookouts on the grill.

PERSONAL STORY OF DAWN HALL

As a little girl of parents who divorced when I was five, my mother who was working three jobs at the time would allow us children to ride the nearby kid's church bus. This was great! A definite win-win situation for both mom and us children. This gave mom some much needed sleeping time while we were away at kid's church and for us children, it was the highlight of the week because we would get a big candy bar when we got off the church bus. (As you can tell I liked sweets even at the age of five, but what kid doesn't?) As a little girl I knew I loved God and He loved me.

My mom remarried when I was about nine. With our new family and the addition of a Godly father came the responsibility of our family to definitely be in church on Sunday morning . . . as a family! This was a neat experience for me and to this day I still have fond memories of all seven of us children piling in the station wagon along with our parents and singing church songs the entire way to church.

Throughout my preteen and teen years I was constantly recommitting my life to God. It was not that I was ever far from God or a rebellious teen; I was actually a pretty good teen. However my teen years were hard years and I would never want to live through them again. I know that if I would have died I would have gone to Heaven. Yet God was not number one in my life.

It wasn't until I was about 20 that Christ became number one in my life. I was alone, sitting Indian style on the floor next to a coffee table reading my Bible. All of a sudden, I began to weep. It hit me like a ton of bricks! Yes, I loved God. I was a Christian, but God was not number one in my life. Tracy was. (Who at that time was my boyfriend.) God did not want to be number two. He wanted to be number one, my top priority. I was never going to have the close relationship God so longs to have with each of us (personally) unless I got my priorities straight first! I knew if I wanted complete peace, love and joy in my life I had to love God more than anybody or anything. From that moment on I have lived with Christ number one in my life. I confessed my sin and promised God, never again would I allow anything or anybody to come between my relationship with God. As I look back now at that moment when I decided to put God first in my life, I am so very grateful! I see people who go through the devastation of finding out their loved one has a terminal illness and they go completely bonkers! I could be wrong, but a part of me thinks it is because they love the terminally ill person more than they love or trust God. I am very thankful that "way back then" I put God first in my life. Otherwise, I too would probably be going nuts knowing my young

263

husband is terminally ill. At the same time I have comfort in knowing if Tracy does die he will be in a far better place, with no more pain. He'll be home in heaven.

TRACY'S AND MY STORY.

We had a fairy tale love story. . . as high school sweethearts, he was the captain of the varsity basketball team and I was a cheerleader and homecoming queen. After marrying, we were foster parents, I home schooled our children and Tracy was a liaison for a tool and die company named Container Graphics. We even physically built our own home.

In November of 1994, the day after Tracy's thirty-second birthday, he was diagnosed with an aggressive cancerous brain tumor the size of a baseball. Emergency surgery removed about a pound of his cancer and left him completely paralyzed on his entire left side. It took months of intense therapy for him to overcome most of his neurological damage. Radiation did not make his remaining fast-growing cancer any smaller and left him bald, weak and discouraged.

The doctor simply said, "go home and enjoy spring. There is nothing else you can do." We were not willing to give up. We knew up front that our insurance would not pay for an experimental treatment that we wanted to try which would cost $20,000.00 to get started and approximately $7,000.00 per month thereafter.

We put everything on the line and refinanced our home to self-publish the cookbook I had been working on for years. Never in a million years did I think I would self-publish my first cookbook to give my loving husband a second chance at life. I had been simply creating low-fat recipes out of passion. I'll wake up at 3:30 in the morning wondering if I can make a high-fat dish low-fat, such as Lasagna Supreme. As an aerobic instructor and facilitator for W.O.W. (Watching Our Weight support group) it was the encouragement of my students which prompted me to write a book. (After I'd been told, "You ought to write a cookbook" at least a hundred times or so I started to believe they were serious!) The truth is I never thought I would, but I figured I'm writing these recipes down for them that I'd created or converted from high fat to low fat . . . why don't I just save them? That's exactly what I did. As a matter of fact it was over 3½ years after I had started compiling recipes before I truly did publish my first cookbook, "Down Home Cookin' Without the Down Home Fat". I know I probably would have never published my recipes if it weren't that I needed to help pay for our medical expenses and supplement our income so we wouldn't lose our home my husband and I physically built ourselves.

The funny thing is, I didn't know a thing about self-publishing books. I didn't even know how to type or use a computer! I taught myself by getting books from the library. Pretty amazing, isn't it? We sold over 138,000 (plus) copies of "Down Home Cookin' Without the Down Home Fat" in 20 months before a "real" publisher took over. God absolutely, positively, without a doubt has had His hands involved in this entire endeavor long before I ever thought I'd actually publish books! It's no wonder why I give God all the praise and glory for the success of my books! I can not take credit. God has done this through me. I'm just the vessel He is working through. It is very exciting to see what God is doing through me and my books! Over $250,000.00 has been raised by others using my books for fund-raising of noteworthy causes. How exciting!!! God is turning tragedy into triumph for His glory! (And I'm happy to give it to Him!) More amazing than the success of my books is the story behind the book... Tracy's residual cancer has shrunk approximately 90% on this experimental treatment. He is no longer paralyzed. He can cycle as many as 30 miles in a day. He even enjoyed white-water rafting and jet-skiing with our family and friends this last summer. He's also happy to be working part-time. We are living proof God is in the business of still doing miracles, just as He was thousands of years ago!

From the beginning we believed God was going to use our most challenging situation for His Praise and Glory! He has done exactly that! We have always believed, no matter what, that everything would be alright....that does not mean we know Tracy will live, because God is sovereign. However, it does mean that we are at peace trusting God, who is in control. Believe me, this is no easy task for me to overcome (trusting God and allowing Him to be in control.) I am the kind of person who likes to know when, what, why, who and how. When you're dealing with brain cancer and $7,000 a month medical expenses there's no way to know the unknown. Doctors only understand 25% of the brain. MRI's (medical photographs of the brain) are not like an X-ray of a broken leg. What the doctor sees on an MRI is a calculated, educated guess. Is what they see radiation build-up, more cancer or swelling, etc.? There are many unknowns. Tracy is absolutely right when he says, "Don't put God in a box and try to figure things out." God is bigger than any problem we have. We have to trust Him and know no matter what everything will be okay.

People often ask, "What is Tracy's prognosis? What are his chances?" Most people with Tracy's type of cancer die at the two year mark. Tracy has passed that and is currently doing better than he ever has since his cancer diagnosis. He was told he had only a 30% chance of living through the surgery (which removed one pound of cancer from his brain.) We've also read that only one out of ten people live longer than five years with his type of cancer. When it comes to Tracy's healing,

Tracy and I don't take into consideration statistics and I'll tell you why. Have you ever read in the Bible, even one time, where God told one of His people, "Well, I give you a 30% chance that I'll heal you." I've never read it. God doesn't work that way. He is sovereign. He is in control. And if it is in God's will Tracy will be healed. That is our hope. That is what we pray for . . . a miracle.

If Tracy should pass away today we feel that he has experienced a miracle. The quality of his life has been so far superior (compared to anyone else we know who has brain cancer) since his diagnosis. We believe Tracy is living proof God is still doing miracles. God is the same God of miracles today that He was thousands of years ago. We do give God all the praise and glory for the success Tracy has had. We believe that God is working through our efforts, our doctors and medicine.

The experimental treatment Tracy is on is self-induced into a cather in his chest which pumps directly into his heart six treatments a day around the clock. The treatment lasts approximately one and a half hours each. He spends about two hours a day changing his I.V. bags and twice a week he gets blood work done. He also sees a holistic medical doctor and each month takes about $200.00 to $300.00 worth of vitamins, shark cartilage, anti-oxidants, etc. He has an M.R.I. done and goes to Houston every two months (because of the F.D.A.'s regulations.) Plus, he sees his oncologist on a regular basis, also. It is a time consuming way of life, but we have to do the best we can with what we have.

We've been told by some people, "God gave you this cancer because He knew you were good Christians you could handle it." Oh boy, doesn't that encourage all of you to want to be a Christian!? I highly doubt any of you are biting at the bit to go through all of the horrible challenges we've had to go through! Others have said," You must have some sin in your life in order for God to be punishing you with this cancer." Listen folks, this is life! Cancer happens to the good, the bad and the ugly! Period.

I would never choose to go through what we are going through, yet we are extremely thankful for all the good that has come out of our most challenging situation! We give "living by faith" new meaning and live it to the max. (Ha!) We've been living on less than half since Tracy's cancer diagnoses and have never been late on a payment! The only bill we've been behind on is for the experimental cancer treatments. It cost over $7,000.00 per month. I think you can see how it's difficult to keep that bill paid in full, especially since Tracy's been on the experimental treatment since July of 1995. All other bills are paid in full. How many of you think you could live on less than half and never be late on your payments? The truth is life is <u>very hard</u> for us but <u>God</u>

is good! I hold onto this truth. Many times it is this truth that gets me through. Tracy and I often say, "We'd rather live with cancer having a close relationship with God and His love, than to live an ordinary life without knowing God."

To follow are some special moments in our life that I'd like to share with hopes that it will be a source of inspiration and encouragement to you. When we found out that Tracy had an aggressive cancer the size of a baseball I cried for at least four or five hours. I remember going outside on our five acres yelling and screaming and just really purging all of my feelings. Thank goodness we live on five acres. If we lived in the city I'm sure I would have alarmed the entire neighborhood! Anyway, I think tears are a way of communicating with God that we ourselves don't understand sometimes. Sometimes people of faith don't express their negative feelings of frustration, anger, disappointment, etc. because they feel if they are a true Christian they shouldn't have these feelings. Instead, they bottle those feelings and suppress them deep within. In all honesty, when we aren't being honest with ourselves about our feelings who are we really lying to? I think ourselves. God already knows how we feel. In my opinion what happens when we don't deal with our feelings and try to get them out, is they act as a blockade and interfere with our communication with God. I think it's important for us to be honest with ourselves and deal with our feelings, so that nothing interferes or gets in the way of our relationship or communication with God.

Even in my darkest times, when I feel like I'm in the pit of the living hell here on earth, I can honestly say that I have never felt far from God. Some may be asking, "How can you be full of negative feelings such as depression, anger, disappointment or hurt and still feel close to God at the same time?" I really don't know. All I know is through all of this, I have never felt far from God. He is my strength. This tragedy that we are going through has not made me closer to God nor farther away from Him. I've always had a close relationship with my Heavenly Father ever since I can remember. Sometimes tragedy draws people closer to God and sometimes it pushes them away from God. For me it has done neither.

Through all of this trauma I've realized that thankfulness is an attitude you choose to have . . . it is not based on what you have or where you are at in life.

Tracy was hospitalized for a total of 30 days. He was in I.C.U. for approximately 5 or 6 days. I'll never forget when he was able to take a shower for the first time after his brain cancer surgery. Up until this point he had been completely bed ridden for approximately 8-10 days except for a couple of times when he was allowed to briefly sit in a chair for a few minutes with assistance. It was such a sad time. Keep in mind that before his surgery he was a strong, athletic, well-built, young man. His

267

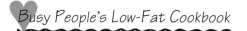

weak tired body which atrophy had taken over was slumped over in the plastic wheel chair designed especially for handicapped people to use when showering. He had lost quite a bit of weight and his muscle had turned to skin and bone. He looked like someone you would have seen in a concentration camp. He got a glimpse of himself (for the first time after his surgery) in the silver flange around the faucet of the shower and he began to cry saying, "I look pathetic."

As a strong Christian woman who loved her husband dearly I did something that I'm sure many of you will judge me for and ask how could she have ever done that? I gently but firmly gave him a little smack on his shoulder, not enough to hurt, but firm enough for him to take me seriously. I replied, "We have no room to be anything but optimistic and thankful. You are alive. You have your memory, (which doctors thought he could have lost through surgery) and you have your right side. (His left side was completely paralyzed.) We have too much to be thankful for to allow ourselves to get down."

I believe that Satan would just love to take a little self pity and use it like a wedge (when splitting firewood) to crack wide open all doubt of God's power and love in our life. He would love for us to feel sorry for ourselves and to pull away from God. I knew we had no room for this and I wanted to nip it in the bud right away!

About four months after this shower incident we had another very traumatic experience! I jokingly tell people, we weren't having enough stress in our lives so we had a house fire. It wasn't a big house fire, (only $3,500.00 damage) but at 3:30 in the morning any house fire is scary!

I had smelled the smoke and three times had incorporated it into my dream. I believe without a doubt that if Tracy had not awakened, I would be dead from the smoke inhalation. I don't know what would have happened to our children.

I had put in a long day as an assistant activities director. Out of sweetness, Tracy had prepared a bath for me. He had lit three candles and put one in each corner of the tub. He was bald from radiation, but had a river of hair growing on the back of his head. I would sit behind him and shave his bald head as I wrapped my legs around his sides so that he could rub my aching feet. That was a fair deal, don't you think?

After the bath we blew out the candles facing the exit. However, we forgot about the candle behind us and never did blow it out. The candle stick caught on fire, along with the bathroom. The smoke alarm never went off. Why? How many of you have smoke alarms in your master bathrooms? Let me encourage you, if you burn candles in the bathroom, get smoke alarms for the bathroom. The reason why our smoke alarm never went off is because our smoke alarms are located outside of our bedroom doors. Our bedroom door was shut therefore all the smoke was inside our bedroom and bathroom.

At 3:30 in the morning I heard this great big ker-plunk! It was Tracy. He had forgotten he was still suffering from neurological damage and was still partially paralyzed on his left side. He heard the crackling of the fire and saw the flicker of the flames in the shower stall across from the tub and immediately <u>tried</u> to jump out of bed to put the fire out. He yelled, "Fire, fire!"

I opened the door to our bedroom and ran down the hallway in the opposite direction of the fire, thinking that we had a chimney fire in the living room because we were heating the house with our fireplace. When I got back to the bathroom to help put out the fire I cried out, "Thank you God, thank you God!" because I knew it could have been a whole lot worse! Now think about our situation . . . here we are living on less than half, my husband has an aggressive brain cancer (and radiation is not making his cancer any smaller) and our house is on fire in the middle of the night. That's when I realized thankfulness is an attitude we choose to have. It's not based on what we have or where we are at in life.

Many times in my life I've felt tested by God. I believe it's because God wanted <u>me</u> to see for myself where I placed Him in my life. Was He number one before anyone or anything? Did I really trust Him?

Another time of testing was when my husband, Tracy, was being transferred to his third hospital. It was eight days after his brain surgery. The doctor had removed one pound of cancer from the middle of his brain. He had been completely paralyzed on his left side ever since the surgery. Tracy's father was helping me transport Tracy from his hospital bed to the wheelchair. Completely out of the blue with no forewarning this strong, Godly man for whom I have the utmost respect, blurts out, "Son and Dawn.... I'd like to encourage you to keep on tithing." In all honesty, I thought to myself, You've got to be kidding me!!! We have no money coming in. Medical bills are piling high. I don't know how we're going to financially make it and you're asking me to keep on tithing? (Tithing is giving 10% of your income back to the Lord.) I was too exhausted and dumbfounded by his suggestion to say anything except, "Let us think and pray about it." In all honesty, it took a lot of energy to keep my mouth shut and not blurt out all of the thoughts running through my mind like wild horses. I was angry that my father-in-law had even suggested such a thing. Yet I knew, with all of my heart, how much Dad loved us. He would <u>never</u>

269

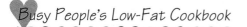

do anything to hurt us or cause us harm. Even though I was confused, exhausted and upset; I knew Dad must have felt pretty strong about this suggestion to bring it up to us in our time of possible financial ruins.

I sought counsel from my mother and friend, thinking for sure they'd agree with me that my father-in-law had lost his mind. Surely, the stress had gone to his head and he could not rationalize clearly any longer! We had absolutely <u>no</u> money coming in. How in the world can you tithe on something you don't even have? A lot of good my mother and friend were! They both completely agreed with my father-in-law and thought we should continue tithing, even through the midst of all we were going through. I could not believe it! Doesn't anyone see the picture? We have <u>no</u> money coming in! Our savings was running through our fingers like water. We were in over our heads with medical expenses. We had <u>NEVER</u> been in financial bondage before. Now I felt like we were drowning in financial bondage! The sad thing was, it wasn't a bit our fault.

After two days of constant thought and prayer, along with millions of tears of confusion, it hit me. It hit me like a ton of bricks! I was all alone. I fell to my knees and sobbed like a baby, but this time with tears of understanding. I could have a million dollars and give every single penny of it back to God. But, if I didn't give it because I wanted to (out of love, thankfulness and obedience) than God really didn't want my money. If we were going to continue to tithe, it had to be, because we wanted to.

My husband once told me, "Dawn, don't put God in a box and try to figure this all out". Tracy is absolutely right! How foolish of me. Just because I can't figure it out, doesn't mean God can't work it out.

The next day I told Tracy what had happened to me the night before. I told Tracy, "I agree with your dad, we should continue tithing". Tracy whole-heartedly agreed also. (Tracy had agreed a few days previously, when his father first mentioned the idea. I on the other hand, was the hard sell!)

Up until this time, we had received no financial gifts from anyone. We were living solely on our savings which was dwindling fast! I was over-whelmed with the outrageous medical cost. We had good insurance, but the out of pocket expenses were adding up rapidly. None the less, I was at peace with our decision to keep on tithing. Not only were we going to keep tithing on income, but if we were to receive financial gifts from others, we decided we'd tithe on those gifts also.

It was so cool! At about eleven that night I arrived home from my day at the hospital with Tracy. I opened my first piece of mail. I couldn't believe it! There was a $20.00 check from my sweet aunt and uncle. Tears of thankfulness ran down my cheeks. The next envelope I opened was from my wonderful cousin and her husband. It was a check for $50.00! I knew, right then and there, these gifts were a confirmation from God that we had made the right decision to keep tithing. Like I said earlier, except for the one medical bill which runs over $7,000.00 per month, we have <u>never</u> been late on any bills. Pretty neat - huh?

It's important for me to convey that when someone in the immediate family (of a close knit family) finds out one of its members has a terminal illness its as if the <u>entire</u> family has that illness. You'll notice as I continue to speak that I say, "When we found out 'WE' had cancer." Please note: I DO NOT HAVE CANCER OR ANY OTHER TERMINAL ILLNESS. I simply imply that this cancer has its nasty hold on my life because my husband and I are so closely entwined as one. For anyone who is blessed with a wonderful Christian marriage, I'm sure you know what I mean. When my husband hurts I hurt. For those of you who don't have a tightly united marriage, it is my hope you someday will. It is a true gift from God and it comes when God's love is the primary focus of your marriage.

For those of us who have a loved one who is fortunate enough to find out they have a terminal illness before they actually die; I consider this knowledge a blessing. Why? Because if they (or you) don't know Christ as a personal savior, now is the perfect time to get things right with God before it's too late! Let's face it . . . after our physical bodies die here on earth, we're either going to heaven or to hell. The choice is ours. The question is, "What will your choice be?" No one else can make the choice for us. As for my family and me, we have chosen to serve the Lord.

My heart goes out to anyone who finds out they are terminally ill. It's hard!!! (Boy is that the understatement of the year!) For those of us who love the Lord I can honestly say it must be easier for us. We have God's loving arm around us at all times to love, guide, and direct us when we seek Him. We never have to feel alone. He is always with us. He will never leave us. We know God is sovereign. We have the hope that God may choose to do a miraculous healing.

For terminally ill Christians not only do we have the hope of a miraculous healing, but also the peace that surpasses all understanding in believing that when we die, we are going to be in a better place than here on earth. We'll be in heaven in ever lasting peace.

Sometimes I wonder . . . if heaven is so wonderful, why do we (Christians) who are terminally ill work so hard at living? That is a good question. Having hands on experience with such a question, my reply is, "because we know how much our loved ones will miss the lost one." As long as we are alive, I believe God is not finished using us.

For those of you who don't have a personal relationship with God, I

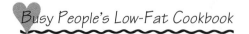

encourage you to do so....at least look into the possibility. There's a "book for a buck" you can order from this book. It will help you with being more educated about God, salvation and eternal peace. Look in the newspaper or telephone book for a Bible teaching church. You have nothing to lose and everything to gain. Of all the gifts I've received in my life, God's gifts of love, joy and peace are the most valuable to me. I want to share them with you. Please mail a self-addressed stamped envelope along with $1.00 per book to:

Cozy Homestead Publishers, Inc.
Attn: FB Dept.
5425 S. Fulton-Lucas Road
Swanton, OH 43558

About Solid Rock

Few things have given me greater joy in life than knowing our family is trying to make a positive difference in the inner city of Toledo by being involved with the Solid Rock program. With a hands-on involvement Pastor Keith and his wonderful wife Shannon focus on the needs of the central city, crossing over both racial and economic barriers.

Through their Kids Church program for children and their youth group for teens they are establishing a moral foundation for the future generation based on Biblical principles.

We are in constant need of bus drivers to transport children to the programs, as well as more volunteers to help in many other areas. Last but not least, child sponsors are needed.

For information contact: Keith Stepp, Solid Rock, 1630 Broadway, Toledo, Ohio 43609 or call: 419-244-7020.

10% of my profits from this book are going towards Toledo's Solid Rock Outreach Program. On behalf of all the children, thank you very much for your support!

Sincerely,

Dawn

INDEX

Index

Index

COOKBOOK ORDER FORM

"Busy People's Low-Fat Cookbook"

These COOKBOOKS make GREAT Gifts! Stock up and
keep some on hand (for those last minute gifts).

Look at chart below for cost of book.

Qty.	Item	Cost Per Book	Total
	Busy People's Low-Fat Cookbook"		
	OH residents add 6.25% Sales Tax per book		
	Add $2 per book-shipping &handling ($3 if only 1 book)		
	TOTAL		

Fill out and send this order form with payment to:

Cozy Homestead Publishing
5425 S. Fulton-Lucas Road, Swanton, OH 43558

VISA, Mastercard, and Discover are Welcome

Call Toll Free 1-888-436-9646

Name _____

Address _____

City _____ State _____ Zip _____

Credit Card/Acct.# _____ Exp. Date _____

Signature _____

DISCOUNTS

#of books	Cost per book	Total cost for all books	2 or more books equal $2 per bk. shipping	Total cost
1	$15.95	$15.95	$3.00*	$18.95
2	$12.50	$25.00	$4.00	$29.00
3 or more	$10.00	$30.00	$6.00	$36.00

*if only 1 book

3 or more books are $10.00 each plus $2.00 per book shipping & handling.

If you would like to know of future recipe books written by Dawn just fill out the card below. When her next book comes out we'll be sure to let you know!

Name _____

Address _____

City _____ State _____ Zip _____

What I liked most about your book:

_____

_____

_____

What I'd like to see more of:

_____

_____

_____

**Thanks for your encouragement!
God Bless & Good Eatin's!
Love,
Dawn**

**Mail To: Cozy Homestead Publishers, Inc.
5425 S. Fulton-Lucas Rd.
Swanton, OH 43558**

✂ —
Cut on dotted line.

**If you've created your own fast and easy,
extremely low fat, and delicious recipe mail to:**

**Dawn Hall
c/o Cozy Homestead Publishers
5425 S. Fulton-Lucas Rd.
Swanton, Ohio 43558**

**Each recipe published will have a write-up
about its originator next to it.**